Hair Trigger 28

A STORY WORKSHOP ANTHOLOGY

COLUMBIA COLLEGE CHICAGO

CHICAGO 2006

FICTION WRITING DEPARTMENT

600 SOUTH MICHIGAN AVENUE

CHICAGO, ILLINOIS 60605-1996

Cover Photograph and Photo Essay
Jeffrey A. Wolin, from *Inconvenient Stories: Vietnam War Veterans Portraits,*
work done 2003-2005, Ink Jet Prints.
Soon to appear in book form by Umbrage Editions.
Jeffrey A. Wolin, ©2005

All images courtesy of Catherine Edelman Gallery, Chicago, the photographer,
and Columbia College Chicago Photography Department.

Hair Trigger 28
Copyright ©2006 Columbia College Chicago
Story Workshop® is a service mark (U.S. Patent and Trademark Office Registration No.
1,343,415) of John Schultz.

Fiction Writing Department
fax 312-344-8043
phone 312-344-7611
email droberts@colum.edu

Columbia College Chicago
600 South Michigan Avenue
Chicago, Illinois 60605-1996

ISBN 0-929911-17-2

Table of Contents

THE DAVID FRIEDMAN MEMORIAL AWARD

The David Friedman Award offers a cash prize to the best story or essay published in *Hair Trigger* each year. Our thanks go to David Friedman's family, which established this fund in fall 2002 as a memorial to their son, a talented writer and painter, as well as an alumnus of Columbia College Chicago and a great friend to the Fiction Writing Department's students and faculty.

Preface & Acknowledgments

WELCOME TO THE TWENTY-EIGHTH ISSUE OF *HAIR TRIGGER*, THE COLUMBIA COLLEGE Chicago Fiction Writing Department's anthology of student writing. Over its long history, *Hair Trigger* has won numerous awards, including first-place prizes in national competitions from three different organizations: the Association of Writers and Writing Programs, the Coordinating Council of Literary Magazines, and the Columbia University Scholastic Press Association. Those of us associated with the Fiction Writing Department are, of course, very proud of the students whose work has been introduced through *Hair Trigger*. Many of them have won individual awards from these national organizations and have gone on to successful careers in writing, publishing, and a variety of other professions.

As with previous issues of the magazine, *Hair Trigger 28* collects prose fiction and creative nonfiction writing by undergraduate and graduate students at all levels. These works come primarily from core classes—Introduction to Fiction Writing, Fiction Writing I, Fiction Writing II, Prose Forms, Advanced Fiction, Advanced Prose Forms—taught using the innovative Story Workshop® approach, as well as from Fiction Seminars, Critical Reading and Writing classes, and a wide variety of creative nonfiction, genre, publishing, and other Specialty Writing courses taught using distinctly successful complementary approaches. The success of the Story Workshop approach and those complementary approaches used in the Fiction Writing Department program is reflected in the broad range of voices, subjects, forms, and cultural/linguistic backgrounds represented in all editions of *Hair Trigger* during its illustrious history, including the edition that you are holding in your hands.

An exhaustive and rigorous selection process is used with *Hair Trigger* to ensure that no excellent story—whatever its voice, subject, or approach—will be overlooked. Student editors in our College Literary Publishing class work over a semester with a faculty advisor who helps them reveal their unconscious as well as conscious biases. These editors, formed into two diverse teams, read submissions and decide which should be passed along to the full group. Those manuscripts passed ahead in the process are read by all editors, who then begin the hard work of deciding which pieces should go into the final book. Instructors may appeal a rejected piece for another reading and further discussion by student editors who, along with Faculty Advisor Chris Maul Rice and Coordinator of Faculty Development Shawn Shiflett, are responsible for making the final decisions. For space reasons, we are unable to include many excellent stories and essays each year; but over the magazine's history, this thorough, fair process has ensured that the best of the best will eventually see the light of day. Respect for the reader, for content, for form, for point of view and language, and vividness of telling characterize the selections printed in this volume, and we believe that the diversity represented in the pages of *Hair Trigger* stands as a distinct and refreshing contrast to the so-called "workshop story" found in many other writing programs. Our appreciation goes to the student editors, chosen for their own ability as writers and readers.

Congratulations to Chris Maul Rice, who was chiefly responsible as Faculty Advisor for supervising undergraduate and graduate student editors in the overall selection and production process for *Hair Trigger 28,* and to Coordinator of Faculty Development Shawn Shiflett, who oversees *Hair Trigger* for the Fiction Writing Department.

Thanks to Chair Randall Albers, Andrew Allegretti, Don Gennaro De Grazia, Ann Hemenway, Antonia Logue, Eric May, Patricia Ann McNair, Joe Meno, Alexis Pride, Shawn Shiflett, Sam Weller, John Schultz, and Betty Shiflett for consulting on matters affecting the student editors' complex editorial selection process—as well as to the many other excellent teacher-writers in the Fiction Writing program.

Thanks to Creative and Printing Services Director Mary Johnson and to John Farbrother and Ben Bilow for cover and layout design. Particular thanks go to Deborah Roberts and Linda Naslund for copyediting, proofreading, and supervising crucial phases of production. Thanks, too, to Joe Anderson, Nicole Chakalis, Katie Corboy, Rob Duffer, Aaron Golding, Conrad Jacobson, Stephanie Kuehnert, Emily Pankow, Jenny Seay, Maurine Stellhorn, and Patty Templeton for their production assistance. And special thanks to Mica "Quark Beyotch" Racine, who has long given us invaluable assistance in production and design of *Hair Trigger* and other projects.

Our profound gratitude goes to Warrick Carter, President of Columbia College Chicago; to Steve Kapelke, Vice President for Academic Affairs/Provost; to Leonard Lehrer, Dean of the School of Fine and Performing Arts; and to Keith Cleveland, acting Graduate School Dean, for their continuing support and encouragement of this program.

We owe a debt, above all, to the over 600 students registered for classes in the Fiction Writing Department each semester, from whose writing the selected pieces in this volume were gleaned.

We sincerely hope that you enjoy the original and inventive work appearing in these pages.

Randall Albers, Chair
Fiction Writing Department

Hair Trigger 28 **Student Editors**
Elizabeth Abruzzo
Frank Crist
Chris DeGuire
James M. Elkins
April Hanson
Joe Tower
Chelsea Laine Wells
Jona Whipple

Hair Trigger 28 **Faculty Advisor**
Chris Maul Rice

Touchdown Tommy

Pat Noonan

THERE ARE FIVE SURE-AS-SHIT WAYS TO TELL IF YOU'RE FROM THE SOUTH SIDE:

1. If ya ever rode a bike one-handed 'cause ya had a case a beer in the other.

2. Your third bathroom is a basement sink, usually right next to the washer and dryer. (Ya have to stand on your tippy-toes, but it's better than waiting.)

3. Alleyways are your salvation from bars that close.

4. The only reason you're not in jail is because of your high-ranking uncle in the police department.

5. You will still fight tooth 'n nail over who had the best grammar school football team, caring much more about this than religion or politics, and you occasionally have to prove your point with a beer bottle to the skull.

He never finished high school and felt getting a GED was a waste a time. He tried to join up with the Marines, but he failed the psychological analysis, not to mention that the cocaine in his system could have covered the Rockies.

They called 'im Tommy the Dishwasher, and for the last nine years he had worked up at Harrigan's Bar as the only dishwasher in the joint. He was up there every day, from twelve noon when they opened the kitchen, until nine-thirty when they closed it up. He wasn't much of a worker, but he never asked for time off and he never missed a day of work, not once. It wasn't that he was committed to the job, he just had nothin' better to do. The breaks he took were short and he used them to smoke dope in the walk-in refrigerator, the pot smoke indistinguishable from the regular deep-labored breaths he took from his short lifetime of smokin' Kools. Sometimes at the end of the night he'd stuff a pork chop or a sirloin steak into his tight, out-of-date, stonewashed jeans and walk out smilin', knowin' he'd have a nice dinner when he got home to his basement apartment. It wasn't really much of an apartment; it was actually the boiler room of the apartment building, but it was cheap and comfy and the barflies didn't mind. He had an old army cot set up next to the furnace. It got hotter than hell in the summer, but in the winter, he never went cold. He didn't have much else down there, a couple of Frank Zappa and Pink Floyd posters and every issue of *Guns and Ammo* since August of '87. He didn't have a couch or a table, not even a refrigerator, he ate on his bed, and company was normally limited to the mice and cockroaches that scurried across the cold, concrete floor, as he looked up from the grilled-cheese sandwich that he cooked on a hot plate that had never been cleaned in the last five years, ever since he moved out of his parents' and into his boiler-room apartment. A deflated football sat at the end of the table. Written on it was S.W.C. Sept., 1985. 11 TDs.

Before Tommy the Dishwasher was known as Tommy the Dishwasher, he was Touchdown Tommy McDonald. He was a legend in the Southwest Catholic Conference, and still is to the many who sit on bar stools in South Side taverns and talk grammar-school football, like an evangelist would talk redemption of the mortal soul.

In the fall of '85 he recorded fifty-nine touchdowns in nine games for the Christ the King Cougars in an undefeated season, eleven in one game, a record that still stands by five touchdowns. His fifty-nine touchdowns are even more impressive, a record by more than forty touchdowns. His twenty-nine hundred all-purpose yards are equally as impressive and mentioned every Christmas by Father O'Reilly, just before the little kids reenact the birth of Jesus.

One year while performing the play, just after one of our little shepherds uttered his only line, "Look, a star," referring to the star that the three wise men followed to a crappy stable where Jesus was screamin' to high hell, covered in hay and afterbirth 'n all sorts of gross shit, surrounded by donkeys and sheep 'n other animals that smelled like shit, one of our other little shepherds yelled, "Touchdown Tommy, where?" Everyone jumped up in spiritualistic amazement, like Jesus Christ himself had came back to life, pulling himself off that wooden cross and walkin' across the godforsaken altar, throwin' down some cardboard, slappin' the sunglasses off the blind guy who lived down da block from me, snappin' em' on his own huge sunken eyes and doin' some sort of gospel-like break-dance for the good people of Christ the King parish, the way people were yellin' and screamin'. A crippled kid in front of me leaped up on his dad's shoulders screamin' how he ain't never seen Touchdown Tommy in the flesh, and the excitement of it cured his legs; the blind guy from down the block got his sight back and the deaf kid no longer needed his hearing aids. After everyone realized it was a false Touchdown Tommy alarm we all sat back with one huge, overall sigh of disappointment. There used to be talk of super-gluing Touchdown Tommy's framed football picture on the crucified Jesus, for it more probably than not did indeed have healin' powers, and this Jesus guy, he ain't healed shit for quite some spell. Father O'Reilly thought about it for a bit, but he didn't want to offend Touchdown Tommy by putting his picture on such a frail and weak-looking Jewish guy, and everyone agreed. Father O'Reilly forgot what he was talkin' about before he was interrupted by the Touchdown Tommy fiasco, so he shortened the mass to only ten minutes in honor of Touchdown Tommy who could never sit still through a whole entire mass. "Praise the Lord for Touchdown Tommy!!!" yelled the good people of the church as they left in as high spirits as ever.

A couple of years ago a petition was started to end the re-creation of Jesus performed by Christ the King's lovely first graders on Christmas Eve, and replace it with the reenactment of the eleven-touchdown game by Touchdown Tommy McDonald. It was practiced for almost a week but there wasn't a first grader coordinated enough to play the part of Touchdown Tommy. Father O'Reilly looked at Billy Sullivan, who was supposedly the most fitting for the role of Touchdown Tommy, with the utmost look of disgust ever brought upon a young boy by a priest and yelled, "YOU!!! YOU ARE THE WORST!!! YOU ARE BEYOND INAPPROPRIATE FOR THE PART, YOU PRANCE WHEN YOU SHOULD SHIFT, AND SKIP WHEN YOU'RE TO STIFF-ARM, YOU PUT WHEN YOU'RE TO GROWL, AND YOUR FINGERS ARE FREE FROM THE SOIL OF THE FOOTBALL FIELD!!!" Father O'Reilly put his fingers to his temples and rubbed them long and hard. He looked at Billy Sullivan and shook his head, first to the left, then to the right, then mechanically from side to side until he calmly stated, "I ask for Touchdown Tommy and you give me this . . . this . . . this SOCCER PLAYER!!!" Mrs. Kelly, the lady who played the piano, fainted when she heard those fateful words, the first graders began to cry, and the statue of Mother Mary came crashing to the ground. Billy Sullivan just stood there in awe; he had never been called such a thing, but to be called such a thing by a priest was atrocious. Later that day Billy Sullivan tried to commit suicide by way of suckin' down an entire bottle of Flintstones vitamins. He recovered and moved to the suburbs, some say to Oak Lawn, others say Orland Park; no one knows for sure.

If we were putting on another lame-ass "baby Jesus" play, anyone could have the starring role. Almost all of the first graders were pasty and frail enough to play the part of baby Jesus, Christ the King being an Irish Catholic church and everything, but none of them had the charisma, the charm, the endurance, or the downright athletic ability it took to play the part of Touchdown Tommy, so a professional actor was flown in. At first, Tom Cruise seemed the perfect fit. He played the football player in *All the Right Moves*, and his athletic prowess was quite evident as he proudly displayed a picture of himself as a former high school wrestler in front of the parishioners on that cold December morning. There were doubts in the hearts of many of the old-timers, and Touchdown Tommy's old teammates said if God himself took the form of Jim Brown, he still wouldn't make a pimple on the ass of the greatest grammar-school football player in the universe.

"I know it will be hard, the hardest thing I've ever done, to play the part of a legend," said Mr. Cruise. "*Legend* also being one of the first movies I starred in, that was back in . . ."

"Get to the fuckin' point, Cruise," said Father O'Reilly, who was extremely nervous and temperamental at the time, being very worried about the upcoming performance.

Mr. Cruise felt he might be losing the crowd, so he flashed his famous pearly whites and all was forgotten.

"I talked to my good friend Ronald Reagan," said Mr. Cruise.

"BOO!" came the reply, Christ the King being a very Democratic parish.

"No, no, no, Ronald Reagan the actor, not Ronald Reagan the president," Mr. Cruise said, as he flashed his billion-dollar smile and all of what he said was forgotten once again.

"Oh . . ." said the crowd.

"Well, I was talkin' over this role with Ronald Reagan…the actor, and I asked him how he psyched himself up for playing George Gipp, ya know, the Gipper, as in "Win one for the Gipper." And he was teaching me techniques that he thought might be useful to portray a legendary football player. When I was about to leave, he brought me in close, put his beautiful lips against my ears, and asked me who I might be performing as. So I told him, Touchdown Tommy McDonald. He gasped at first and then clutched his chest. "Don't do it," he yelled to me, "it will ruin your career; if God himself came down from heaven and possessed the body of Ickey Woods he couldn't play that part. This part will ruin you, Cruise, RUIN YOU!!!" Well, at first I was a little worried about what ol' Ron told me, but then I thought about it for a minute, looked in the mirror, and said, "Hey, you're Tom fuckin' Cruise, you can walk on water, baby, you've been a stock-car driver, an agent (in many forms), a greaser, an Irish immigrant, and even played a football player before. You're invisible, baby, you're Tom fuckin' Cruise, you can walk through walls, fuck ya."

At that, he pointed two fingers in the air and cocked his head sideways. We stared at him in wonder for a couple of minutes until he flashed that trillion-dollar smile again. Then we cheered to high hell.

"Tom fuckin' Cruise," he whispered.

All was goin' well until Tom went over to Coach Connoly's basement to review old highlight tapes of Touchdown Tommy. They had only gotten through the third game of the season when Coach Connoly, who was sittin' next to Tom Cruise, saw a light flicker in Tom's hand.

"Mr. Cruise, I didn't think you were a smoker," said ol' Coach Connoly.

"Only when I'm nervous, coach, only when I'm nervous."

On the night of the performance Mr. Cruise failed to show up. He wrote a letter of apology to the priest and the parishioners. It was short and to the point and read, "I have come upon many roles as an actor, this one terrified me, many regrets. Tom Cruise." He was no longer Tom fuckin' Cruise after that, just plain, old, boring Tom Cruise.

His picture is propped up in a glass display case at Christ the King church to this day, above the '94 and '95 Southwest Catholic Conference champions, and in between a picture of Pope John clutching rosary beads with a stern look of religious contempt written all over his pasty white face, and a painting of the Virgin Mary holding a dead Jesus as blood pours from the crown of thorns that was placed on his head by Roman soldiers. Pope John seemed almost jealous of Touchdown Tommy's accomplishments, and even though Jesus rose from the dead three days later, he sure as fuck never scored eleven touchdowns in one game!

He's smiling' in the picture, not a smile of happiness that comes from a great birthday or the birth of a firstborn child, but a smile of complete and total arrogance that comes from accomplishing something nobody else had before, something nobody else had even touched, even slightly grazed, not even vaguely sniffed, like a fart passin' in a violent breeze.

His back is propped up against the bright yellow goalpost; a football is held like a loaf of soft bread and seems to be growing between his shoulder pads and the dark maroon jersey with the number twelve in bright grass-stained white. His white helmet, tucked under his other arm shows the battle marks of the season: the yellow and black from Saint Cajedan's, in which, during the opening game of the season, he scored five touchdowns, all on the ground; then the green of Saint Denis where he got six touchdowns, three in the air and three scurryin' between the tackles; next he burned Saint Linus for five scores; and during homecoming week, he blazed through the trenches of Ridge Park, burning Saint Bernadette during the Cougars' first home game, earning his biggest battle mark—a dark blue dent when he went helmet to helmet with a tiny safety as he went in for touchdown number seven, his final of the day.

It was only midseason, and Touchdown Tommy already had twenty-three touchdowns to his credit. It seemed overwhelming when the *Beverly Review* ran an entire front page dedicated to the great accomplishments of everybody's All-American, Touchdown Tommy McDonald, the pride of the South Side, but then, when we thought his publicity couldn't grow any larger than the local paper, the *Sun-Times and* the *Chicago Tribune* dedicated full-length pages about his performances with color photos of him stiff-arming opponents to the ground as he ran through defenses that were solely dedicated to stopping him, and eventually Mike Ditka, the head coach of the Chicago Bears, came to see him play, and their Defensive Coordinator, the famous Buddy Ryan, the father and mastermind behind the legendary 46 defense offered his guidance to the coaches of Holy Redeemer, who were next on the Christ the King Cougars and Touchdown Tommy's hit list, in stopping this boy wonder.

If you thought having Mike Ditka there watchin' him play put a butterfly or two in the iron-clad stomach of Touchdown Tommy, ya probably ain't worth yer weight in shit, 'cause it just infuriated him that this jerk Ditka was steppin' into his limelight, plus they had this Ryan guy, who took the whole week off coachin' da Bears, during a Super Bowl season, mind ya, to instruct these Redeemer pansies in stoppin' him from scorin' so he could tell his grandkids he stopped a true force of nature. Holy Redeemer got the ball first, and Touchdown Tommy kicked off. He looked over at the Holy Redeemer side-line where he saw Buddy Ryan wearin' Redeemer red studyin' a clipboard and wearin' a huge headset. He looked up on Longwood Drive and swore to Christ he saw Mike Singletary and the Fridge sittin' on top of an old Dodge truck with binoculars and walkie-talkies, relayin' what they saw in the offense back to ol' Buddy Ryan. Touchdown Tommy looked back over at the Fridge and Singletary, then at Buddy Ryan, then towards the sky, up towards the heavens, spit a huge black stream of Red Man chew that split the uprights of the goalposts forty yards away, and smiled a black-toothed grin that could've froze hell twice over. The whistle blew for the kickoff, Touchdown Tommy looked out the distance towards the return man, mouthed the words "fuck this," spit on the ground, and kicked a blooper that was high enough to break up clouds that traveled ten yards to the millimeter. Hands on both sidelines saluted, fighting the sun and looking into the air as if they were observing a lunar eclipse. Taking advantage of the rather high kickoff, Touchdown Tommy ran full speed towards the defense. Half of them ran straight for the sidelines in fear of life and limb, retreating in their red uniforms as if they were the French army. The other half, the gutsy fellows who knew no better, tried their best to maintain their positions, but ya can't fight off a tank with brass knuckles, and Touchdown Tommy slobber-knocked each and every one of 'em and got back just in time to catch his own kickoff. He tucked the ball underneath his shoulder pads and ran backwards the whole way, sticking the ball in the direction of Buddy Ryan, who proceeded to vomit uncontrollably.

When he got to the end zone someone threw a piece of cardboard, where Touchdown Tommy performed an impromptu break-dance much to the delight of the crowd who shook their heads to the rhythm of the music that was echoing loudly from the boom-box in the corner of the end-zone. It was, after all, the 1980s. Touchdown Tommy scored seven more touchdowns in the first half, taking off the second half and lying on the sidelines, getting shoulder massages from Redeemer cheerleaders. Buddy Ryan offered no comment in the post-game interview, but tears in his eyes were evident as his grandkids looked on in shame. The next week he scored six touchdowns in a game versus Saint Barnabas, in which he only played the first quarter, and followed it up with a measly five touchdowns in the first game of the playoffs. People started to worry if Touchdown Tommy was losing skill when he only managed that five-touchdown game, and if that was a cause for concern then people really started to bite their nails to the quick after a season-low four-touchdown performance in the last playoff game versus Saint Gerald. Next up, in the Southwest Conference championship game was Saint Denis, and word around the South Side was that they had loaded up the team with ringers. People were worried, and Touchdown Tommy just casually blew off his critics.

"I'll show him," he stated in a post-game televised interview after the Saint Gerald game. "The best is yet to come, yes sir, my best is yet to come . . ."

I was sittin' up at Harrigan's Bar one night drinkin' Budweiser 'n Crown 'n Cokes. It was past three in the morning, and my cousin Johnny K and I were talking' grammar-school football at the end of the bar. I played on Christ the King's '95 S.W.C. championship football team and he played on the '94 winning team. Pictures of both our teams rested soundly in a glass display case at Christ the King on the middle shelf. On the top shelf there's a picture of the Pope with a stern-jealous expression written all over his face. Then there's a picture of Mother Mary holding a dead Jesus. Between those pictures is a photograph of the greatest grammar-school football player ever to play the game. I was losing the argument, because we had one loss to our record, a two-point defeat to Saint Michael's, who we later beat in the championship game and I sucked down another Crown 'n Coke in anger, because I remember how Mike Scrobouten didn't block on the extra point, destroying our perfect season, and it still kills me to this day. We started talkin' louder and louder until Harrigan, the owner of the joint, walked over towards us. He was drunker than a hundred Black Hills Indians on relief check handout day and slurred his words.

"Maaan . . . I seen both yur teams play, 'n you guys weren't no nothin' compared to that '85 team." He swayed back and forth as he spoke, like grass blades under a circular wind that managed to maintain balance when it seemed almost impossible. "It was dat October aftanoon, and the sky was one big fuckin' cloud that stretched as far as the eye could see. It was windy and had drizzled lightly, but the night before it poured down angrily and da field was better than a virgin's pussy on prom night. Every goddamn person on the South Side was there, from Bridgeport to Beverly, from Midway to South Shore. Everyone came to see to see Touchdown Tommy, ya know; some thought he was washed up, came to see a dying legend, 'n others, well, the true believers came to see an artist."

"So, how was it—the game?" I asked.

Butch looked into my eye as if he had just caught me taking a shit on his living-room carpet, and kind of leaned a little too close, a drunken close-talk that makes you agree with whatever the person says as the whiskey-whispers hit you like train smoke.

"He scored eleven touchdowns dat game, eleven goddamn touchdowns, my friend."

"No shit, Butch, everybody knows that. I learned that shit before the Lord's Prayer, but I want to know about the *game*, I want to know more about his performance," said Johnny K.

"I just said, are ya deaf? I just told ya."

Butch looked confused. He looked confused and irritated and drunk. He looked incapable of recapturing a memory of five minutes ago, let alone a memory that happened almost twenty years ago as he sipped away at whiskey 'n water, spilling a generous amount on the collar of his shirt.

"How bout some detail?" I begged, "No one ever talks about the performance, just that he scored eleven touchdowns, 'n everyone was so busy watchin' the game nobody bothered to videotape it."

"Details, details, ya fuckin' kids, dat's all ya want is yer little details. Ya gotta understand der's just things that go beyond explainability. Moments like those just can't be put into words or prose, they remain indescribable, moments that are only meant for those who bore witness, who become a spectator to a breathing god in shoulder pads. I can describe the moment all my kids were born, all goddamn eleven of them, and I had eleven as a tribute to Touchdown Tommy, as a way to show my appreciation, and I can describe the moment I first fell in love (with a '57 Chevy), and how I felt when all the kids were born, but an event of dat magnitude, of an eleven-touchdown game, God couldn't even explain."

I handed Butch a cocktail napkin because his eyes started to mist up in the corners as he remembered that day, and he handed it back to me because my eyes started to mist up because I hadn't been there, and then we kind of stood in silence among the barroom whispers and whiskey mirages that encompassed our thoughts, wrapped around them like a noose, strangling our perspectives and angles until Johnny K broke the silence that wasn't at all awkward, like a moment of silence to remember, to pay somewhat of a respect for no other reason than we were drunk at three o'clock in the morning and feeling awfully sentimental, that sentimentality that only lasts a few seconds and sometimes leaves you with a terrible sense of embarrassment the next morning. But we knew this couldn't occur; we knew that there are sentimentalities that are as hard as concrete, as ever-present a fixture as the sun, the stars, and the moon.

And Johnny K spoke, "So, where is he now, ol' Touchdown Tommy?"

"Usually washin' dishes in the back," responded Butch.

Me and Johnny K laughed at the anecdote 'n sucked down Budweiser's 'n Crown 'n Cokes, until Butch's wife came 'n closed down the bar.

Her Birthday

Frank Crist

THE DREAM LAST NIGHT INVOLVED A CAR. IT WAS SOME KIND OF BIG, OLD CAR—perhaps the Cadillac that I just got from my grandparents—definitely a grand-parent's kind of car, which was filled with, no surprise here, my grandparents. It wasn't always the same set of grandparents—at times it seemed like there were seven or eight people in the car at once—and whoever was speaking would most often be female, changing from Anita, to Lucille, to Mardel, to Irene. They were yelling at me because we were lost in some nebulous ghetto of Chicago, boxed in by a parade. We were trying to go to lunch, but everywhere we went, the streets were cordoned off by the parade. Blocked and buggered at every turn. Ah, yes, the car was a sort of burgundy color. So, instead of just sitting there and watching the parade like we probably should have, I kept turning down side streets, which turned into alleys, which turned into dirt roads. These, in turn, would turn into dead ends, or paths through people's yards with great gaping holes in them, or piles of rubble and debris that were impassable.

Somehow I kept managing to go. Out of Humboldt Park and into Wicker Park, but it wasn't easy. I would drive down embankments, around roving tribes of gang-bangers; I think at one point I even drove through a restaurant, carefully steering around white-tableclothed tables laden with fine wineglasses and silverware and white napkins. That was ironic since we were trying to find a restaurant, but that didn't occur to me then.

None of this phased me, however. I wasn't in any sort of a panic, rather a calm, collected kind of confidence. There was grumbling from the grandfolks all around me, all worried and bothered that we were driving through someone's yard, or a nasty alley, or a condo construction site where we'd crawl down one wall into the still-exposed basement foundation, and somehow make it up the other side, even though it was at least four feet high, and go about our merry way. I was the foil to their worry, telling them that everything was OK, and that they should just sit back and relax, I'll get them to their lunch, no problem, and it'll be good too, with tortellini and ragout and spaghetti and nice, warm bread, covered in salty butter, and this stopped their grumbling after a bit, but there would always be another obstacle, something else to maneuver around, or above, or below, never ceasing, and every time we would get close to getting back onto a legitimate street where we could drive around like a real car full of real people, there would be that damned parade, always that damned parade.

Slowly, as with all dreams, this one fizzled out, and my closed eyes became aware of breathing that wasn't mine. My hands found warm flesh that didn't belong to my body, and my penis realized that it was pressed up into the warm buttocks of the birthday girl. Ah, the birthday girl, I thought, in that moment when wakefulness and dreaminess collide. What a mess, that birthday girl. It was her big one—twenty-one-years-old against all expectations—and she'd spent the night with her head in a bucket. I congratulated myself for that one, feeling responsible, and rightly taking responsibility, for showing her such a good time. You can't have a twenty-first birthday without ending up with your head in a bucket in the middle of the night, rather, all night long. That's the routine: you go out, have drinks, people buy you drinks, the bartender makes you fancy drinks for free, you have some laughs, you realize that you're finally sitting at the bar that's been long denied to your curious self; you close down the bar thinking, *I'm finally legitimately drunk*, you stumble all the way home, laughing your head off, kicking all the light poles because they just voted for Bush and got him re-elected, and as soon as you get back to your date's house, you fall to the ground, delirious, maniacal, cackling, and wasted, and I watch, and I know that this is the calm before the storm, the whirling wind of the hurricane, and I can see it in your face, and I try to make you eat a berry-berry Danish to take a little of the edge off, to get something into your stomach, otherwise I know you'll dry-heave all night long.

And it comes, the big vomitous night. Hurl. Retch. Spit spit spit. The prolonged regurgitation of nothing left. Have a drink of water. Sip. One more. Sip. And out it comes as quickly as it went in. Drink more. Always drinking. Always retching it back up. Because it's your goddamned twenty-first birthday, and even though you're drunk as shit, a hare's hair away from the dry heaves, you're having a good goddamned time, because now you know that you can go out and do this every night for the rest of your adult life if you so choose. Twenty-one. The wait is over.

I opened my eyes and saw that she hadn't moved an inch after about ten hours of comatose sleep. She was a dead lump of girl meat, still shimmering with alcohol fumes like spilled gas on a black car in the middle of August. I was a bit sweaty and I realized it was because I had been absorbing these fumes from her all night long. Absorbing them and having drunken-driving dreams with the grandmothers. I was a little drunk the night before, not too terribly so, and when I realized that she was too trashed to make a choice about which birthday present option she wanted, I undressed myself and crawled into bed with her, taking pity on her state, which was also a bit volatile since every time I rubbed up against her to give her at least some kind of birthday fuck, her head would insert itself directly into the bucket next to the bed, and another paper towel would be torn from the roll and clumsily applied to an errant bit of berry-berry Danish that had found its way into a nostril or onto her neck. I took pity on her and just let her sleep it off, and when I closed my own eyes, I didn't think I was drunk at all, but I started getting a little dizzy. It was just one trip around the world, then I was fine, but I thought for a second that we'd have to be two heads in the bucket, as if encouraging each other, goading each other, two racers competing for the finish line of dark, sweet, catatonic oblivion, where the body simply gives up on the mind and sets about the difficult chore of grinding up all the poison we'd spent all night ingesting, cursing ourselves all the while and promising the dark and clouded mind that it would suffer in the morning with a flaming case of alcoholic diarrhea. Thanks, our bodies would say to us, thanks a lot, you drunken assholes, now your emotions will suffer the pain of your over-toxified livers. Your bodies will die, but not without putting you in a bad mood first.

Her choice for her birthday present was simple, if unsuccessful. I gave it to her while she was on the floor in a fit of spastic laughter, before she started saying, "I'm so dizzy," as though it was a mantra. She lay on her back and I squatted over her, my hands on my knees, my head resting on my arms, staring into her eyes with a devilish grin. "I'm going to give you your choice because it's your birthday," I said, which made her immediately apprehensive, which was exactly what I wanted her to feel. She was my toy. She had given herself to me, pledging me her very life, and it was mine to do with as I pleased, which I always did. But, since it was her birthday and all, I wanted to give her a choice, which was not so much an empowerment as it was another subtle form of torture for a drunk, drunk girl. What choice? she asked with wide eyes. You can either sleep with my cock inside of you all night long, I said, hard and stiff, filling you inside, not fucking, but feeling me deep inside of you all night long, coloring your dreams with passion and ecstasy. I let it hang there. I'd offered this up to her before, and she'd swooned at just the thought of such a thing. I let her have sex with me without a condom on the condition that she never ever let another unsheathed penis enter her, and she always did as I instructed. Her eyes rolled in her head and she hummed and moaned thinking about her first option.

Or, I continued, leaning into her a little, piercing her with my eyes, and having the satisfaction of knowing that I had her, and that she would do what I wanted, now and forever, that she was mine and mine alone, and even though I let her fuck other people, her heart and soul and body truly belonged to me, for my pleasure, for my satisfaction, willingly and forever. Or, I said, I will beat you all night long, and you can scream as loud as you want, but you'll wake up tomorrow with fat, purple lash marks all over your body. She was excited by the first option, but this put her over the top, and she groaned at the conundrum of what to choose, what to choose. She giggled and grabbed at her breasts, arching her back a bit, rolling her eyes, imagining what a night under my belt would be like, a pleasure thus far denied to her, knowing how savage I would be with her, finding that line where the pleasure of the lash becomes pain, riding it, staying right on it, and then going way, way beyond it, giving her a real nightmare, a situation of real torture, of real terror, and letting her scream and scream until she finally just gave up and took it. That was the look in her eyes.

Oh my god, she said, why do I have to choose? Can't we do both? No, I said to her. You can choose either a night of continual pleasure, or a night of continual torture. Since it's your birthday, I'll let you decide. She giggled nervously, still pulling at her breasts through her shirt in a kind of unconscious way, torn in her decision, and seemed about ready to talk it out with herself, as though speaking her options aloud would help her decide, but I cut her short. I'm going to smoke a cigarette, I said, running a finger delicately down the bridge of her nose, watching her eyes close, absorbing every moment of the simple contact, and after I smoke this cigarette, you're going to tell me what you've decided. I rose up off her, sat in the chair next to my desk, and rolled a cigarette.

Of course, none of either came to pass. Halfway through the smoke, that Satanic chant of, I'm so dizzy, or, I'm feeling dizzy, or worse yet, I'm feeling really dizzy, and finally, I need to go to the bathroom right now, and guiding her past the piles of dirty laundry—you don't want to pass out in those clothes, I said, they're pretty disgusting—and raising the lid to the toilet, and instructing her that under no circumstances was she to make a mess in my bathroom, just to make sure that she keeps her head firmly within the bowl, and getting a glass of water to prevent the dry heaves, and watching chunks of Danish eject, all yellowy and purplish from the berry-berry, and popping the question to her one more time—You can't pass out on me to avoid the question—and knowing that was exactly how this night was about to go, and more dry heaves and drinks of water, and still I was pretty amused, because, hell, it was her twenty-first birthday, and I'd feel pretty sore if she wasn't vomiting her guts up all night long anyway. She deserved it. It was her birthday.

Carrie and Jenna

Nicki Brouillette

THE EXPECTATION WAS SEX, LIKE THE SUMMER WOULD REFUSE TO END UNLESS our virginity was lost. In less than a week, Jenna and I would be freshmen, Chris would be shipped off to the boy's military academy downstate, and Mikey would spend every free waking moment at varsity football practice. I'd wound up with Chris by default. Chris was Mikey's best friend and Mikey was Jenna's boyfriend and I was her best friend and so somehow it made sense to draw the final line and match up a corner and make a neat little square. Except that Chris was not my type in the least. Not that I had a type back then, really, but if I had, Chris certainly would not have been it.

"So are you nervous?" Jenna asked on the big day.

I was lying sideways on Jenna's bed, flipping through a magazine while she stood in front of the dresser mirror experimenting with different shades of her sister's makeup. Jenna had the kind of face that didn't need coloring, really. Her olive skin darkened above her eyes and her lashes were naturally thick, black, and long. She wasn't too tall like I was, and as her sister Angie put it, she had started to fill out. What wasn't filled, Jenna stuffed.

"About what?"

"Carrie, you know, about tonight. Like, do you think it'll hurt?"

"Why would it? It's not like they're fully grown men."

I left out the part about us not really being fully grown women either, because Jenna only would've argued. She would've pointed to the things strewn about the bedroom she and her sister shared: from the selection of various sized curling irons whose cords twisted over the vanity to the perfume bottles resting in the mirrored tray, to the high-heeled shoes lining the carpeted floor of the closet, to the lacy, stringed underwear busting out of the drawers, and she would have claimed these things as evidence. She might've even dragged me by the arm into the bathroom and shoved a box of tampons in my face to give me the concrete biological proof of our womanhood. And then I would've had to remind her of how, at the beginning of the summer, I had helped her pack all her fluffy stuffed animals and frilly curtains into tightly sealed boxes, how I took down all those posters of puppies and kittens and helped her paint the pink walls a moody gray. And then she would say something about how that was only the start of our transformation and now it was time to complete the process, to *blossom*, or *become butterflies,* or some shit that she would've picked up in one of those girly teenybopper magazines secretly designed to get guys laid. I knew this because we'd gone through it all before.

"Carrie, men are fully grown as soon as they're done with puberty. That's, like, a fact. I read it."

I did not doubt that she had read it, because all summer long Jenna had been taking little preparatory trips down to the library and checking out books on anatomy, the Kama Sutra, and anything written by Henry Miller. The librarians never batted an eye because Jenna was, by all accounts, the town slut's kid sister.

"Whatever." I looked up from the magazine. "Hey, don't you think Chris kind of looks like a scarecrow?"

"My god, Carrie! You are sooooo picky. Personally, I think you guys are cute together."

I was not being picky. Chris's blue eyes bulged from his head, not in that cute boyish way, but more like there was something wrong, something genetic or like his mother had drunk too many bottles of cheap wine when he was in her womb. There wasn't anyone around who could confirm this, though, because his dad had disappeared when he was still a little kid, maybe with another woman, maybe to prison—no one really knew—and his mom had dropped him off at his uncle's house one day and hadn't ever come back. It was sad in a way, and sure, I felt bad for him, bad enough to let the guy put his arm around me. Nowhere near bad enough for sex.

"Are you kidding me? Have you seen the guy without his shirt on? His chest looks like, like one of those metal grates that cover up the sewers."

"Wait a second," she snapped. She spun around, dove at the bed, tore the magazine from my hands, and lunged right in my face. "You're not chickening out on me, are you?"

"No," I lied.

"Because you can't, you know. We made a deal. You don't want to go to high school and be one of those girls that nobody'll ask to prom or homecoming, do you? Because that's what'll happen. Look at all the boyfriends Angie has. Look at all the flowers she gets. She'll get to marry whoever she wants."

"Carrie, everybody thinks your sister's a slut."

"They do not. Only girls think that. All the guys adore her. And it's not like you and me are friends with other girls anyway, so we have nothing to lose."

"It's not nothing. We're losing our . . ."

She clasped her palm over my mouth. "Don't say that word. You know I hate that word. We're becoming women. I mean, unless you don't want to, unless you'd rather be one of those girls who carry those folders with the pink unicorns on the covers and wear the T-shirts with the little hearts and flowers that they paint on themselves."

I put my palms on her shoulders and gently shoved her off me. "I have *never* been one of those girls."

"OK, OK. You're right. You haven't." She sat down beside me and twirled the frayed end of my pigtail. "It's just, you know, we've been best friends forever and I thought this was something we could do together."

"I'm not having sex with you if that's what you mean."

"Carrie!" She popped up and went back to the mirror. "My sister was fourteen when she did it." Her voice softened. "And anyway, Mikey's in love with me. It's like in Health class how they're always saying we need to abstain until we find that special person, well, Mikey's it. He's the one."

Mikey was the only reason I went along with it, or the talk of the big IT. Jenna had had a crush on Mikey ever since she spotted his grainy black-and-white photo in her older sister's yearbook. He had a wide grin, a patch of coarse fuzz on his chin, and a stiffly gelled hairdo that reminded me of the plastic pompadour on my old Ken doll. Mikey also came with a car, this rusted-out Trans Am that you could hear coming from miles away. Unlike anyone else Jenna and I knew, Mikey lived in this thing called a subdivision that had a fancy name and everything—Oakwood Estates or some crap like that—and I think that car and that big two-story house were at least half the reason Jenna wanted him so bad. Like she thought that having him on her arm would make up for her dumpy prefab house and the fact that every librarian, teacher, and mechanic could name five guys that Angie had slept with, like she could walk down the main road toting a fancy football player and just forget what she was.

Which is why I was really getting gypped in the whole damn deal. Chris was just another reminder of what I was: the girl who would always get the leftovers.

"Yeah, well, Chris sure as hell ain't *the one*."

"Listen to me, Carrie, he told me he loved me." I looked up at her dark eyes through the mirror. They were glassy and, at the same time, utterly grave. Her mouth remained a flat line.

Love can be a powerful word for a girl, a word like some hallucinogenic drug or a loaded gun—hell, it can be like that for a grown woman. But for Jenna and me, it was even more than that. We used to joke about how if we took her psychotic mom, set her up with my drunk of a dad, then each cut off a side of our dinky houses and pushed them together, we might be able to fake like a normal family.

I knew whatever Mikey told her when they were alone was bullshit. But I couldn't say it. I was her only friend and if I made those tears overflow and stream down her cheeks, Jenna wouldn't have anyone left. And for that matter, neither would I. All I said was, "Consider yourself lucky that the hot one fell for you and you're not stuck with the scarecrow."

"He's not *that* bad."

"Why does it have to be tonight, anyway? There's still like a week before school starts."

"I told you already," she whined. "This is our last opportunity. My mom is going to that wedding or whatever, so if she comes home at all she'll be, like, way drunk, and nobody's ever home at Chris's house so you guys can stay there and everything'll be perfect."

"Yeah, nobody'll be there except . . ."

"Except for who? Oh, my god. Ray? Are you serious? He'll be so stoned out of his mind that he won't notice anything."

"It's still gross." Ray was Chris's cousin. I didn't know how old he was exactly—some days he claimed to be thirty, others sixteen. He was out of school, more likely a dropout than anything else, and if he had any sort of job at all it was to coerce Chris into doing stupid things—smoke maple leaves, burn off his arm hair, eat catnip—in which case his only income was amusement. "And anyway," I told her, "Ray totally creeps me out."

"How is that possible? He's just some loser," she said, pulling up her long brown hair.

"Yeah, well, every time I go outside or into the sunroom, he's sitting there in that same stupid lawn chair with barely any clothes on and he, like, stares at me with his little slit eyes."

"That's just the way his eyes are, Carrie. He's a pothead. It's not, like, he can help it. Besides, if it weren't for him, who would buy us booze?"

She went to her sister's side of the closet and pulled out two skimpy shirts. "Which one?" She held up a low-cut mesh red tank top and then a black sheer scoop-necked shirt.

"Um, if you're gonna wear the white pants, I'd go with the red. Black is so wintery." Sometimes I could not believe the shit that came out of my mouth. Jenna's brainwashing had taken full effect.

I buried my face in the magazine as she changed and finished her make-up. She sprayed on so much perfume that it seemed to suck all the oxygen out of the room, and I had to scoot up real straight to try and get my nose above the sharp scent of flowers. My eyes began to redden and water.

"How do I look?" Jenna asked, twirling around.

Honestly, she looked like crap. The fabric of her sister's shirt hung droopily over her shoulders and sagged at the neckline, bunching into these awkward folds in the area where the shirt was used to containing two full-sized breasts. She'd smudged black lines around her eyes and blotted hot pink lipstick over her mouth so that her face looked like some over-exposed photograph, all eyes and mouth. I did not point these things out, though. Jenna was my best friend so I only sneezed, forced a smile, and said, "You look great."

"I do, don't I?" she agreed, spinning back toward the mirror. "You know, I bet I could pass for at least sixteen. Aren't you going to get ready?"

I tossed the magazine aside and sat up to look at my reflection in the mirror. My dirty blond hair was braided into the same stiff pigtails I'd worn since first grade. Where my face wasn't sunburned, it was spotted with tiny freckles. I gazed down at my clothes, at my violet ribbed tank top, my fading jean shorts, then at my pale, razor-nicked legs. Uncertainly, I replied, "I am ready."

"Oh, OK . . . Hey, do you want to borrow one of Angie's push-up bras? If you leave it on, he'll never know the difference."

"No, thanks."

Jenna stuck her index finger between her teeth and sucked in some air, as if this action aided her thinking process. She snatched a wand of mascara and jumped onto the bed. I winced and leaned away. "Come on, just a little," she said, unscrewing the cap. "Carrie, hold still."

She brushed my lashes a few times and leaned back, tilting her head and looking at my face like it was her canvas. Her mouth shifted from side to side in concentration. She went back to the dresser. "Jenna, that's more than enough. I don't like stuff on my face."

"One more thing." She smoothed back the loose strands of my hair that were forever dangling in my face and pinned them in tiny plastic bow-shaped barrettes. "Now you can see your eyes."

I had to admit, I looked better, sort of. My clumpy eyelashes felt heavy now, like the lids of those dolls that open and close depending on which way you turn them. I practiced blinking in the mirror, but stopped myself when Jenna noticed. Who the hell was I trying to impress, anyway? It's not like I was actually going through with any of this.

"You ready to go? It's getting dark already," Jenna said, slinging her purse over her shoulder. Why she needed a purse to walk across the alley to Chris's house, I did not know, but I rose, shrugged, and followed her out the door.

Outside, the idea of sex was everywhere. It was suspended in the thick, moist August air, and it clung to our skin as we passed through it. It was hidden in the shape of our houses, in the prism-like frames and added-on tin roofs and screened-in porches that faced into one another like pursed lips stretching toward each other to kiss. It was in Jenna's walk, in the way she thrust her hips from side to side as she staggered in her platform sandals across the uneven gravel of the alley. And the setting sun was like a timer counting down to the main event. There was no escape.

Halfway across the alley, I turned my head back. I could see the lights still glowing in Jenna's house and in my own next door, and I couldn't help but wonder why we were heading into the darkness of Chris's house so eagerly.

Jenna pulled open the door of the sunroom, though it wasn't a sunroom really. It was a bunch of mesh screens framed by flimsy steel and attached to the vinyl siding at the back of the house, but we tried to make it sound more luxurious. We tried to make ourselves feel like we were worthy of a fancy name like Oakwood Estates, too. From the looks of it, though, you could see right away that we weren't. The muddy clay ground had been covered by prickly green Astroturf, and because there was just one utility outlet on the back of the house, the only source of light was the neon blue tube in the center of the caged metal bug-zapper. The windows above the kitchen sink faced into the sunroom, and out of them dangled wires that snaked across the ground into the far corners of the room where two box speakers sat. The ends of the wires were all stripped and frayed from people tripping over them, and the sound from the stereo inside constantly faded in and out. The tops of the speakers were littered with half-drunk soda cans that had been forced to serve as ashtrays and bongs. The only seat in the so-called room was a single metal lawn chair cushioned by alternating orange and red plastic strings that remained under the bug-zapper, and in which Ray was a permanent fixture.

Because Ray was forever shirtless, I often imagined that if he one day left the chair, his back would not only show the indentations of those wide plastic strings, but it would be striped orange and red too, like some drunkenly acquired joke of a tattoo. Ray didn't look up when the rusty hinges of the door creaked open, but I could see him squint his glazed eyes like he was trying to decide whether the noise came from inside his head or the outside world. Finally, he pitched his head backward, his wavy, chin-length hair fluttering back behind his ears, and grinned maniacally. Ray's face resembled Chris's in certain ways. He had the same gaunt cheeks and pointy sliver of a nose. His lips were plump and swollen, like someone had quite recently smashed their fist into his mouth, but when he grinned, those lips stretched up from cheek to cheek, showing all his jagged little teeth. Unlike Chris, Ray had stubble that sprouted up in patches covering the bottom half of his face like a muzzle.

Jenna crouched down in front of Ray the way people do when addressing small children. "Are Chris and Mikey here?"

He smacked his loose lips together like an old man without teeth. "Mikey? Ohhh, riiight. Mikey, Mikey, Mikey. No, dude, not here. Chris is inside, though. Yep, inside the house." He nodded and then waved his hand through the air like he was presenting a prize. "Take a seat. He'll be out in a minute."

Jenna sat in the corner that faced into the alley, and I plopped down on the floor beside her, squeezed so close that our knees were touching.

The speakers faded in and out. Ray contemplated the crackle of the bug-zapper over his head and lit a joint. Jenna clucked her tongue against the roof of her mouth. I tugged the bottoms of my shorts over my thighs and heard bottles clinking together. Awkwardly, Chris emerged from the house.

He bent over, held the door open with one foot, cradled a myriad of cough-syrup-sized bottles of schnapps in one arm, and dragged a case of beer along the floor behind him. The case went thumping down the two stairs, and the door sprung shut. Sadly, when Chris stood upright I could almost see why Jenna would say we looked cute together. He was tall and pale and lanky, and so was I. He was shirtless, showing off his sewer-grate chest, and his long nylon shorts slipped down past his waist so that you could see the lines under his hips pointing down like arrows to that region where I vowed never to go. He'd been lifting weights ever since he started hanging out with Mikey, but it hadn't done any good. Mikey had that kind of thick muscle that made it look like there were small animals clinging to his biceps and shoulders. Chris had nothing but bones.

"Refreshments," Ray uttered, "cool."

Without looking at either Jenna or me, Chris tore into the cardboard case and passed Ray a warm beer. He walked up to us and held out two bottles of schnapps. We grabbed them, and immediately, Jenna ordered, "Trade me. Mikey likes it better when I smell like peaches."

Chris cracked open a can of beer and struck a pose as he sipped, thrusting his hand onto his hip and tipping his head way back. He tapped his foot and gulped as if he was counting out the seconds to ensure that he took a manly enough drink. After he'd wiped his mouth with the back of his hand, he gazed down at the empty strip of Astroturf between the door and me and took a step forward. I crossed my legs Indian-style so that my right knee stretched all the way to the doorframe. Defeated, he moved back and slumped down on the step beside Ray's chair.

With Chris and Ray side by side, I could see the difference in their eyes. Chris's eyes, though they repulsed me in their own way, maintained their innocent blue and, because of their largeness, seemed to roll over everything he looked upon as though longing, but unable, to touch it. Ray's, on the other hand, were squinty and black. They were all pupils, like two black holes that would suck up everything he saw, warp it in his mind, and send it back and out in the form of the tiny red veins that clawed across the glossy whites of his eyes. I avoided looking directly at Ray the way you avoid looking directly into the sun, for fear that he would take me in and I would be forever lost.

Ray took a long hit from the joint and slouched back in his chair, opening his eyes wide. "That's riiight. Tonight's the big night, eh? Now remember, kids, you have to use protection," he cackled

Chris's big eyes widened, and he elbowed Ray's leg. As Jenna struggled to twist the cap off her bottle, she said, "We aren't kids, Ray."

Somehow, it didn't faze her that Ray knew that we were all silently scheduled to have sex. I wrapped my arms around my waist, but quickly let them drop. If anyone should have to know, it might as well have been Ray. He didn't talk to people, and no one bothered with him. His world ended at those mesh screens.

"Aren't you a feisty one? Good for you, cous. Good for you."

"Excuse me, but I happen to be *Mikey's* girlfriend."

"Mikey? Oh, yeah. Muscle-head." He turned to Chris. "No worries, dude. You're better off with the quiet one. Quiet chicks are wiiiild."

"I'm wild," Jenna pouted, giving up on the bottle and handing it to me.

"No offense, kiddo, but you're all talk. I've known…"

"I am not all talk. You just ask Mikey how much talking we do."

Ray had stopped listening, his attention drawn to the noise of an engine sputtering and gravel spitting away from tires. Chris kept taking quick little sips of his beer. A few moments later, Mikey's black Trans Am squealed to a stop in front of the sunroom in the alley. He got out, slammed the door, and checked the handle to make sure it was locked. Jenna's bouncing leg kept knocking into mine. Mikey swatted away a swarm of gnats that flew above his head and came through the door twirling his car keys around his index finger. He heaved a heavy sigh meant to indicate that he'd had a rough day, a rough day in the life of a varsity football star with a daddy-bought Trans Am. I didn't buy it.

"Hey, Mikey." Chris finally spoke, rushing to hand him a beer.

"'Sup, dude?" Mikey extended his fist and the guys slammed their knuckles together.

Jenna swooned upward, thrust her hands into her back pockets, and stayed posed that way until Mikey noticed her.

"Babe," he said, slinking his free hand around her waist and pulling her close. He cocked his head so far to the side that it was parallel with the horizon and dove for her lips. Their heads swiveled back and forth for a few seconds too long, and when they broke apart, Mikey looked around at the rest of us like we should all be jealous.

"I missed you," Jenna cooed, running her fingertips over his chest.

He gazed over her head and stepped around her toward Ray. "Did you get the shit?"

"Not shit, my friend. Mar-i-juan-a. Narcotics, man. Here." He tossed a plastic baggy containing seven or eight joints in the air and Mikey caught it in the crook of his arm, pulling it gently to his side like a football.

"How much?"

"I don't know. Fifty?"

"Fifty bucks? Are you shitting me?"

"I do not shit you, man. Not you."

"Dude, I'm Chris's best friend. Why you wanna play me?"

"It breaks down like this. There's the, uh, rolling fee, 'cause I know your thick fingers can't roll no beauties like that. And then there's what I like to call the pretty-boy surcharge. But if you've got some other source, if one of your *other* white-trash friends has a sweet hook-up, then I'll take 'em back, smoke 'em myself, no questions asked."

"You can borrow money from me," Jenna offered.

Mikey sighed again and dug into his pocket. He peeled a fifty off a little wad of bills and flicked it in the air. The bill fluttered down, landing at Ray's feet.

Ray stared at it for a second before saying, "Dude, I'm hurt, I really am. Chris, grab that for me, would ya, buddy?"

Obediently, Chris popped off the step and retrieved the cash. While he was up, Mikey took his seat and Jenna sat down on the stair below him, nestling her body between his spread legs. She pitched her head backwards and looked at him upside-down. "Did you miss me?"

"Yeah, babe, of course I did. You know, I mean, I haven't seen you since, since what? Yesterday?"

Jenna smiled and curled her arms around his leg, resting her cheek on his knee. "I know. Exactly. That's so long."

At that, I cracked open one of the bottles and downed a big gulp. Chris inched over to Jenna's former spot and eased down onto the floor. I looked at him sideways. "You smell like beer."

His bony shoulders folded into his chest. "Sorry." He slid his empty can onto the speaker and hesitantly reached for the bottle of peach schnapps. I quickly thrust it into his hand so he couldn't accidentally brush my leg, and then I scooted to the edge of the doorframe.

"So aren't you guys excited about school starting?" Jenna squeaked.

"I'm ready for football. We're *so* going to State this year."

"I'm not going to school," Chris sulked.

"Well, it's a kind of school. You'll still have classes and stuff."

Ray chuckled. "Oh, yeah, and my little cous here just loves to learn, 'specially when it's with a bunch of dudes. Better make tonight count. It's gotta be good enough to jerk off to while you're all cooped up."

"Shut up, man."

"It's not going to be that bad," Jenna explained. "At least it'll be real easy to stay faithful to the people who really matter."

Chris glanced at me and I snapped my head toward the alley.

"Now, me, on the other hand," she continued, "I'm gonna have to join the cheerleading squad just to chase all those other girls away."

Mikey nearly choked on his beer. He coughed a few times and said, "Don't you trust me?"

"It's the girls I don't trust."

He wrapped his arms around her stomach and kissed the top of her head. "You ain't got nothing to worry about, babe. Cute little freshman like you."

"What's that supposed to mean?"

"Jenna, baby, where's your drink? Chris, pass me some of that peach shit." Chris crawled across the floor and handed Mikey an unopened bottle. With ease, Mikey twisted off the cap. "See how I take care of you?"

"Carrie's gonna try out for cheerleading, too, aren't you? Carrie and I do everything together."

"Everything," Ray drawled, leaning forward.

I took another sip. "I don't know. I'm not sure if it's really my thing."

I could see the fear bolt through Jenna's eyes, and she indignantly arched her back. "We had an agreement."

"What the hell are you talking about? You never mentioned cheerleading."

"Whoa, chicks getting heavy."

"Carrie, you *know* what I mean." She put her palms on her knees like she was ready to spring forward.

"I do not. You're flipping out!"

"She's right, babe. Chill, OK? This is no time for fighting." Mikey tilted his head and planted little kisses all over her neck. "Chris, maybe you should go put some mellow music on."

He glanced over at me like a puppy looking for approval and I agreed. "Yeah, go."

Mikey went on whispering in Jenna's ear or blowing in it or slobbering in it or whatever the hell he was doing, and I tried to keep my eyes down. If I looked up I would've seen Ray staring through me in a trance. The way he stared actually made me hope Chris would hurry. He breathed in and out heavily, puffing his chest out and arching his back as though there was a doctor pressing a cold metal stethoscope to his skin and coaching, *Inhale, and again, and again*. He ran his fingers through his swirls of chest hair down to his leg hair and the wiry strands on his toes. It was like watching someone have foreplay with himself.

I took many quick swigs from my bottle before Chris returned. Coming through the doorway, he stepped on Mikey's hand, but Mikey didn't call out. He simply slipped his hand into the space between the bottom of Jenna's shirt and the top of her pants. Chris sat back down, his leg touching mine, and I glared at him until he scooted back into the corner. I continued drinking my schnapps, and he opened another beer for himself.

"So," he tried, "how's things?" His voice was flat, not deep like a man's but not as squeaky as a boy's either. It came out restrained, traveled in a straight line, and dispersed before the last syllable sounded.

"Fine."

"Cool. So . . . are you ready to go back to school?"

"Not really." I raised my eyebrows, turned my head, and drained down the rest of the schnapps.

"Um, this music OK?" The speakers faded out.

"It's fine, kind of old, though."

"This is classic shit—stuff, I mean."

"You can curse, you know. I don't care. It's not like I'm some fucking little Catholic schoolgirl."

"Schoolgiiiirls," Ray drew out, grinning that ear-to-ear, putty-lipped grin.

Chris inched closer and I inched away, maintaining a grip of Astroturf the width of my leg between us. "Should I change it?" he asked once the speakers faded back in.

"Don't. It's fine."

Jenna giggled and slapped Mikey's arm. I watched him hold the bottle of schnapps up to her lips as the tips of his fingers crept under the top of her pants. As I took a swig, Ray nodded and Chris smashed his lips into my cheek. The bottle clinked against my teeth and liquid dribbled out of my mouth. I shot Chris a squinty-eyed glare, but he had already recoiled into his spot.

I had kissed Chris, like a real kiss, only once before, drunk on malt liquor in the dark. It wasn't entirely repulsive. His lips were soft and he let his mouth stay sort of slack instead of puckering so stiffly and pressing so hard that you feel like your teeth might buckle inward the way most boys do, or at least the one other boy that I'd kissed. The best part, if you could call it that, had been the part right before the actual kiss when we were just about nose-to-nose and his warm breath hit my face. I gasped in that instant as though trying to gulp up all his air. I liked that feeling.

"I saw your dad the other day," he told me.

"Oh, yeah?"

"He didn't look too good. It was at the convenience store. He got his car stuck up on the curb somehow . . ." I could feel more heat rushing into my sunburned cheeks. "And he was like, yelling at some guy 'cause he thought the guy swiped his cigarettes . . ."

"Where's your dad again, Chris? I forgot," I snapped.

"Probably dead," he listlessly replied. "How about your ma?"

"She's dead."

The sun was gone. Mikey had gotten Jenna's shirt tugged up so that her tanned belly was all exposed. The bug-zapper continued to sizzle and snap above Ray's head, and every once in a while the noise would command his full attention for minutes at a time. Chris slid closer.

"Are you drinking beer again? It smells."

"Sorry."

I passed him the schnapps. "We can share."

"I've gotta go to the ladies room," Jenna said, standing up. "Carrie? You coming?"

I pushed myself to my feet. We never actually went inside Chris's house, but I never knew if it was because we didn't want to or because we weren't allowed. I imagined it was the kind of house where you deliberately left your shoes on and maybe even covered your hands in gloves to avoid touching whatever dust or mold or garbage was lying around. Jenna clasped my arm.

"Can I come, too?" Mikey joked.

"You're coming back, right?" Chris worried.

"We'll only be a minute, and you," she winked at Mikey, "will get your turn later."

We walked across the alley in the darkness and went back in Jenna's house. This might seem like a pain in the ass, but when you think about it, it was probably the same distance from the living room to the bathroom in any normal house. I stood with my arms crossed and my head tilted against the bathroom door as Jenna shouted from inside.

"Did you hear him?" she called.

"Hear what?"

"Mikey! He said it again."

"I was trying not to pay attention. What did he say?"

The toilet flushed and she whipped open the door. "He loves me!" She threw her arms around my neck and rested her head on my shoulder. "Carrie, you are like my best friend. I love you—not like I love Mikey, but like my sister. I love you more than my real sister." Her eyes had grown large and lingering.

"We don't have to go back over there, you know."

"What are you talking about, silly? I'm horny. Mikey did the second-base thing like right there."

I did not know what it meant to be horny. I did not know what it meant to do the second-base thing, nor did I want to know. Jenna dragged me back across the alley. When we returned, the guys were all smoking pot and there were clear plastic-wrapped condoms in every color of the rainbow strewn all across the ground.

"Pick a color, ladies," Ray grinned and then added, "Remember, boys, green means go."

"Green," Jenna shrieked, raising her arm up like she was signaling the beginning of a race. She staggered back and caught onto my shoulder for balance.

I uttered, "Red," and Chris dove toward the pile, snatching a red condom. If he puts that on his dick, I thought, I will bite into it like I am trying to get to the center of a cherry Tootsie Pop.

Mikey stood up, pinching a condom between his thumb and index finger. With the joint in his other hand, he swaggered up behind Jenna, wrapped his arm around her neck like he was putting her in a chokehold, and brought his other hand up to her lips, nonchalantly resting his forearm on her chest. "Go on, babe, take a little hit."

I sighed and sat down in my corner. Jenna giggled and swayed, but Mikey had a firm hold on her. I couldn't tell if she was drunk on schnapps or drunk on Mikey and the stupid idea of love. I hoped for her sake it was the former. She took a big pull from the joint, and Chris, standing anxiously behind her, grabbed it from Mikey's hand. Jenna coughed, and Mikey let go of her. He patted her back as she doubled over and melted down to the floor. Chris dashed to my side and handed me the joint as though he were offering me an engagement ring.

I held it like a cigarette, but I didn't take a drag. "You smell . . ."

"Like beer, I know." He nodded and held up a new bottle of peach schnapps. He took a long gulp. "There. Happy?"

"Thanks."

"You gotta smoke it," Ray instructed. "Don't get high if you don't smoke it."

"Ray, you sure this ain't gonna show up if they make the team take a piss test?"

"I told you, man, this shit's like stealthy, undetectable and all that. No worries."

Chris wrinkled his brow. "There's no such . . ."

"Shut up! I said *stealthy*, dude." Ray laughed.

He looked down at me, shook his head, and then something strange happened. Ray slid out of his chair. I wanted to ask him to turn around so that I could see if his back was striped orange and red, but I'd never really spoken directly to him before. He crawled over to my side and sat against the door. I figured he'd been in that chair so long that his legs had atrophied and no longer functioned. I grabbed the bottle and threw my head back for a big sip. I was stuck, sandwiched between the scarecrow and the pothead.

"You've never done this before, have you, kid?" I shook my head. "Well, lucky for you, I am the master. Now first of all, there's no sense letting it all burn away like that. Won't do you any good." Ray's voice took on a soothing melodic quality. "What you gotta do is take a nice, slow drag. Do it slow; otherwise, you'll burn your lips. You gotta get the smoke way down in your lungs and hold it there as long as you can like you're underwater or something. You'll probably want to cough." He pointed at Jenna, whose eyes were still watering from all the hacking. "But you just gotta fight it."

He propped his elbows on his knees and waited. I followed his instructions step by step, holding the smoke for a whole fifteen seconds before I coughed and it went spluttering out of my nose. I gave it a second try.

Ray nodded and went, "Good job. Next time, we'll go over etiquette."

Jenna was on her feet again, sort of. Mikey had her by one arm. "I'll take you to the bathroom," he told her.

She rushed over to me and squatted down. "Carrie! I'm going to the bathroom. This is it!" Her smile was so large that it forced her eyes shut.

"Do you want me to take you?"

"You're so silly." She kissed my cheek. "Good luck! Stop over later, OK? Much later."

She popped up, spun around, and let Mikey latch onto her arm. Ray moved aside and Jenna and Mikey walked out the door. I couldn't see them go, but I heard the sound of Jenna's sandals crunching over the gravel. The crunch seemed to echo inside my body, seemed to be the sound of my very own bones shattering into pieces. My skin felt sensitive, like when you have a fever. I tried to decide whether or not I was high. It took a few seconds, or a few minutes, or it took a while, anyway, but it finally dawned on me that I was alone. Alone and in between Chris and Ray. My best friend was in her moody gray bedroom losing her . . . becoming a woman. My eyelids felt heavy again, not just from the clumpy mascara, but heavy with wisdom. I had to shut out the world and wait for it all to be over.

Chris passed me a bottle and I took a big swig and he scooted closer. I laughed. He was trying to get me drunk so that we could have sex. I gulped another sip, thought, *Fat chance, motherfucker.* Chris's leg was touching my leg, but I didn't bother to move because the only place to go was into Ray's lap. Standing up didn't seem like such a good idea. It seemed like a lot of work. I was trapped by a scarecrow and a pothead and by the darkness. My heart raced, beat against my rib cage like it was trying to escape. I stared at the bug-zapper. The light was blue, blue like the sky and the sea and peace and tranquility. I listened to the singeing of the little bugs' wings.

Chris opened a new bottle and kept shoving it into my hands, and I kept drinking from it automatically because I was thirsty and because that's what you do when there is a bottle of liquor in your fist. No one spoke, but the bottle went from person to person and so did the joint, followed by what I think was a menthol cigarette. Whatever came my way went into my mouth like I was some infant exploring the world. Really, we were like a coordinated assembly line of infants. From time to time, Chris would peck at my cheek and my head would sort of bobble back and forth and Ray would give a big thumbs-up. Once, Chris caught the corner of my mouth with his big, full lips and I scrunched my head into my shoulders. I was about to yell at him, but something about him looked funny so I stopped, and instead, I stared. His skin appeared yellow, and as I watched him it was like the yellow pallor of his face mixed with the neon blue light of the bug-zapper and Chris went green. He stood up quickly and bolted inside the house.

After the door had slammed, Ray called, "You all right there, buddy? Shouldn't mix beer and that syrupy shit."

I moved over to the stair so that I could see Jenna's house. The light was on in her bedroom, but the curtains were drawn closed. I tried to listen for any sounds, for any moaning or the creaking of bedsprings, but I couldn't hear beyond the hum of the bug-zapper. Ray was at my side again. He pulled the rubber band out of my hair and ran his fingers through the thick waves. It felt nice, like warm beads of water trickling down my head.

"You're pretty," he said, like he'd never seen me before. I giggled. "You are. Prettier than the other one. Too bad Chris is sick." He undid the other rubber band, took out the barrettes and fluffed my hair over my shoulders. Absently, he touched his fingers to my lips and just as absently, I kissed them.

My head was swimming. I thought that I should probably move, that I should run out the door and into my house and dive into bed and stretch the covers over my head, but Ray's lips were on mine. Ray, who might have been thirty or might've been sixteen, was kissing me. He had his hand on my chin and his tongue was doing acrobatics in my mouth. He pulled away and I should've fled then, but I pitched forward instead. I swallowed in all the air he'd left behind and then, eyes closed, I found his lips again. He put his palms over my cheeks. I wasn't thinking about who he was or what he looked like. I forgot all about the squinty eyes and jagged little teeth. I focused on the warmth, the warmth of his breath, of his hand as it slid down my neck and cupped my breast. He kissed my cheeks, kissed the fluttering lids of my eyes. He called me smart, called me pretty, told me I'd go places, and it stopped mattering that he was Ray, the aging pothead loser. He wrapped his arms around my waist and pulled me into his lap.

My feet dangled, not quite reaching the floor, and he held me close. I draped my arms around his shoulders and rested my head in the crook of his neck. His hair tickled my nose. I felt myself being lifted up as his lips ran down my neck and I wanted him to carry me far off and away, but he took me only as far as the center of the sunroom. He lowered me down onto the prickly, green Astroturf. Only faintly did I realize what was happening. It was too absurd to be real. It was like some fucked-up dream that I'd sort out in the morning lying half-awake in the safety of my bed.

I felt his hairy chest against my biceps. His body blanketed mine in shadow. I couldn't see the neon light or Jenna's house. He kissed my bare stomach and my shorts seemed looser, felt two sizes too big. Under my back, there was a pile of condoms. His mouth was against my mouth and his shorts were no longer on. His hand slipped into my shorts and then into me and I winced and bit down on his lip until I tasted blood. It felt like he was rubbing away the layers of my skin, and I wondered if this was what it felt like to be horny or in love. I wondered if it was the same thing people called pain. I wondered if pain was what becoming a woman was all about.

Ray dug under my back and opened a condom. It smelled like the dentist's gloved hand. He rolled it on, but I didn't dare open my eyes. I didn't want to see it. He tugged off my shorts, then my underwear, and he wedged his whole body between my legs. My hip nearly popped. He thrust himself inside me and I bit down on his arm. My eyes watered. It felt horribly unnatural, putting something like *that* in *there*. As he wiggled around, it got easier, but not by much. I squeezed my eyes tightly shut. I did not want to know if he was making one of those awful faces with his mouth open wide. My teeth were still sunk into his arm, and the fake grass rubbed my back raw. I stayed as still as I could and I counted: one, one-thousand; two, one-thousand; and tears rolled out of my eyes. By fifteen, one-thousand, it was over.

The condom came off with a snap and I remembered where I was, who I was with. I patted the ground until I touched my shorts, then my underwear, and, as quickly as possible, I slid them both on. Ray was already back in his chair. Before I'd gotten my shorts buttoned, the door opened and Chris staggered out, holding a glass of water canted sideways so it spilled. He looked at me for a moment, at my messy waves of hair and my bunched-up shirt. His big blue eyes were glossy. They no longer seemed to bulge from his head but, rather, his eyes retracted, like he wanted to pull his sight back, to become blind. He righted the glass and looked at me pleadingly, as if he was a child and I'd just taken away his favorite toy. I shifted my eyes to my feet. Really, what I'd taken away was his chance at being a man. I stood awkwardly, as though I hadn't yet put my clothes on. Chris's head tilted to the side, and the corner of his mouth lifted up into a half-smile that was somehow both apologetic and sad. He walked toward me, and his hand extended into my down-turned gaze.

"Are you thirsty, Carrie?" he offered meekly.

I took the glass and briefly looked up at Chris. "Thanks," I uttered, gazing back down into the water. I ran my hand along my back, plucked a still-wrapped condom off my sticky skin, and let it flutter to the ground. Ray was slumped back in his chair, his squinty eyes now all the way closed. I handed the water back to Chris. "I better get going. I'm, um, not feeling so well."

"I know," he nodded.

"What?" I snapped.

"Nothing. I just hope you feel better is all. I'll see ya later."

"Yeah, see ya."

He leaned against the doorway and I staggered out into the alley, my legs—my everything, actually—kind of numb. Mikey's Trans Am was gone. As I slipped into the house, I thought about how pleased Jenna would be that I'd actually done it, but when I got into her room, she was lying face down on her pillow and her body was shaking as she sobbed. I could see the black streaks on her sheets from where the mascara had gone streaming down her face. She was clutching one of her teddy bears that we'd packed away at the beginning of the summer. I turned off the light and sat down beside her, resting my hand on her shoulder.

"Did you do it?" she sniffed, lifting her head.

"Well . . . I . . ."

"I couldn't do it, Carrie! I don't know why. I just couldn't. It was about to happen, and then all of a sudden I couldn't let him touch me. I didn't even want him to kiss me, and I tried to explain it to him . . ." She paused and heaved in some air. "I don't know what's wrong with me. Carrie, what's wrong with me?"

"Nothing's wrong with you, Jen."

"Yeah, well anyway, he dumped me. Actually, he didn't even dump me, really, because this whole time he had like a whole other girlfriend."

I lay down and draped my arm over her back.

"She was at a cottage or something for the summer. . . . So, how was Chris?"

"Nothing happened," I told her as I stared out the window.

Jenna's breathing slowed and she laughed. "Guess we're still caterpillars."

"Tomorrow we can go buy school supplies with unicorns all over them."

"No. We're not like that."

"You're right, for once. . . . You know, I always thought Mikey was an asshole. What kind of guy more than five years old still goes by *Mikey,* anyway?"

"Why didn't you tell me?"

"'Cause he was still pretty damn good-looking. For an asshole."

I wiped some tears from her face and she glanced up at me all sticky-eyed. "Why did he have to say he loved me, Carrie?"

"Because he's a bastard."

"But," her lip quivered, "if he's a bastard, why did I love him?"

"Well, see, honey, all men are bastards. Eventually, you give up and pick one to love. Now, you get to pick a new one. You should consider yourself lucky. Some women end up married to the very first bastard they love."

Jenna giggled at my pseudo-motherly tone, but really, in that moment, I felt almost motherly. I felt like I should tell her a few things about life, like sex was about as profound as brushing your teeth, like being a woman was no different than being a girl. Doing it didn't change anything. I felt shitty before and equally shitty after. But I said nothing. Jenna rolled over, curled her legs into her chest, and closed her eyes. Her makeup had all rubbed off on the pillowcase, and as she drifted into sleep, I realized it wasn't her face I was jealous of. It was her hope that some guy or some action would change things, would fix her life and our shitty little town and her family and her house. Jenna still had that sort of blind faith, and if there was anything that made her a girl and me a woman, it was that.

This Ain't No Disco, This Ain't No Foolin' Around

Sheba White

JOANNE SAYS, "HAVE YOU HEARD THIS THING CALLED *PUNK*?" AND I THINK I SAY, "*Punk,* what the hell is *punk*?" And then, of course, because Joanne is my very best friend and I trust her immensely because we are both fat and ugly little girls and therefore waste our time with pretense, she says, "You know…Oi Polloi, the Sex Pistols, the Damned, and oh . . ." But then, this is where Joanne rolls her eyes back in her potatoey head and licks her lips like she does when she's eating toast with peanut butter because that is her very favorite, toast with peanut butter. Somehow a log of the soft, gooey white bread passes between her thin lips every day. "With extra butter please," Joanne says, "and creamed peanuts." She doesn't like the chunky kind, really can't stand the hard bits in the chunky stuff, but she'll eat it if she must.

Joanne flicks her shoulder-length brown hair back from her eyes, because she is into that Flock of Seagulls-kind of hair that stays in your face and covers all the bad things fifteen-year-old girls feel the need to hide, like, well, like your face. So Joanne gets sick, then, of looking at me looking at her with bewilderment at this definition of *punk,* and she adds like a television expert—the ones they drag in to comment on everything nobody wants to know—"Oh, you know, my brother listens to the stuff all the time. Really loud stuff with lots of cursing," and then, "you want to hear it?"

So we go to the other room and kneel on the floor in our socked feet. "Oh, shit, we've got to be careful," Joanne says as she slowly tries to put on THE ALBUM that is going to clear everything up—Oi Polloi, the Sex Pistols, the Damned, or something like that—without getting her greasy fingerprints all over it. It belongs to her brother Mike, who as far as I know is all about dressing up in torn clothes and maintaining stringy hair in oily mounds and having some kind of mental condition called schizophrenia that makes him throw things at his sister and spit on his father or bite people who "obviously want the best for him." Besides being just plain stupid, that Mike. So now here is Joanne, with her butter-stained and potato-shaped hands that she wipes on her polyester Arby's pants like she's protecting the Holy Grail of albums or something.

So I get all fussy and say, "Well, goddamn it, Jo, put it on, already," like her dad does when he wants her to turn the TV dinner in the oven, or grab him a can of Hamm's, or sometimes even to rewind his nudie tapes on the VCR. "Well, goddammit, Jo," and Jo's got this kind of waddle on account of so much fat; she just keeps on rocking back and forth on her feet, which look like cotton flippers peeking from under her butt. She's just kneeling there in front of the stereo and wiping her hand and adjusting the knobs on the turntable, "for better sound," she says. Says you can hear more that way. Says that her brother likes it high and distorted, the speakers vibrating the porcelain dancing French-girl figurines on the corkboard shelves. Says it calms him down to hear it with the tenor way up and the speakers at something like level eight.

"Oh, for chrissakes," I say, until I hear what she means; I hear razors cutting through the fat of being fifteen and being ugly and being . . . well . . . little nibs in the pit of the worst years of our entire life, if you must know. But this sound, it's like a man screaming into me, turning my body upside out, and I think I'm gonna . . . I think I'm gonna puke all over Joanne's father's orange and mocha deep shag carpet circa 1973.

"What, what?" Joanne says on volume six, because really she can't hear a word at all without her hearing aid, which for some reason I never think to ask why she had, but I know it must have something to do with her father because he likes to whack her hard until she comes out of his room crying and blubbering something about the fat lady singing, or when pigs fly, or some such thing, and looking for her favorite peanut butter knife.

"I said," I continue, forming my lips into an O, as if Joanne can suddenly read lips, being deaf in one ear, "where did he get this?"

"Who?"

"Your brother!" I say, my mime more emphatic now. "Where did your brother pick this up?"

"Oh," she says, again the expert, "he must of stole it from one of his friends."

Now I know that's a story and a half because Joanne can see the form taking the shape of how I want to say things from now on, and she's just being jealous or cool or whatever, because she can't seem to connect to this sound the same way I can. But I don't care, 'cause at fifteen, when everything is so fat and ugly like Joanne and me sitting on her father's orange and mocha shag carpeting and Joanne framed all in Arby's polyester splendor that is the color of dried blood and mustard and she's eating peanut butter and toast and all, which I can't stand, just so you know, I think *Shit, nothing can get uglier than this.*

But here it is, this man screaming like a buzzsaw in my head or a balloon exploding in my stomach or something like a tire popping, not deflating, but blowing out at highway speed, and all I could think, ya know, was that I was fifteen and already I felt like yelling like that to Joanne, to her fat dad who watched the nudies, to Mrs. Larsen who tried to convince me in class that Egyptians were white, and Brady Hisch who laughed at me because I had my period. I wanted to scream so maybe somebody would come running to listen.

Jessie Eager has that kind of name that turns somersaults in your mouth, so I think I'm in love. I tell this to Joanne and she says, "Yeah," like a sigh, one day when we're on the MCTO heading nowhere in particular, and she adds just about what you'd expect the wrong sidekick to add, "yeah, take a ticket," because she knows that I know that she knows Jessie Eager is definitely going to be my man, even if I've seen him exactly two and a half times with her schizoid brother Mike. Only I want her to say something like, "Love is for suckers," 'cause that would be the punkest thing to say and we've just watched *The Decline of Western Civilization* for like the billionth time where this kid has a line like that. We've never been in love, can't even get near it with a pair of gloves and a warm nursey smile, but we still know that we're in the right vicinity when we think about it.

Joanne is wearing her trademark army green coat, and her bangs swoop across her face like a tidal wave. She nicks my leg with her Chuck Taylors and winks, "He is a babe, yeah?" I want to punch her right then. And not just because she never knows how to dress for anywhere, which means that you don't put on a coat and scarf like you're going *somewhere*, but that you underdress, as if you couldn't care where the fuck you're going, 'cause wherever it is, you're gonna feel pain, or better yet, numb, or even better, you'll die. I want to punch her for being so fat and so frickin' supportive—the wrong sidekick.

So I change the subject: "He's a lush."

"Mmmm . . . not so much," she says, the ends of her bangs finding their way into her mouth so it comes out all muffled like "nonesuch."

"Yeah, much," I say, "a real toaster," which means that Jessie Eager has been known to fall down drunk wherever, doesn't matter if it's covered in rat dung and bum piss, like a regular town drunk, that Jess.

Joanne gets a look on her face that tells me she is thinking of peanut butter again. If it weren't for her eating, Joanne wouldn't be such a bad broad. She has thighs like nutcrackers and an overbite that looks as though someone left pats of butter in the place where her mouth should be, yeah, but she also has a nice round face and catlike eyes that she plays up like a real goth, only it is July and the heat through the windows makes them look more like some ancient movie star, like Gloria Swanson in that one old movie I could stomach—because it was cool, ya know, how the reporter ended up floating in that pool and he's telling you the story and all—or like she beat herself up with her irregularly sized fists overnight, beaten, but not dead, not exactly punk, yeah?

"Nice guy, though, really nice guy."

"Yeah, whatever," I spit out at her sulking frame and watch the same exact house on the same exact piece of lawn surrounded by the same exact squat little shrubs pass by our window. I'm getting this tight, trapped feeling just looking at it all, the land opening up like a wound when I want it to be tight and fast and like a gazillion things flying about me like cement and steel insects. "How can they live out here?" I moan. "I mean, how can they stand it?" I make my best, disgusted Gloria Swanson face to emphasize my contempt at the boondocks we travel through to get to the city, the MCTO going halfway around the world to pick up the old mall ladies with their gazillion shopping bags and sweatsuits and thermosed coffees, even though we live only five minutes from the city's border.

"Yeah, it's really sad," Jo says, "I told my dad that that's when I'd run. I swear to God, it's when I'd definitely run. You're not getting me out to the boondocks, I told him. I'd rather eat nails or join the Republican Party. Or better yet, I'd rather fuck Ronald Reagan, that's like the two combined, innit?" She says "isn't it" in her best fake British accent, which is how we feel real punks talk. And we both look at each other and laugh, 'cause that's exactly how it is, me and Jo, for like forever now and forever then, and fuck the poseurs who don't know it.

★ ★ ★

Jessie Eager is in an alley behind McDonald's with bits of puke stuck to his spiked leather jacket and brown stiff head and thick pulpy lips, but even that doesn't stop me from loving him.

"You take his left leg, I'll take his neck, right?" Some kid with a dirty gray coat is instructing Joanne and me how to pick up a drunk. It goes something like this:

1) Turn him on his stomach so that

a) he will not projectile-vomit on you should he wake up in the middle of said project and,

b) if he should start vomiting it will end up on the ground and not be lodged further into his throat where he may,

c) in his drunken state, choke on his own bile.

2) Avoid any part that may kick and swing.

Joanne and I each grab a thigh and fake retching noises when we hear the suction that Jessie's wiry body makes when his clothing is released from the vomit on the gravel.

"This is so punk rock," I say to Joanne, because it truly is the most punk-rock moment we have had that summer, and that includes drinking our first beers under the crumbling train bridge, stealing candy from Montgomery Ward and spitting it out in neon chunks on the security guards when they caught us doing it, and cutting our hair into perfect three-inch triangular wedges that we stiffened with a bit of egg white and cheap cans of hairspray into little pyramids on top of our heads. We look like DayGlo Weebles in all that McDonald's neon glow, me and Jo.

Only Joanne looks at me with genuine fear on her doughy face, and I can tell that she has this soft concern for Jessie's chunky dribble. "Dammit, Jo," I say, "he's OK, just a bit out of it, don't look so stressed, Beaver," which is short for Betty, which is short for lesbian or girl skater, neither of which Joanne is, but it sounds funny anyway and it usually makes her laugh.

But Jo is not listening; she's so damn caring. I want to drop Jessie right there on the pavement, mid-puke, and kick Jo for giving a shit about things that don't matter and not about the things that do, like, for instance, who is seeing us carry Jessie Eager's drunken body out of a McDonald's parking lot and how can we turn this into major punk-rock points in our favor? And, of course, I'm thinking about Jessie Eager's muscled thigh against my waist like that. And I'm thinking: "Yeah, this is Mrs. Jessie Eager." And I'm thinking he'd say, "This is my old lady, Katie," or "My old lady, Katie, will get you a beer," or

"My old lady is some ball-breaking bitch," and sort of scratch his thick brown hair with a fake seriousness you'd imagine an actor playing someone Irish in a movie doing. "Ah, that Katie," he'd say. Only it turns out, no one is watching.

The blowout comes over Mia Peck. You could fit two Mia Pecks into one of our legs, ya know? So of course I'd fall in love with her. Mia Peck is a real sidekick, a real punk. You can tell by the size of her pyramid, which she measured at a good foot and two-thirds above her scalp, the nonchalant way she eats her food, and the way she has of looking through you when you're talking, as if she's heard it all before. "Nothing's shocking," is Mia Peck's way of looking at you, and "I'm so bored just looking at you," is the only other way she has of acknowledging your existence. So of course I was in love. Who wouldn't be? Then she adds: "I've slept with Jess once, it wasn't great, he's got a limp dick," so of course I was in hate, too.

Joanne says to me, "So you're hanging out with Mia a lot lately," and I know where this is going. I try not to get mad, but I do anyway.

"Since when were you my ma?" I ask. Joanne's face turns barbeque red and I can see her wanting to say something equally painful, but being as how there's not one evil bone in her body, which is why I can't hang out with her anymore, she can't seem to come up with anything sharp enough to hurt me.

"That's cool," is all she says. "I mean," she stammers, hair in peanut butter mouth, "Mia's cool and all," which comes out something like "Mia's cruel s'all," on account of her hair chewing. And I give her a look stolen straight from Mia's book, page 4, which looks something like this:

> Mia's book page 4
>
> Are you for real?

The coolest thing about Mia is that she knows everyone and everyone wants to know her, and those that don't are shit. "Fuck Mia," *blue triangle, runny nose*; "Where you been?" *red skirt and cowboy boots*; "Shit, Mia, I lost your number," *dirty T-shirt and faded, ripped jean jacket*—she just looks right through them all like they're just ripples in hot air, like she's some blaxploitation star walking the hood during the opening credits.

The uncoolest thing about Mia is that she drinks a little too much, and when she drinks too much she's even more viciously lovely, her hand droops under her perfect breasts like someone with palsy, her blue eyes look like a baby seal's, all watery in the center and crusted at the edges. Besides, when she's drunk like that she gets special in Olympics ways, like Special Olympics—you want to clap at the absurdity of it and you're a little sad, too, 'cause you feel like you shouldn't be watching, like maybe you should be getting off your own ass and trying to do something to save the embarrassment of it all.

And fuck, if the boys still don't look her up and down knowing-like, like "I've had her once and she wasn't that good, either," kind of looks and kinda sad, too, the way they look at her, like the dolls Joanne and I disfigured when we were kids to the point where you couldn't move an arm without the head falling off, and we couldn't get rid of those dolls and we couldn't love them either, me and Jo.

"Yeah, so there's this show," Mia is saying, "that we're all going to . . ." Mia talks like this, like everyone is always in agreement with her and everyone is part of her group and everyone wants to do everything with her . . . "because this band is playing and I've slept with one of the guys"—Mia has always slept with one of the guys, including schizoid Mike—"and supposedly, they're opening for Dag Nasty," I'm telling you, Mia knows everybody, and everybody always knows her, including bands from California, fuck, she's cool, "and he'll get us in for free. Dag Nasty is the shit," she says, because she mostly talks like someone from somewhere warmer, though she's from Minnesota. So we go.

But being somewhere with Mia is not like being somewhere with a real person, ya know? Every two seconds someone comes up and wants to talk with her, and you're sitting there and someone wants a drink, or someone knocks your drink over, or someone is taking a drink from Mia's soft pink lips, all mildewy with black lipstick and Hamm's, and the only thing you can hear under the music grinding in your ear is this buzzing sound, like a beehive, as everyone and their grandma tries to inch in on Mia. "Mia's Katie will get it," is the only other thing you hear as you go and get it, whatever it is. But they know your name, cause you're with Mia, even if maybe now you're the bad sidekick.

"So, there's this little kid with a big gun, and he's waving it around," says Jess, leaning into a wall covered with spray paint at some kid's basement party. What kid? I don't know; it doesn't matter, because this is what Jess says, "and his dad comes down like a real jerk and the kid gets so spooked that he just up and shoots his dad right in the gutter of his neck." Hahaha, hahaha, haha, goes all the laughter around him, 'cause Jess is taking his broken-bottle bleeding fingers up to his neck and feigning asphyxiation, and smearing blood all over his throat, which makes me kinda see why Joanne's dad can smack her, ya know? 'Cause sometimes people can remind you of something else, or someone else, or sometime else that you don't want to think about.

Like Jess with his kneeling on the floor like that? And with his eyes glistening with glassy pure nothingness like that? And all I can think of is Joanne and the look she gave me when I told her that she was just a fat cow anyway and I was letting her out to pasture with all the other heifers, and then I just got off the MCTO in the middle of that sameness, all that nowhere—it was so punk rock—and watched as Jo's Flock-of-Seagulls hair made like a Nike swoosh through the bus's window, but her face stayed the same as Jessie Eager's now, like something had crawled up in there and died. I can't stand that look, just so you know, so I frown at Jess.

"You're so pent up," Mia says, one corner of her mouth bent down like a hanger. "Jah," Mia says, cause she's all drunk, and when she's drunk she speaks Swedish Rastafari, "Jah, man, Katie tight tittie. Are you my little Katie tight tittie?" And she flicks my chin with her fuck-off finger and passes out against some kid's cement basement wall standing up, because she's that frickin' punk, Mia, passed out with pale blue lids like a baby or those pictures of Jesus— making what she said even funnier. Haha ha. Haha ha haaaa, like a frickin' Greek chorus, these kids.

So I stand, too, only kinda looking stupid, like that reporter's body floating in all that clear pool water at the end of *Sunset Boulevard*, and all the photographers snapping away, ya know? And all I could think of was how awful he musta felt face down and all and knowing that the photographers were getting the worst possible shot of him, 'cause up 'til that point, he thought he was one of those beautiful people, he was like me, yeah?

And I want to ask someone this, but who? In the middle of an all-nighter where someone gets punched and someone else cuts his face in half going through a balcony window, when one of Mia's rejects has his scabby hands down the front of my skirt and is kneading the place where a stomach should be, but there's only more fat, when Mia's nose starts to bleed for reasons that I don't want to know, when I'm feeling like the water is closing in on me and all I can see is the bottom, I wish I could turn to someone and ask, "This is so punk rock, innit?"

When the Saints Go Marching Out

Ira Brooker

AUTHOR'S NOTE: I FINISHED THIS ESSAY IN JANUARY OF 2005. SEVEN MONTHS later, I was horrified to see my every dire prediction come to fruition. Escalating property and insurance rates are driving the locals out of Hampshire, there is a stranger living in my grandmother's house, and Hurricane Katrina has forever altered the face of New Orleans. I certainly take no joy in that kind of prescience. In February 2005, my wife and I made our first return visit to New Orleans since moving away in mid-2003. It was Mardi Gras, our favorite time of year, and we were thrilled to see how little had changed about the city we'd come to regard as home. We wandered the streets of the Riverbend neighborhood, visiting old haunts and getting misty with nostalgia. As it turned out, that visit was our goodbye to New Orleans as we knew it. It will be rebuilt, certainly, but a significant portion of the city's soul and carefree spirit cannot be restored. We now know that the worst can and will happen. It's a valuable lesson, to be sure, but I can't think of many harder ways to learn it.

New Orleans is doomed. That's not an embellishment or a figure of speech; it's a scientific fact. Whether it's coastal erosion or a level-five hurricane that finally does the job, time is eventually going to catch up with "the city that care forgot." For me, a former resident and eternal devotee of that singular city, that's a dreadful thought. For the past three years this country has had to acknowledge that the places and people we hold dear could be ripped from us unexpectedly at any moment, and that knowledge has turned us into a paranoid, easily-led society. How much more macabre, then, to know that the place you love not only could but almost certainly *will* be destroyed, and that you will only be able to stand idly by and watch it go?

Losing New Orleans is doubly tough because there are simply no other places quite like it. I saw things during my two-year tenure that I could never have hoped to see anywhere else in this world. The spiritual high as I watched a band of Mardi Gras Indians come bursting out of a tiny jazz club and got caught up in their impromptu parade down Frenchmen Street; the celebrity junkie's adulation as John Goodman was called up on stage at Jazz Fest to accompany the great Pete Fountain in a rousing take on "When The Saints Go Marching In"; the smug superiority of watching flabby, khaki-draped tourists who weeble-wobbled their way through the French Quarter gathering armfuls of postcards from places they wouldn't even bother to see. Gumbo might be the most overused metaphoric image in New Orleans, but it's also a fairly apt one. All of the conflicting yet complementary levels of weirdness make for a tasty, city-sized stew whose recipe can never be replicated.

To be completely honest with you, when I first got to New Orleans I hated it. Hated, hated, hated it more than I had ever previously hated anything in my entire life. I was miserable, depressed, actively praying for that level-five hurricane. It was just so far removed from anything I'd ever experienced before. Spending your formative years in tidy, polite states like Wisconsin and Minnesota in no way provides you with the cognitive tools needed to comprehend a seething, slouching orgy of a city like New Orleans, and I was overmatched.

See, one thing that I think often escapes the notice of visitors and itinerants is that we're not just throwing this party to celebrate your arrival. You can spend a four-day weekend hoisting mixed drinks and gawking at mansions and exposing your breasts, then head back to your humdrum existence at home. But for us, this is the humdrum. There are hundreds of thousands of folks exactly like you waiting in the wings, and we're expected to pitch the same shindig for each and every one of them. Ever heard a comedian complain how people will come up to him while he's eating or watching a ball game and expect him to be "on"? New Orleans is like that; we always have to be on, fulfilling your every lurid fantasy. Because if we aren't on you won't come back and you'll tell your friends not to come and the tourism cash flow will dry up, and you can't support a whole damned state off shrimping revenue and a couple of off-shore oil rigs.

That's a lot of pressure for a twenty-two-year-old newlywed coming from Minnesota, a state where sense of humor is regularly beaten out by wary stoicism in those "What do you look for in a mate?" polls, and I was, quite frankly, not up to it. It's a whole different culture, completely unlike anything anyone who hasn't lived there has ever experienced, and it takes a major psychic toll. Add to that the confirmation of my longstanding fear that a B.A. in English Lit would actually render me less employable than I was going into college, and you've got the recipe for a full-scale existential meltdown.

Mardi Gras came just in time. To tell the truth, I was not at all looking forward to my first Carnival season. I'd heard a lot of the lore and I knew all of the songs and some of the traditions, but to me it sounded like just a two-week amplification of the party-all-the-time attitude that was driving me crazy already. Still, I went along with it, because how can you live in New Orleans and not at least give Mardi Gras a try?

And I loved it. Maybe not wholeheartedly at first, but little by little the weirdness and wildness thawed my chilly demeanor. My first parade was a revelation. The moment the first float rolled into view, fifteen feet high, bedecked with blazing pastels and laden with dozens of masked, bead-flinging riders, I thought, "Now here is something I've never seen before." For a while I maintained what I thought to be a healthy disgust for the swarm of soused morons clamoring to catch those useless beads and trinkets, but eventually curiosity got the better of me. I raised a tentative arm as a sparkling blue band came tumbling at me end over end, and when it came close enough I closed my fingers around the bubbly plastic baubles and snatched it out of the dusk. It felt good. More than good, really. Exhilirating. Who would have guessed that the release I'd needed for going on six months could come in the simple catching of a five-cent string of beads? I slid my prize over my shaggy head and took a couple of steps forward, eyes scanning the oncoming float for potential projectiles.

That's the type of experience you just couldn't hope to duplicate, and it's tied inextricably to this one-of-a-kind place. I know that I can hold onto my memories and mementoes for as long as I live, but if New Orleans were to disappear, those memories would be forever tainted by an emptiness as unique as the place that once occupied it.

My wife Myra does not share my passion for places. There are some certain spots that evoke a sentimental reaction from her, sure, but Myra is a scientist. She looks at things with a colder, more analytical eye. Her specialty is aquatic ecosystems, so she has spent many hours in the Louisiana bayous observing firsthand some of the threats that may eventually destroy New Orleans. She's explained it all to me in horrific detail.

Back when the nation ran on the back of its shipping industry, the powers that be decided they couldn't risk having their factories and company towns wiped out by a flood. To prevent that sort of tragedy, the U.S. Army Corps of Engineers built a system of dams and levees starting around St. Louis that would keep the river flowing true. Unfortunately, in the process the engineers also made sure that all of the vital soil and nutrients that made up the famed Mississipi Delta would be flushed into the Gulf of Mexico instead of collecting and strengthening the banks. As a result, there is no longer any barrier to keep out the encroaching tidal waters. Every year the Gulf eats a larger and larger chunk away from Louisiana's swampy coastline, by some estimates decimating as much as twenty acres annually. At present, there is no feasible method of combating this coastal creep. If it continues unabated, the water will eventually make its way into New Orleans.

Myra has seen it coming. She's been up to her knees in bayous where the fish populations are slowly dying from the steady leaching of salt water. It saddens and frustrates her, but she knows that at this point most of the damage is irreversible, and she accepts that. I wish I could share her detachment, but my artistic temperment doesn't allow me that kind of remove. When New Orleans goes, Myra will be sad, but she will accept it and move on. I expect to be inconsolable at first and permanently damaged in the long run.

The corroding coast is a frightening thought, but at least there is the possibility that the threat can be averted through new scientific advancements before the worst has happened. That is not the case with hurricanes. We've all seen terrifying news footage of the destruction hurricanes regularly inflict on the Gulf Coast. Just last summer we watched as Hurricane Ivan eviscerated much of Florida and Alabama. I felt awful for the people living in those places, but in my heart I was thanking the powers that be that Ivan had changed his course at the last minute and spared New Orleans. However much damage places like Pensacola and Galveston sustain, they will be able to rebuild. When the big one hits New Orleans, that will not be an option.

And the big one will hit. It's just a matter of time. Storm watchers are consistently surprised that New Orleans has not been struck by a level-five hurricane—the strongest recorded type of storm—long before now. Every year the Gulf Coast is threatened by two or three large tropical storms, at least one of which inevitably hits New Orleans. These tempests do plenty of damage and make life miserable for a couple of days, but by pure luck the city has so far managed to dodge a truly cataclysmic storm. When that level five finally hits, and researchers say it most definitely will, that'll be all she wrote.

By the rules of nature, New Orleans should not physically exist. The highest point in the city is five feet below sea level, which means the waters of Lake Pontchartrain, the large body of water that borders New Orleans' north side, are actually higher than the city streets. By all rights the land should be an uninhabitable morass. Whatever inspired those first French fur trappers to establish this waterlogged swatch of swamp as a permanent settlement is beyond me, but somehow they made it stick for going on three hundred years. The bugs have never quite been worked out, as demonstrated by the constant buckling and potholing of every paved surface in town, but for the most part the water stays put.

And that's exactly the problem. New Orleans owes its dry-land status to a complex system of levees and pumps designed to keep water from getting in. Unfortunately, this also means that, should the water ever find its way over these barriers, it will have no way out again. The city will essentially become a giant bowl of stagnant water about ten feet deep. The pumps will be no help. Already, anytime the area gets significant rainfall, they back up within an hour. During even minor tropical storms, about half of the city streets become impromptu waterways. Interestingly enough, the lower-lying stretches of Interstate 10, ostensibly the vicinity's primary emergency evacuation route, are consistently among the first to flood.

The levees will provide protection for a time, but there is only so much a wall of earth can do against a wall of water. I used to live two blocks from the levee. There's a small paved road running along the top of it where I often went running or bicycling in the evenings. Further down the road are a couple of riverside parks, one for dogs and the other for people. The city has done its usual excellent sham job by turning the levee into a place for fun and enter-tainment instead of a constant reminder of how thin the membrane is that sep-arates residents from watery annihilation. But when I would go running after a tropical storm, there was no ignoring it—it just doesn't take much to make that water rise. That's why houses on the river side of the levee (yes, there are a few souls bold enough to dare nature that way) are built on fifteen-foot stilts.

After bigger storms like Lily or Isadore, the residents need every inch of those sturdy two-by-fours. If I took another run a few days later, I'd see an eerie forecast of what lies in store for New Orleans. Pools of stagnant, stinking water fostered new legions of tiny black mosquitoes. Receding waters revealed unruly piles of driftwood and other, less organic debris. The packs of mutated, mutilated wild dogs that usually kept to the safety of the tidal forest during daylight now lounged about in the sun, feasting on washed-up rodent carcasses. I shuddered to think what they might find to eat when the whole city flooded.

The obvious question is, if this kind of apocalyptic vision is really inevitable, why do people stay in New Orleans? If you're asking me that, you've obviously never lived there. It's tough to convey that unique New Orleanian mindset to an outsider without making us sound like a bunch of simpleminded hedonists. But heck, there are worse things to be than simple-minded hedonists, so here goes.

Use the phrase "Big Easy" around a native and you're likely to get nothing but a raised eyebrow and a cold shoulder. Nobody likes to hear his hometown reduced to a stupid catchphrase, and most New Orleanians are fairly resentful of that centuries-old image of their city as the nation's whore, a place where you can pay your money, have your fun, leave a mess, and get the hell out with no repercussions. But the truth is, "Big Easy" is a pretty accurate phrase when it comes to the town's overriding attitude. New Orleanians just don't get too worked up about much of anything. (There are a few exceptions, as evidenced by the city's constant contention for the title of America's murder capital.) While the stereotype that we all sit around all day on our gigantic porches with a pot of gumbo and a case of Dixie beer is not true, we are by and large more willing than most people to sit back, relax, and hope our problems work themselves out. For proof, walk around a residential neighborhood and take a look at the lawns. You'll notice there aren't very many of them. Growing grass requires regular mowing and maintenance, especially in the summer months when being outdoors in Louisiana is most intolerable. The residents have found a way around this predicament by planting their lawns with low-growing shrubs or just filling them in with decorative rocks. The elaborate, time-consuming manicured lawns of the North are few and far between. Another example: I describe the famous New Orleans architecture as "sustained decay"—even many of the nicest buildings look as though they're perennially right on the verge of collapsing upon themselves. This is partially due to a sweltering climate that makes brand new materials look like they've recently been salvaged from a Civil War shipwreck, but the general spirit of maintaining the minimal level of effort necessary to survival plays a big role as well.

The hurricane situation is similar. Everyone in New Orleans has heard the reports. It's no secret that the city is probably not long for this world, but other than packing up and getting out, there's not much anybody can do about that. It's much less stressful to simply plan on worrying about it when the time comes. It's not too bad an attitude on an individual level, but the same kind of thinking infests local government. Those measures that could possibly help—shoring up emergency relief supplies, revitalizing the pump system, building nonflooding escape routes—generate a lot of talk, but the odds of anything concrete being accomplished before the hurricanes hit are not promising.

The New Orleanian sense of humor tends toward the macabre, so when the storms are rolling in there is a general air of dancing in the streets of Pompeii. Full-blown hurricane parties are not unheard of, with old friends swilling sangria by oil lamp behind boarded-up windows. Since half the towns-people consider themselves romantically doomed Tennessee Williams charac-ters, they don't find it hard to giggle all the way into Armageddon. If anybody in town actually sprinkled conversations with French the way they do in the movies, the whole thing would be dismissed with a rueful "C'est la vie! Laissez le bon temps roulé!" I myself can testify to the singular thrill of slipping on a rain jacket and taking a stroll in the opening hours of a tropical storm. Standing on the levee trying to separate the gray of the river from the gray of the sky, straining against a wind that would knock me down if I didn't resist, relishing the slap of angry raindrops against my face as I wade through the shin-deep waters of a deserted Freret Street, knowing all the while I could easily find myself homeless or worse by morning—it's a fatalistic delight like nothing else I can imagine.

There are, of course, the other, stupider types who consider hurricanes a personal affront best dealt with by refusing to back down. I recall a particularly weaselly former boss who threatened to fire any employee who fled during the government-recommended evacuation for Hurricane Lily. These John Wayne types, although overrepresented by the media in their quest for images of back-wards Deep South good ol' boys, are hardly indicative of the general attitude. These people will be the floating bodies on the TV news when the big one finally hits, a role most New Orleanians are too sharp to take on willingly.

We're trained from early on to deal with people dying. Death is all over TV, movies, books—it lurks in every facet of our daily lives. Even if we're not very good at dealing with it, every relatively sane one of us is acutely aware of his or her impending mortality. But nobody tells us that places can also die.

Perhaps I attach more importance to place than most people do. I know I drive my wife mad every time we move with my mooning over the last place we lived. It's just part of my mentality, I guess. Nearly every memorable moment in my life is inextricably wrapped up with the place where it happened. A co-worker flashes a brand new engagement ring and I'm on one knee in the moonlight on an abandoned wagon bridge in Winona, Minnesota. Kevin Garnett takes an elbow to the face on TV and I'm in a high school bathroom in Onalaska, Wisconsin, watching the blood pour from my mouth into the sink at an alarming rate. "Rave On" comes on the radio and I'm in a seedy museum in Lubbock, Texas, barely able to breathe as I gaze upon a display of Buddy Holly's discarded guitar picks.

I will return to some of these meaningful places someday. Some of them I will never see again. But whether or not I have any intention of revisiting any given place, being told that I can never go back there, that the place that evokes so much for me is no more—that is existential torture of the highest degree. I define myself by these places. When they disappear or change fundamentally, I feel as if some part of my being has been ripped out. Even though my memories remain intact, there is something about an irreversible alteration to the original template that sullies the entire experience, like the asterisk attached to Roger Maris's sixty-one home runs in the baseball record books.

There are many things I love about New Orleans—the food, the music, the architecture—and I will miss them dearly when they're gone. But even more so than all of those evocative things, I'm concerned about losing the place itself. It's a difficult concept to explain. I'm defining place as sort of a peculiar mix of concrete and abstract. Perhaps a brief analolgy is in order: My grandma checked into the nursing home last month. She's eighty-eight, and she wanted to go. She recently fell and broke her ankle and had to crawl across the basement to call her sister to come help her out. My mom went to stay with her for a couple of weeks to get her things in order. While cleaning up around the house, Mom found canned goods dating back more than a decade and a wardrobe riddled with holes and stains. So obviously, it's a good idea to get Grandma out of the house and into an assisted-living environment.

I'm notoriously bad at dealing with change, and all of this has me pretty shaken. What's surprised me, though, is that it isn't the idea of Grandma's impending death that worries me most. I've lost grandparents before. It's a tough thing to go through, but at least I have some experience with that kind of loss. What I'm really dreading is the loss of Grandma's house.

That little house outside Ham Lake, Minnesota, has been a constant for me as long as I can remember. It's where my brother and I woke up each Christmas morning and waited impatiently for the adults to get up and allow us a crack at our stockings. It's where Grandpa had his endlessly fascinating metal shop and smoke house. It's where the clanking boiler in the basement fueled any number of vivid childhood nightmares. Now that Grandma is moving out, I don't know when or if I will be inside that house again. Even if a cousin buys the place and keeps it in the family, there will be fundamental changes that will eventually relegate the house I used to know to the realm of memory.

That's more or less how I feel about New Orleans' predicament. Thinking of individual elements that will be lost to me is scary, but imagining the entire city disappearing is just too immense, like trying to describe eternity. Some things are just supposed to be as they are, untouchable, immutable, but it seems that those are usually the things that change most drastically.

When I was living in New Orleans, I'll admit I fell into the "Eat, drink, and be merry, for tomorrow we must die" mind-set. The approach of a tropical storm was scary, but it was also a rush, like driving too fast on a country road. When you're living somewhere, particularly somewhere you love, it's near impossible to imagine that place being gone someday. Now that I'm living elsewhere, though, I can step back and see that threat with clear eyes. And it scares the living hell out of me.

It's the waiting that's real torture, an infernally compounded kind of waiting. Hurricanes are not like tornados. You know when they're coming for days, sometimes weeks in advance. I spend all year waiting for hurricane season, dreading what kind of storms the Gulf will conjure up this time around. Once the first hurricane is reported, I wait for something to form in Louisiana's general vicinity. Then I wait to hear what direction it's heading in. And if it's going New Orleans' way, all I can do is wait to see what kind of damage it's going to do.

This past summer, when Ivan was in the news every day, with the estimates of potential damage growing more dire with every report, I sat glued to the TV biting my lip in agony. My wife Myra says looking at me at those times really frightened her because I looked so fragile, like I was ready to burst into tears at any moment. And I really was horribly worried. We still have good friends living down there, but I wasn't too concerned with them. I knew they'd all clear out in time. I was worried for the city, worried in much the same way I am about my grandma's house.

★ ★ ★

As I said before, Myra is not nearly as distraught about the plight of our former abode. She loved New Orleans, too, but regards it more as a neat place we once lived than the Holy City I have built it up to be. Nonetheless, she is going through a similar experience with her hometown. She grew up in Hampshire, Illinois, until recently a quiet, rural community of 1500 people. In the last few years, however, the forces of sprawl have cornered little Hampshire. The housing developments are being slapped together quicker than I would have thought possible. The town's population has doubled over the last five years and is predicted to quintuple within the next five.

Just about every weekend we make the forty-minute drive from Chicago to Hampshire to see Myra's dad. Every time we near the township limits, we see another former cornfield going under the bulldozer's blade. Myra's face grows dark and she begins mumbling curses under her breath. The newspapers have started referring to Hampshire as a "far northwestern suburb," a phrase that makes her near catatonic with rage. For the time being, the old section of town where her dad lives remains intact and unchanged. Block's Grocery, with its six aisles of beautifully limited selection, remains the hub of the business district. Old-timers like Myra's dad still drink at Chuck's Pub, while young folks like Myra's former classmates go across the street to the Corkshire. Local elections are still dominated by Republicans running unchallenged. But Myra sees how this is going to play out: the yuppies will keep moving in, looking for a place where they can pretend they're living in the country and still keep a relatively easy commute to the city. As the newcomers begin to outnumber the old guard, they'll start reshaping the town in their own image. New referendums will be passed. Local landmarks will be bulldozed. The chain stores will move in. And before long they will have made Hampshire virtually identical to whichever pre-fab suburban nightmare they fled from in the first place.

It's stories like Hampshire's that make me almost glad that a more violent fate waits for New Orleans. As Neil Young said, it's better to burn out than to fade away. Our nation has spent the last five years cowering in the face of unseen foreign invaders bent on destroying our most cherished places, but we'd already been doing a rather effective job of it ourselves for quite a while. Just ask the displaced street people of post-Giuliani Times Square, the long-idle autoworkers of post-GM Flint, Michigan, or the cash-strapped shop owners of post-Wal-Mart America. As much as it saddens me to think of New Orleans' taverns and art galleries marinating in ten feet of toxic water, the mighty live oaks withering as their roots soak in various poisons, the steel rails of the streetcar tracks twisted and scattered along the ruins of St. Charles Avenue; I would be even more horrified to see a glorious dive restaurant like the Camellia Grill shuttered to make way for a T.G.I. Friday's, or to watch the crumbling shotgun houses of the Ninth Ward plowed under in favor of shiny, split-level condos. Likewise, it pains me to think of my grandma's house undergoing an extreme makeover at my cousin's hands, until I think of the remote plot of farmland Myra's uncle owned and worked when she was younger currently the site of a bustling Home Depot.

I won't be so alarmist as to suggest that America is on the path to eliminating the concept of the meaningful place altogether, but I will say it is becoming harder and harder to find places to cherish. I know that things fall apart and time fades away, that the death of places is as old as civilization. But at least ancients like the Greeks and Mesopotamians left ruins, fragmented remnants of the places that once were. That may be that the best New Orleans can hope for is to become the modern Atlantis, a curious trove of cultural artifacts for years to come. But what ruins will Hampshire leave as it is swallowed up and homogenized? If Myra visits her childhood haunts twenty years from now, what touchstones will be left to ignite those cherished memories? Or to instill new memories in the next generation of Hampshirers? There are still some items one can't purchase at the local strip mall.

There's no avoiding it—places die as surely as people, and once they're gone they're just as impossible to bring back. Maybe it's too early for me to be shedding tears for New Orleans or Grandma's house or Hampshire. Maybe I should follow the conventional wisdom and use this time to cherish what I still have. Right now, though, the thought of each place only reminds me of how soon it will be gone, and what a loss it will be when that happens. I think I can be excused if I mourn a little prematurely. After all, there are no funerals for places.

Into the Eye of You

Chelsea Laine Wells

My father was a man who spent his entire life dying. Inside he was a six-year-old whose mother had just been killed by cancer. He was a ten-year-old whose father told him every day that he was and always would be worth nothing. He was a twenty-year-old who found drugs and latched on like a drowning man. He was a thirty-year-old who was so far gone on cocaine and crystal meth he believed people were living in his attic. He was a fifty-year-old who had systematically lost everything and had no one to blame but himself. He was a fifty-three-year old in a motel room with a gun in his mouth, finally letting go.

You took everything from me, you bitch. You brainwashed the girls and turned them against me, and now they're as heartless as you are. They don't love me, they don't give a shit if I live or die. Every day of my life is shit and it is your fault, all three of you.

In so many ways, it is just like every other letter he wrote my mother, or me, or my sister—the blame and bitterness, the self-pity, the justification of countless hostilities. I read it standing at the foot of my mother's bed. Towards the end of the second page I am so angry I'm just skimming his words. I barely see the last line—*It's really incomprehensible to me, but no more*—or the lack of signature.

"Don't you think it's odd he didn't sign it?" my mother asks me from the head of the bed, where she sits grading a stack of papers. His words fail to arouse any anger in her, the cutting edge of them dulled from years of use.

"Not really," I snap. "You know what I wish? I wish he would die. I wish he would just go and shoot himself in the head like he's constantly threatening. Then he'd finally be out of his fucking misery and the rest of us would be a hell of a lot happier. I mean that. I *mean* it." I can feel the blood in my face and my heartbeat in the hollows of my throat. My hands shake as I refold his letter and shove it back into the envelope. "You know I mean it, don't you?" I demand.

She nods slowly. There is an old sadness in her eyes. She wishes I would forgive my father; she tells me again and again that she forgave him years ago for the betrayal, the lies, the infidelity, the drugs, the screaming fights, and she's much happier. She's at peace. My answer is always that a father is a very different thing from a husband, and she quietly concedes. "Yes, I know you mean it," she says, and I turn away from her. I walk into my room and put the letter into a drawer with all the other ones just like it. So much anger and misery and blame bleeding from his round, scrawled handwriting, I can almost feel it coming off the paper like heat. All my life he had threatened suicide, holding it like a knife against anyone he felt had wronged him or anyone he thought might listen. He used to tell me he would do it while I was at school. I was the first one home, so it would be me who discovered his body on the living room floor, his head bleeding into the rug my great-grandmother had woven close to a hundred years ago.

"You'll know it's your fault that I'm dead," he would say, staring evenly into my eyes every time, "because you didn't love me enough." He wanted those words driven into me like a stake, he wanted them to take root like a disease and worm into every part of me and color everything that I thought, every action I took. Over the years, I had learned to discount this, as much as anyone can learn to discount something that damaging.

I shut the drawer, and the phone rings.

My mother answers. I hear her normal hello, her upshift into pleasant familiarity as she greets my stepmother, and then silence. I walk back into her bedroom. I watch her put her hand over her mouth, and I know. She raises her head to meet my eyes.

"He's dead, isn't he?" I say—a statement.

She nods.

"He shot himself," I say.

She nods. In that breathless second I understand that the universe is not strong enough to survive under coincidences of such terrifying extremes. No, I killed him with my words. And two floods open and tumble down inside me. There is shock, a cold water tide of it plunging into every exposed cavity and corridor, and then there is the warmer element, the stealthier one, threading like fingers of smoke into the darkest and truest places. It is relief, the bone-deep, bloody relief of a loose tooth yanked out at the root: he is gone.

When it started I was standing behind my mother, heedless, thinking about birds. She was watching my father, dead-steady, her face settled into a familiar mix of anger and resignation. Around us the living room seemed normal at first glance—the dim yellow light over the dining room table, shabby brown couches that were more comfortable than the expensive furniture at other houses I'd been to. But the air was thick with a tension as tangible as water, and nothing was OK.

"Why won't you take your hand out of your pocket?" she asked my father, and her words were steeped in calm, but with a sharp underlying edge. Her back was perfectly straight and her chin was thrust forward, as though she was shoring up an immense inner weight.

My father said nothing. Under the dim living-room lights his arms appeared browner than they really were, his hair darker and thicker. He looked younger, except for his eyes, which were a thousand years old. His left hand was thrust deep into his pocket, his head bowed. With jerky, irritable motions of his right hand, he sorted through the junk strewn across the dining room table. He ignored her, entirely, as though there was no one else in the room.

I watched them both, looking from one to the other, feeling tense in a familiar way. I was nine years old and so accustomed to my parents fighting that peace made me uncomfortable. Still, there was something abnormally upsetting about this fight in particular. I felt it. My stomach was a fist.

My mother said it again.

"Why won't you take your hand out of your pocket?"

And again he ignored her. His motions on the table grew harsher and more random, purposeless, a vague, forceful shoving of the items collected there—coins, lighters, matchbooks, Life Savers, a dollar-store Swiss army knife. His shoulders were hunched unevenly, held rigid with the right higher than the left, the guilty hand dug deeply into his pocket.

Invisible, I turned halfway towards the birdcage behind me. It was home-made, a smaller equivalent of chicken wire stapled to a raw wooden frame, and the birds inside were losing their feathers. One of them screamed and attacked his mirror in a frenzy of confused hostility. I found an uneven edge of chicken wire and pressed my fingerprint into the point of it as hard as I could.

With seemingly impossible composure, my mother asked the question a third time, the words worn smooth and soft as stone under water.

"Why won't you take your hand out of your pocket?"

My father shoved too hard, skittering a lighter over the edge of the table. It landed noiselessly on the carpet.

"Because I don't want to," he snapped without looking up. His voice was so tight, so alive with fury, an animal straining at its slender tether, that I removed my finger from the wire and silently circumvented the couch into the living room. I sat limply on the side closest to my parents, curved against the back, my arms boneless and useless, and I watched the two of them, three feet apart across the surface of the table, somehow a thousand miles away from each other.

"You hocked your wedding ring again, didn't you?" my mother asked. I looked at her hands; they cupped the decorative wooden knobs on the back of a dining room chair, rhythmically tightening, twisting, releasing. Otherwise she was motionless, her face still set in that stone-carved expression of anger and resignation.

My father gave no response. He started shoving things into his other pocket—matches, the knife. On the couch, in the long aimless corridors of my mind, I thought about storms spilling from a clear blue sky, spinning out of rainbows sharp and brilliant enough to blind people.

"Didn't you?" my mother asked.

There was a swift and startling burst of motion as my father jerked forward and slammed the palm of his right hand against the table. "It's none of your fucking business," he spit at her. My mother did not flinch, but the first fissure of emotion opened in her voice.

"How could it not be my business?" she said. "It's our *wedding* ring."

"I didn't do that," he said, clipped, staring down again at the table.

On the couch I thought about the boy down the street who I had a crush on; I thought about climbing the tree in his front yard and how if I pushed him from the cradle of its branches he would hit the ground and die.

"Then take your hand out of your pocket," my mother countered.

"It's none of your fucking business what I do."

"Why do you do it?" she asked him. "Why do you keep doing this to us?"

"I'm not doing anything to you," he shot back, lifting his small, bloodshot eyes to meet hers, and his voice was harder, harsher, almost a shout.

On the couch I thought about what dress I wanted to wear in my coffin—the yellow one with the full skirt—and I wanted my koala bear on my chest, under my crossed hands. I thought about the lid closing over me and how quiet it would be in the ground.

"You're doing it to all of us," my mother said. Her voice had also risen in volume, but was plaintive.

"I'm not doing *shit* to the girls," he said.

"*Yes,* you are, you being on drugs affects—"

"I am *not* on drugs," he shouted, leaning over the table again, and she shook her head, looked at the ceiling, her hands tight on the dining room chair.

On the couch I thought about cutting my finger and submerging it in the creek next to my grandmother's house, mating my blood with the current and sending it out into the world.

"Will you listen to yourself?" my mother implored. "Will you look at yourself?"

"Kiss my ass," my father said. He shoved everything on the table into his pocket, haphazardly, and his left hand slipped out unthinking. My mother saw, and I saw the naked band of white on his ring finger.

"You did hock it," my mother said. She sounded flat and defeated. "You hocked your wedding ring for drug money. That's great."

"No, fuck you, I didn't hock anything," he said, and his words were laden with disgust and irritation.

On the couch I remembered what my cousin told me about graveyards—that when you pass them you have to hold your breath or the souls will suck into your body. For the first part I always obeyed, my lungs tight and fighting inside me, and then I let the air tumble out and I breathed deeply, tempting the dead.

"Oh, you didn't? Then where is your ring, exactly?"

My father changed his tactic. "I'll get it back," he said. Every word was broken off sharply, splintered like wood. The letters of them were meant to cut.

"Sure you will," my mother said.

"Kiss my ass," he told her again.

On the couch I thought about ghosts walking our sleeping house with lidless eyes and distended mouths open so far that the jaws dangled, dislocated, against heart-empty chests. I thought about their bare feet and their cunning, and about the dark, still shape I always saw out of the corner of my eye when I brushed my teeth in the front bathroom. It watched me from the doorway.

"No, thank you," she said. Her hands were loose against the chair. She looked down; there was nowhere else to go within this fight. "Why bother getting it back?" she asked him bitterly. "It obviously doesn't mean anything to you."

"That's bullshit." He checked his pockets for cigarettes, preparing to leave.

"It's all bullshit, isn't it?" my mother said.

"It's all fucking bullshit," he shot back. "It's all fucking bullshit."

On the couch I thought about the times that he did not come back, the nights he was not at home, and the calm, half-easy, half-anxious anticipation of his return. I thought about the phone ringing and what it would be like to learn of a car wreck that way, or an overdose, or a heart attack, or suicide. I thought about the calm settling like dust over everything and cementing into permanence, and the door never slamming again, and the angry ignition of his car dead forever.

"Go," she said, and moved a weary hand. "Just go," and she padded softly into the kitchen.

My father said nothing. He moved through the living room with his keys in his hand, brushing past me like I was furniture, his hard, red eyes up and focused ahead. He gripped the knob and turned it, forcefully, and then kicked the screen door from where it stuck in the frame. A stifling finger of Texas night nosed in, the smell of baked concrete letting go of its heat, rich grassy outside musk, the dying cinders of daytime. The door was yanked shut, so hard that the impact rattled every window and cracked through the ceiling like a whip. The screen screamed back into place. The ignition of his car caught.

My mother came back out from the kitchen and sat next to me. She gathered me against her side and held my head with one hand. "I'm sorry, baby," she whispered against my hair.

My eyes drifted to the phone. I said nothing.

I don't know what to do with my hands. They fret and falter at the hem of my shirt, at my pockets, at each other, until I trap them against my sides under crossed arms. A breeze comes up and shoulders its way through the small corridor in which I stand, between my car and an official white panel van. It is December in Texas, sun cutting down through the clear day like water. There is an unhurried chill to the air that translates into the edges of the dry leaves, the pooled dark banks of shade. My head is cocked and I am listening to the woman standing opposite me. She works for the hospital to which my father donated his body. She strikes me as a former camp counselor, maybe, in her white polo shirt and stout khakis, her flat brown shoes, her short, curly wash-and-go haircut. She is thick and seems rooted to the ground, like a small tree trunk. Her face is a scrubbed-clean palate for the solemnity that is undoubtedly essential in her line of work.

At this point, less than two days after his death, I know very little, except that since he was not officially married to my stepmother, I am the legal next-of-kin. Therefore, I am in charge of everything, which is a double-edged sword. On one hand, it keeps me in constant motion. On the other hand, I have no idea what I am doing, and I never know what to expect.

"We had to discard his clothing," she says. She speaks with a sort of ceremonial gravity, using the word clothing instead of simply clothes. "It was completely saturated with blood."

I nod, accepting this information as though it means nothing. On the other side of my mind I am thinking, how interesting, that they assume I would not want my father's blood.

"Here is an inventory of what was on his person at the time of death," she says, handing me a typed form. I glance at it and see that, among other things, it includes a laundry list of the discarded clothes. "If you could just sign this form stating that you received his personal effects," she goes on, and passes me a clipboard and a pen bearing the same hospital name as is stenciled on the side of the white panel van behind her. I sign. Somehow I will have to get used to signing documents verifying my father's death.

She retrieves the clipboard and the pen and turns away to lean into the front seat of the van. I fold the list into a perfect rectangle. The integrity of the corners is important to me. I match them up with utter precision and slide my pinched fingers along the crease, then again, then again. I am as steady as life itself, a constantly beating heart, a metronome. I am steady.

The woman turns back towards me, holding two things. In one hand is the carbon of the form I signed. In the other is a clear plastic bag containing, among other things, the bottom plate of my father's dentures.

Time is hellishly deliberate at this point, segmented like a millipede, each second isolated from the next. I accept the form without looking at it. Instead my eyes are snared on the hideous incomplete grin standing upright among a mundane jumble of coins and lighters. She holds the bag delicately by its twisted top and there is air trapped inside, ballooning it out. My father's teeth rest within like a goldfish fresh from the pet store.

I take the scant weight of the bag into my hand and let it hang there at my side, touching nothing. I was not prepared for its contents. I wonder if she was fooled by my wooden calm. I wonder if she does this so often that she has ceased to notice the subtleties of people's faces, the taxidermy stiffness of their limbs.

As I stand there not looking down, she gives a speech I have already heard about the process of donating one's body to medical science, the sacrifice of it, the confidential nature of the research that will be conducted on my father. Too raw-nerved for subtlety, I spit into her words like an axe; I need to know.

"Is there only half of his dentures," I ask, inside recoiling heavily at the actual word, "because the top part was destroyed?"

She blinks at me, allowing a fissure to open in her veneer of professionalism. She says, quietly, "Yes. The gunshot destroyed it."

"It took the top of his head off," I say. My voice is so even.

"Yes," she says again, and then gestures towards the bag dangling from my hand, although neither of us move our eyes to look down at it. "There was quite a bit of blood. We washed his things three times but there are still traces of it everywhere."

"OK, thank you," I say and begin to turn towards my car.

"I wouldn't let you see his body," she says abruptly, and I look back at her. Something strikes me about her statement, but I don't know quite what. "I wouldn't let you see it even if you wanted to," she says, and her gaze is steady on mine. I don't know what to do with that, so I thank her again, and open the car door. I hide the clear bag and its contents under a newspaper the second I am inside and feel an immediate relief. I don't want anyone to see it—not her, not the people driving home after work towards dinners and disappointments. I join the absentminded flow of their traffic, wordless.

Only later will I rethink the encounter, the woman's last statement, the word *transport* stenciled under the name of the hospital, and realize that all along my father's body was three feet away, toothless and half-headed, in the back of that white panel van.

"Hello, is this . . . Chelsea?"

The hesitance at my name, and my stomach tightens up; never again will I trust phone calls. "Yes?" My voice is inflectionless. I pace in the narrow, glassed-in foyer of the willed-body-program building attached to the side of the hospital like a tumor, and press my cell phone against my ear so hard it burns. My eyes fix on a midget Christmas tree set up in one corner. There are faded presents around the base of it, dust collected in the loops of the bows on top. There are hardly any ornaments, just strings of lights, the multicolored ones. It does nothing to muffle my voice bouncing from the glass doors to the brown tiled floor, so every word I say is trailed by a faint comet-trail reflection of itself.

"This is Sergeant Tim Ingram with the Mount Pleasant police department," says the voice. His words are deep and slow and Southern in a way that reassures me.

"Uh-huh."

"I'm the detective who's assigned to your father's case."

"Oh." I stop and straighten. Moments ago, when my cell phone rang, I had been on the line with a judge from the Mount Pleasant court system, providing official authorization to release my father's body from Mount Pleasant's custody, despite the fact that he was already in Dallas. So he was no property of the Dallas County coroner's office, soon to be turned over to the willed-body program for research. He'd been dead for three days. The sheer conceptual motion of his inert body made me dizzy. "Was I supposed to call you?" I ask Tim Ingram. "I didn't know I was supposed to call you. I have no idea what I'm doing," I say, and then give a short, desperate laugh.

"No, no," he says quickly. "Actually, I don't really need to contact you. I mean, I just wanted to call to see if you're OK."

"If I'm OK?" My eyes go to the glass door and the early evening darkness behind it. I see my image there and glance quickly away, to the reflection of the Christmas tree. The lights look blurred, as though I am seeing them through water. It is beautiful in a small way that makes sense to me at the moment. I know intellectually that it is harder to cope with death during the holidays. That's what they say, isn't it? But I don't feel that. Death is death is death, I keep thinking, with a surgical detachment.

"I wanted to tell you I'm real sorry about your dad," he says softly.

"Oh," I say, "thank you." That's all I can manage to get out.

"Now listen," he says, "anything you need, I want you to call me. Any questions you have, anything you want to know, any problems, I want you to call me."

"Thank you. I will." There is crying somewhere inside me, echoing up towards my throat. It isn't about my father, though; it is the kindness of this cop calling after his work hours to ask me if I am OK. Death is a gift in this way: it reveals all the unknown kindnesses in people you never would have seen otherwise.

"I'm in the office five days a week, from eight in the morning to five in the evening, and if I'm not there someone will know how to contact me."

"OK. Thank you," I say again; my God, that phrase is so small and inadequate.

"I have a daughter named Chelsea," Sergeant Ingram says suddenly, and I have to put my hand against my eyes and push hard, painfully, to keep myself steady.

"Oh, yeah?" I say, and laugh a little.

"Yeah," he says.

"That's nice," I say. Nothing coming out of my mouth is deep enough, broad enough, anywhere near strong enough to convey what I feel. What I want is to touch him but he is several cities away, in the small town my father chose for his death.

"Yeah," says Sergeant Ingram and then hastily, almost as though he is embarrassed for having told me his daughter's name, he says his goodbyes and we hang up.

I immediately save his phone number into my cell phone. Then I stand there next to the Christmas tree, the dark on one side, the fluorescent-lit reception room on the other, my mother and the willed-body-program counselor waiting with clipboards of forms requiring my signature. I stand there and look down at nothing and relive the exact East Texas inflection of Sergeant Ingram's accent until I can't anymore.

My father's obituary appears in the newspaper on Friday the 13th. That morning I get a call from a friend of mine and learn that the restaurant she opened less than a month ago burned to the ground overnight, on the one unprotected day between the old insurance policy and the new one. She has lost everything. Her voice is distant and stunned. She sounds like a shocked second of silence after a car wreck or a lightning bolt or a gunshot. I understand this silence; for days I have been walking around in the sickening vacuum of it.

After I hang up I think two things. The first is that this day has begun on an ominous note. The second is that my father would love the fact that his obituary premieres on a day like this, on Friday the 13th.

I call my stepmother later to tell her how it came out because I promised I would. We have had several conversations over the past week, short, brittle exchanges that center on the business side of this entire ordeal. Obituaries, flowers, the memorial service. Nothing more.

She asks what picture I used and I tell her one from the late sixties, a hippy picture. He is twenty or so, smiling this broad, genuine smile that I hardly recognize. There is a leather cord tied around his forehead and a parakeet on his outstretched finger. It is obvious that he loves whoever took the picture.

"That's real good, sweetheart," she says. Her accent stretches each and every word out until the seams of it strain. Her sentences have the unhurried feel of a deep, hard yawn that pulls from the back of your throat to quake your entire body. I am reminded of Tim Ingram and wish for one wistful second that my voice sounded like that. "We put one in the Greenville paper, too. It's not written as good as yours, I'll bet, but it's something."

"I'm sure it's great," I tell her.

"And we used a recent picture, one where he was wearing that bandana on his head he liked so much, the one with the skulls and crossbones on it."

"Oh yeah," I say. I know the one. I know too much of it.

"I guess he was . . . I guess he was wearing that when he . . ."

Patty's voice thins and trails off and I feel a sudden white rush of panic. Jesus Christ, Jesus Christ, I do not want her to cry, but it has nothing to do with her unhappiness. I am not concerned about that. I can't be. Selfishly, I do not want her to cry because I know I will not be able to summon the strength to comfort her. I accepted his belongings. I released his body. I signed all the forms. I made the decisions. I wrote and submitted his obituary. I planned the memorial service. I blew up and framed pictures of him. I called everyone he ever knew. I cannot comfort Patty. If I have to comfort Patty, I will break apart.

"Maybe he was," I say quickly, knowing full well that he was wearing that bandana, and that it was shredded by the shot that killed him. It is listed on several of the many forms I have signed: one head rag, black, destroyed. "So, anyway, save some of those Greenville obituaries for me and I'll keep some of the Dallas ones for you, and I guess I'll just see you on Sunday at the memorial service, OK?" I block her with a wall of words to keep from hearing the tears in her voice. Everything inside me has risen to the surface like water. I am an elevator, I am reeling with that tickly vertigo, the crawling butterflies of falling and falling and falling. Underneath me my foot is slowly going to sleep but I can't move to relieve it. Instead I bear down on it, coaxing out the pain. Patty's moving slowly towards goodbye, so I charge past her, step on her, and end the phone call before she has a chance to get out the entire word. I can't help it. I cannot be responsible for her. I'm the legal next-of-kin. If I break apart, who will do everything?

I hang up the phone and sit there on my mother's bed and catalogue in my mind the things I have to do. Constant motion. I stand up.

Mount Pleasant, Texas, is officially named one of the one-hundred best small towns in the United States. Every Saturday night there is a city-wide jamboree with live country music. Every December the high-school choir holds a Christmas concert and dessert potluck. Every Valentine's Day there is a father-daughter dance at the civic center. In the heart of the town, the roads are cobblestone and the streetlights look like something out of a Gene Kelly movie. Small businesses have striped awnings and doors propped open with cinderblocks. Old war veterans in lawn chairs sit outside the barbershop, watching cars pass and exchanging terse nods with the customers as they go inside. In

Mount Pleasant, men and women still get their hair cut in separate buildings, no crossovers. The drive-in movie theater is still operational. The woman who sells you tickets calls you sugar or honey. The bank has a marquee with a digital clock and temperature readout that seems to show the temperature a beat or two longer than it shows the time, or maybe that's just the feel of the town tricking my mind. Maybe it's the atmosphere of this place, the genuine sense of ease settled in the pit of the town's stomach—maybe all of that got into my blood and made the exact time seem less significant than the quality of the air.

The police station sits in the center of the town, trying to be unobtrusive. It is a small, square building attached to the courthouse. I park my car in the tree-lined lot and walk inside with my heart in my throat.

The woman at the front desk calls me honey. I tell her that Sergeant Tim Ingram is expecting me, and she says she'll run and get him. I sit on a wooden bench along one wall and conjure up the memory of the last time I was in a police station—when my father was arrested for drug possession on a family vacation. That, too, happened in a small Texas town—Jefferson, Texas. His birthplace, Farmersville, bore a striking resemblance to both Mount Pleasant and Jefferson—small, rural, sugar-coated and frozen in time and as stereotypical as a movie set. I wonder if his death and arrest were couched in some sort of subconscious revenge towards Farmersville.

A door leading to the back part of the station opens, and Tim Ingram sticks his head out and smiles at me.

"You Chelsea?" he asks, and it is strange to hear his voice, his accent, in person. Tim Ingram is short, blond, and powerfully built. I know without asking that he played football in high school, and that he excelled at it; he probably could have gotten a scholarship to Texas A&M, but he didn't want to leave his hometown. He is dressed like a cop on a television show—gray slacks, a tie, and a short-sleeved white shirt. He does not have a gun or a holster and I wonder if this is deliberate, if he thought ahead and decided that I would be more comfortable without a gun in the room. Already I have fallen into a sort of hero worship of this man and I am startled by his actuality. Even his name has become an icon of what he is, his full name, and I cannot force myself to shorten it. He is Tim Ingram, like a superhero.

I follow him down a couple of hallways and end up in his small, cluttered office. He pulls out a chair for me and holds the back of it until I sit. My hands are cupping my elbows, and my fingers are dead cold. Over and over I am thinking, he saw my father's body.

He sits slung back in his desk chair, stretched out, his arms up and his fingers laced behind his head. In this position his biceps flex until I am sure his sleeves are going to burst at the seams. He smiles easily and fully. Although his gaze remains focused on me at all times, he has a nervous blinking tick. Every ten seconds or so he blinks rapidly as though there is something in his eyes. I cling to this idiosyncrasy; I lean towards that eventual moment when he blinks. It makes me love him.

I am here because he invited me. We have talked several times in the week since my father died. Sometimes I called him with a question or a list of questions; sometimes he called me just to check up, just to make sure I was OK. Once he told me I could come up to Mount Pleasant and talk with him face-to-face and he would tell me everything I wanted to know. The idea of this answered some deep, wrenching hunger inside me, so I accepted, and we set up a time, nine days after my father's death. The memorial service was just days ago. It had felt like a distraction to me, a ritual for everyone else. My closure had nothing to do with that preacher I had never met or my father's extended family, many of whom did not know whether I was Devon or Chelsea. My closure was here, worming my way into the scene of the crime.

I am nervous sitting in his office. I am terrified he will think I'm sick for asking about all the awful things I want to know. This is not the first time I have expressed this fear to him, but I can't help myself and the words tumble out.

"I just want to apologize for the questions I'm going to ask," I say, staring at the space of floor between us, trying not to appear as though I am crawling with embarrassment. "I don't know why I have this need to know this stuff. I don't want you to think I'm a gore hound or something."

Tim Ingram shakes his head, lowers one hand halfway, and makes a gently dismissive gesture.

"Listen," he says, "when I was seven my dad died in an explosion working on the Alaskan pipeline. All they found of him was one arm with his watch still on it. They didn't tell me much on account of I was so little. But when I got older I started wanting to know details. My mother didn't understand it, but I went looking for all these details about the accident. It was all I had, you know? It was closure. This is your closure," he says. "I understand that."

I nod for a moment, still fixed on the floor, unable to look up at him. Inside me a well of tension is slowly draining. Tim Ingram has just given me permission to obsessively reconstruct the details of my father's last days, the condition of his body, everything. Over the next two and a half hours, under the shelter of his permission, he will supply me with the details to do so.

I look at him once I am under control. "Thank you," I say, these shallow words that ultimately do not touch the lifelong gratitude I will have for his kindness and his absolution.

He takes me through it, minute by minute. My father checked into room 112 of the Comfort Inn right off the highway on the morning of December 8, 2002, a Saturday. The motel staff remembered my father as happy, talkative, padding barefoot around the grounds and riding his motorcycle up and down the highway. They remembered that he bought stamps the night before he died—to send out Christmas cards, he said. Tim Ingram asks if he sent me one.

"Actually," I tell him, "what he sent out were a bunch of suicide notes. Really bitter, angry, suicide notes."

For a moment Tim Ingram is speechless, as though the contrast between suicide notes and Christmas cards breaks his heart. "Oh, don't tell me that," he says, then softly, "I'm so sorry." And through his reaction, for just that second, I feel it—apart from my voracious, emotionless need for knowledge; I feel how tragically far off the mark my father's last impression was from his actual state of mind.

He tells me about the maid who found him, how she screamed and ran into the parking lot. The girls at the front desk called the police department. Tim Ingram happened to be on call that morning, so he responded, and was greeted with what he called the most gruesome crime scene he'd ever come across in ten years of police work. My father's face and head were gone from the nose up. His scalp had split and flopped down on either side of what was left of his skull to rest on his shoulders. Every inch of him was drenched with blood. He was bolt upright in a chair, his left hand open on his thigh, his right hand resting close to his groin and clenched in a fist with the thumb overlapping his index finger. Evidently he had activated the trigger with his left hand, despite the fact he was right-handed. His feet were bare and splayed, and his toes pointed up, off the floor, in a parody of surprise.

On the surface of the table were deep scratch marks that showed the unusual trajectory of the gun. After it went off, it flipped away from him, scarred the table, and then wedged between the front and back of the chair opposite him. The barrel pointed straight at the ceiling. Tim Ingram says that the gun's upright position, coupled with my father's ruined head and perfect posture, was the eeriest thing he had ever seen.

There was a note on the bedside table with my father's name, my step-mother's name, her address and phone number, and instructions to notify her and give her everything in the room. Next to the bed were two garbage bags, tied shut, filled with presents. One of the paramedics, a seasoned professional

Sergeant Ingram had known for years, had to leave the room to vomit as they were carrying out my father's body.

"Your father's case started out as a murder investigation," Tim Ingram tells me. "Every suicide starts out that way. Now, of course, it seemed real obvious what had happened when we went in there, but you can't be too careful. So we've looked at every angle of it, and there's just no denying that your father took his own life."

"Anyone who knew him could have told you that," I tell him. "This has been years in the coming. He did a lot of threatening."

Then he wants to know about my father, which touches me. I explain his background with drugs, his endless depression and anger and self-hatred, his sense of humor and astounding generosity.

And I ask a thousand questions. I ask about the gun and what will happen to it. Tim Ingram tells me where he got it, when he got it, how much he paid. There was no evidence that he sawed it off in the room so he must have done that before, at home, most likely so that it would fit in his motorcycle saddlebag. He tells me that it is illegal because it is sawed off, and that it will be melted and destroyed.

"We haven't done that yet, though," he says. "We still have the gun in evidence, here at the station. Do you want to see it?"

I sit stone-still, exploding inside with nerves. Do I want to see it? Of course I want to see it. "Yes, I'd like to see it," I say stiffly. I am bolt upright in my chair, my back arched slightly, aching. The gun is here. The gun is in the same building as I am.

"How do you want to see it?" Tim Ingram asks me. He picks up the phone and holds it there, waiting.

"From a distance," I say. I imagine touching it and my stomach rolls over. It is not the thought of touching it that scares me, though. It is how much I want to touch it that scares me.

He dials a few numbers and then speaks into the phone. "Hey, could you grab that gun from the Comfort Inn suicide last week?" he asks. "It's set to be chopped and melted down but I need to see it first. Just bring it into the hallway."

Tim Ingram hangs up and looks at me. His eyes weigh my reaction, but gently, and I think suddenly what a good father he must be to his daughter, also named Chelsea. I hear approaching footsteps.

"Is it out there?" I ask quietly.

"John?" Tim Ingram calls past me.

"Yeah," someone answers.

"Yeah, it's out there," he says to me. And then he waits.

I let go of the arms of my chair, realizing as I do that I've been gripping them so hard they are slick from my sweat. I stand up and turn halfway to hold the doorjamb of his office. And I look out into the hallway.

A cop dressed just like Tim Ingram is standing ten feet away, holding a black gun about two feet long. I listen to my heart beat for a while. Tim Ingram is silent behind me but I can sense that he is sitting forward in his chair for the first and only time. I stare at the gun but cannot make myself absorb any details of its appearance. I cannot think of anything to say about it. I cannot feel anything about it. Intellectually I know that this is the object that killed my father, but I can't make myself react in any negative way. I want to touch it. I want to know if it is hot or cold. I want to find out if it would leave powder or grease or blood on my fingers. I want my fingerprints on that gun. They belong there.

Finally I nod and come back into the office. I hear the footsteps of the man recede behind me. Tim Ingram leans back in his chair again, slowly, and folds his arms behind his head. Pretending normalcy, I go back to my obsessive catalog of questions—exactly how he looked with his head gone, quotes from the people who remembered him, what happened when they moved his body out. But now I am sheathed in a layer of cold that was not there before.

For two and a half hours Tim Ingram tells me everything I want to know, patiently, calmly, and in extreme detail. The satisfaction of it is like eating. I grow increasingly exhausted and wonder how I will manage the long drive back to Dallas.

Just before I leave, I fumble in my pocket for the folded clipping of my father's obituary that I saved for Tim Ingram.

"I don't know if you want this," I say, handing it to him with clumsy fingers. "It's not a big deal. I just thought maybe you should have a different last impression of my dad than that body being carried out of the room."

"Thank you so much," he says, looking closely at the picture, the cord around my father's head, the green-bellied parakeet. "Is this your dad in the sixties or what?" He is smiling and I smile with him, the feel of it unfamiliar on my face.

"Yeah, back when he was a hippie," I say. "I love that picture because he looks so happy." I watch him read the obituary.

"This is real nice," he says. He folds the thin strip of paper with his thick, careful fingers and tucks it into his breast pocket. "I keep a scrapbook of every case I've worked on and I'll put this right in there. Thank you so much."

"No, thank you. I can't even tell you," I start, and then stop and shake my head. I am not ready to cry yet, and certainly not in this wonderful man's office. "Thank you for everything," I say.

Tim Ingram hugs me when I leave. "Now listen," he says, "you know you can call me anytime about anything, right? Even if it's been ten years and you have some little tiny question that you've already asked me fifty times, you can call. And when I retire the department will still know how to get hold of me and they'll give you my number." I am nodding, gathering myself mentally, trying to prepare to leave this man and the temporary comfort he has provided. He pulls out a card and writes his email address on the back of it and has me write mine on another. "I might email you sometime," he says, almost shy, and I am reminded of the first time we talked, when he blurted out that his daughter's name was Chelsea. "If that's OK," he says quickly.

I tell him that it is, it's more than fine, that I would like to keep in touch. We have this strange and indelible bond, Tim Ingram and I. Locked in his mind is an image I will spend my entire life struggling to reconstruct.

Two years later, Tim Ingram is still checking up on me. Every few months I get an email just asking how I am, how I'm doing in school, what the weather is like in Chicago. Seeing his name in my Inbox fills me up with affection and grief and amazement that he remembers me. But really, the point is not that he remembers me; the point is that he remembers my father. I care more about that than anything.

On my way home that day, I pull my car over onto the shoulder across from my father's Comfort Inn. Everything Tim Ingram said is echoing down the length of my body like physical shockwaves, looping ceaselessly, and I'm absorbing the impact of it again and again. I put my hands on the steering wheel and my head on my hands, turning sideways, to stare at the calm face of the motel. Cars whip past me and I imagine I can hear, distantly, the blissful furious thunder of my father's motorcycle as he rode it around and around the night before he died. The ghost of it is so heartbreakingly close, for a moment it seems to be just outside my window and I almost raise my head. But I know there will be nothing there, so I close my eyes and I can feel the vibration in my spine, in my stomach. I know his ghost lives inside me. And I know that, somehow, I have to release him.

In the end, all that is left of him are his teeth. They are in the sealed plastic bag I signed for, jumbled together with the flotsam of his other belongings. The plastic bag is hidden inside a paper one. I go into my mother's bathroom and kneel on the floor and put the whole thing on the closed toilet. I tip up the end of the paper bag and ease out the meager remainder of my father's belongings. It is the first time I have seen the teeth since I accepted them from that woman, and I find that I cannot look directly at them. I keep my eyes to one side, as though they are a solar eclipse.

When I lay the bag flat, the teeth slide towards the middle. Carefully, I slide my fingers under the bag, and through the plastic, grasped against my palm, the lighter, the pocket knife, the blood-coated cross earring, the gold chain, the cheap digital watch. I lift my hand so that the teeth slide to the opposite end of the bag and everything else stays in place. Some change that I am not able to secure goes with them. Without touching the teeth I use my fingertips, over the plastic, to slide each coin down to the other end of the bag. It takes an endless, aching amount of time, crouching there by the toilet, my knees against the cold porcelain. I am not willing to do it any other way. The teeth were at ground zero of my father's suicide, and I cannot touch them.

When I finally have everything separated I lift the middle of the bag and cut it straight across. I breathe through my mouth. I am terrified of smelling gunpowder or blood or nicotine. As soon as the bag is halved, I Scotch-tape closed the part that contained his teeth, pick it up, and drop it back out of sight into the paper bag.

For the first time, I closely examine the rest of what the bag contained. His earring, a long dangling cross with a skull at its center, and his gold chain are both caked with blood, every link and crevice stiff with it. The lighter, the pocket knife, and watch are all coated also, as though they had been dipped in paint and then hastily shaken off. Every coin is rimmed in blood.

I stand at my mother's bathroom sink and rinse everything in water so hot it hurts all the way up to the bones in my wrists. The soap-scummed white porcelain holds the brown tint of his blood as the runoff passes over it, so I stop and scrub it out with toilet paper until it is spotless.

The blood clinging to my father's belongings is stubborn. Finally, I give up. I use paper towels to dry everything and put it all into a Ziploc bag. Only after the bag is sealed do I realize that I am still breathing through my mouth, so I stop and inhale tentatively through my nose. Under the fragrance of soap is the faintest trace of cigarette smoke. I tell myself it is from his watchband, not the teeth, not the teeth, *not the teeth*. I gather everything up and leave the bathroom to hide it all in a drawer, my hands raw and dry from the hot water. Later, hours after dark, I retrieve the paper bag and a backpack with everything I need inside it and get into my car.

Driving, I think back to when he got dentures. My father's teeth were always bad despite meticulous dental care. He brushed three times a day. He flossed after every meal. He gargled. Ultimately, he fought a losing battle. The dentist just kept pulling them, one by one, moving further and further towards the front of his mouth, until finally there was no other option. He came home that day and told my mother and then went straight to bed. We tiptoed around him the way we always did, but this time he had a legitimate reason to be so upset. The house breathed uneasily at this change in the usual.

After he got them pulled, he had to heal before he could be fitted for dentures. I was young but I remember my distinct horror at imagining a mouth with no teeth, the foreign swollen softness, the thick, blood-marbled spit, the new emptiness and space, a tongue worming blindly and finding nothing but tender root and raw tissue. Having no teeth changes the framework of an entire face. In all my life, I never once got used to seeing him without them. I never once got past my initial horror at the idea of it.

I park my car on a tree-sheltered street alongside a deserted playground. I take everything I brought out to the middle of a picnic area, where there is a low cement base of what used to be a streetlight. Quiet is everywhere, physical as fog. The gravel holds bits of glass like dull jewels. I kneel in front of the base and lay the paper bag in the middle. One part of my mind has refused to think about this aspect of dealing with my father's death, but another, deeper part refused to let go of it. Once I decided what to do it seemed so simple; it seemed there had never been any other option.

I take a hammer from my backpack. Using both hands I raise it and through the paper and plastic bags, through the haze of hesitance I feel forming at the edges of my mind, I bring it swiftly and directly down onto the teeth.

I don't expect it to be easy, and it isn't. The teeth are not made of glass, or porcelain, or anything so fragile. The first several blows do nothing except tear the paper and plastic bags so that I can see the grin of them, still perfectly intact. And the tear marks are in the shape of his teeth—literally, they are bite marks. The teeth are fighting back, biting into the swing of the hammer, into the force of my will to destroy them. I slam the hammer down harder, right into the top edge of the teeth. Gradually they start to fracture but not in sharp, defined pieces. It is almost as though they are made of very hard wax. The edges of the teeth dull, almost curl; they separate reluctantly from the whole in pieces with curved, smooth edges. The tissue pink of the gums I split with the claw of the hammer, and then I switch to the claw of the hammer entirely, chopping everything into smaller fragments until the scattered pile is unrecognizable.

And the worst part is the smell. Not in the sense of offensiveness, but in the sense of privacy. There are few places more private or intimate than inside of the human mouth. Standing there in the deserted park with my father's teeth crushed before me, breathing in the moist sour cigarette and body smell, is closer to him than I ever wanted to be. Not to his death—it is closer to his *life* than I ever wanted to be. I feel embarrassed for him, and hysterically apologetic, and I know I will cry about it at some point. Crying is something I continue to put off for the time being, though, like ignoring a letter you desperately do not want to read. It may be sealed but it's still in there, waiting for you.

I set about the task of cleaning up the teeth. Carefully, I sweep the remains to the edge of the cement base and into a cheap plastic dollar-store box he once gave me. The fragments clatter like poker chips as they fall in. I use tape like a lint roller to pick up every invisible shard from that cement surface, going over it three or four times. I refuse to leave any part of him behind. Then I wad the tape and the plastic and paper bags that his teeth bit through into the plastic box so that the fragments will not rattle as much. I put the lid on the box and tape it in place, then tape over the entire box so that the original red surface and poorly rendered flowers are no longer visible.

And it is over. The end of him is destroyed and controlled. I did it for both of us. For me, I destroyed the teeth so that the last remaining piece of him in this world was not something that horrified me.

For him, I destroyed them because they were witness to the flower of furious blood and fire that ended his life; I destroyed them because he wanted no witnesses.

"Well, hi, babygirl. This is Daddy."

"I know. Hi, Dad."

"What are you doing?"

"Mom and I were just about to go out to eat." I always planned my escape route, quantified the time I had available before he got his hopes up. "We decided we want soup because it's cold."

"Oh. Well, I just wanted to know how my babygirl was."

"She's fine." I made my tone flat and expressionless. Edged everything with a rind of impatience; it kept him at bay.

"What'd you do at work today?"

"Nothing. Same ol'." I cultivated silence. Showed no interest.

"When do you think you and your sister could come up and see me? It's only a forty-five-minute drive up here."

"I don't know. She's never home from college and I'm pretty busy. And it's more like an hour."

"Maybe I could come see you, we could go to Country Burger. And maybe then we could see a movie?"

"I don't know. When? I mean, maybe, if it works out time-wise." I always deflected everything. One sign of weakness and he'd trap me into it.

"I just miss you so much. I miss you so much."

"I know. I miss you too." No emotion.

"I just love you so much, babygirl, you're everything. You know that, don't you? You're everything."

"Yeah." How many times had I heard that before? By then it should have been meaningless to me.

"Well . . . I'll let you go if you and your mom are going out to eat."

"OK."

"All right, babygirl."

"Wait, Dad—" And then the weakness—when it came, it was always sudden, from nowhere, and I couldn't control it. "Is it snowing up in Greenville?"

"Oh yeah, it snowed a little this morning."

"And are you still riding your motorcycle around?"

"Yeah! Oh yeah, I ride it everywhere. Everywhere."

"Aren't you cold? Do you bundle up, I mean?"

"Oh yeah—I have that nice vest, and a nice coat Patty got from Wal-Mart for real cheap, and one of those woolen ski masks to go under my helmet."

"So you're wearing your helmet? Good."

"Yeah. Yeah, I always do." He paused, almost as though he was as uncomfortable with receiving my interest as I was with giving it.

"OK." Back to flatness. I gave him scraps; he could survive on those.

"OK, babygirl. I love you. Bye-bye."

Always bye-bye, like a little boy.

"Love you. Bye." And I cut the connection. Never waited for him to do it first. He wouldn't.

And that was the last time I talked to him.

The woman behind the reception desk has blond hair pulled back into a ponytail and tired blue eyes. She glances up as I come in. I approach the desk awkwardly, my hands in my pockets, unsure of how to broach this subject. I look back at her children on the couch by the window, flung out in postures of boredom, their coloring books open and ignored. There is an open bag of goldfish crackers on the floor.

"Hi," she says, and I look back at her.

"Hi," I say. I can feel my heart in my head. Since I don't know what to say, I decide to be blunt. I move closer to the counter so that her children can't hear me. "Last week a man died here," I say, and her eyebrows immediately draw together, a concerned look, and my stomach drops at the notion that she talked to him.

"Yeah," she says. "That was awful."

"He was my dad," I tell her evenly.

She draws in a breath and, for a moment, is speechless.

"It's OK," I say immediately.

"I'm so sorry," she whispers, leaning towards me.

"Did you talk to him?"

"Well, not much, but he was always around—that whole weekend, I mean. He seemed like such a happy guy. He walked around here barefoot and talked to everyone."

"That sounds like him," I say, and there is a spark of something inside me— something between regret and grief. He was relieved, I think; he was light with relief. "I wondered if I could see the room," I say, and I can feel my face grow warm. I am terrified of coming off as a gore hound, or a sympathy hound.

"Oh, honey," she says doubtfully.

"I know. I'm sorry." I wish Tim Ingram was here to explain it to her. He is so close, five minutes away, but I feel that I have already imposed on him enough. I need to do this alone. I steel myself and continue. "I just need to see it. There's not a lot of closure with suicide," I say, and to me the statement smacks of self-pity. I start to feel sick. "I know it seems awful."

"Are you sure?" she asks. She looks like she wants to hug me. She looks like she would rather not give me the key, and I start to get nervous.

"I am. I'm sure," I tell her confidently. Hear how clearly I enunciate my words? See how strong I am?

"They're sort of remodeling it," she says, reluctantly. "They're tearing the walls out, and the carpet, everything, and rebuilding it all."

"Oh," I say. I want to ask if this is because of the gallons of blood, but I don't. "Do they do that . . . every time?" I ask instead.

"Yeah, every time someone dies in a room they tear it all out," she says. She steps so softly on the word *dies* I barely hear it. I am nodding, coping.

"So is it okay if I go in there?" I ask. "Room 112."

She keeps her eyes on me as she hands me the key. "Are you sure you're

OK, honey?" she asks me.

"I'm sure," I say. "I am. Thank you so much. I'll bring this right back."

I wave at her children on the way out; they stare blankly at me, like cats.

There is a sagging mattress propped up against the window of room 112. I slide the key in and find the door already unlocked, so I push it open.

The room is largely gutted. Furniture is pushed up against the walls and the carpet is gone, revealing gritty, plaster-dusted cement. Directly across from me is the enormous mirror outside the bathroom, and my reflection in it, backlit and hovering like a ghost in the open doorway. He stood in front of this mirror with his cheap camera and recorded those final images of himself. They were the last exposures on the roll, afterthoughts.

For a moment, I stand there, locking eyes with myself, and allow my heart to slow to a normal heart rate. He died here. This is where he died. This is where he sat, where he exhaled his last breath, where he bled slowly and silently into the ridges of every coin in his pocket.

Tentatively, I step inside and close the door behind me. The silence is riotous, as though the room will ring forever with the brutal plunging wake of the gunshot. I move a little farther inside. I am walking on my tiptoes, as though I don't trust the floor to hold my weight. As though this is a fragile dream place that cannot be expected to behave rationally.

My eyes crawl the walls, up to the ceiling, and for the first time I see the minute specks of blood still there. The inside of my father's head. Dots, dashes, scrawled carelessly like hurried shorthand. Or like red stars shooting all in the same direction, towards some infinitely important and unreachable point in space. I stand there with my head tilted back and follow their path but they lead nowhere. That blood was left for me to see. I am breathing deeply, freely, with relief. This is as close to the center of his death as I will ever get.

I move my gaze down the wall again, studying it, and find another smear close to the floor. My father's knife is in my pocket. I take it out and kneel before the spot, right behind the place where he must have died. I push the point of the knife into soft plaster and dig a hole around it until I can pry out the entire piece. I stand without dusting the grit from my knees.

On the table behind me is a Gideon bible. I open it to page 1210 because he died on December 10th and place the plaster carefully inside. The Gideons put bibles in motel rooms for people who need them. I need this one. I wonder if he read it. With only a twinge of guilt, I put the bible in my backpack.

There is a reason that I am here, beyond voyeurism. I need to know if he remained in the room. I need to know if he was somehow trapped here. Violent deaths often leave the spirit of a person confused, caught in the place where they died. I don't want this for him. This would be hell, and I can't stand the idea that God neglected him to hell just for being so desperately unhappy. So I look for him.

I close my eyes and breathe and listen to the silence. I feel for him with my heart. The room is still and quiet and my pulse stays even. I open my eyes and say his name.

"Dad?"

But there is nothing. He is gone.

Do you know, Dad, that I have swallowed your death like food? I see your head in my mind's eye as clearly as if I were standing there in the room with you when you ruined it. I made that sweet Southern cop tell me exactly what you looked like, exactly how much of your face and skull were missing, exactly how much of the room was coated with the inside of you. A seasoned paramedic had to leave the room to vomit. There was so much blood it was in ridges, each separate ridge, along the edge of every coin in your pocket, and four thorough washings did not remove it. The movie versions of people shooting themselves in the head—grotesquely inaccurate. Monstrously understated. Maybe because none of those people used a double-barrel sawed-off shotgun.

Do you know that I know these things? I don't know whether or not I want you to. You suffered enormously at both your hand and mine, and in the end I felt left out. I went looking for the horrific details of your gore because I wanted to match you, step for step. I wanted to claw my way into that room, into the eye of you.

Do you know that I have your ashes in my desk cabinet? You can hear the chalk-hollow click of bone fragments when your container is tipped. I don't move you much. Sometimes it catches me, the knowledge that I own your body in this form and that you live in my apartment. Sometimes I feel you in there. I know the ashes are you, just changed, same as the half-headed corpse that made that poor man vomit when he took you out—that was you, too, just changed, forged into something else in the crucible of your answerless misery. I imagine that the dimensions of the inside of my desk cabinet stretched surrealistically long, like a hall, to hold your dead body, prone and obedient now on its back among your old yearbooks and my general clutter, carefully arranged to keep you from view. Although you no longer have eyes to look at me. But you don't need them. You are always with me. I remember, when I picked up your ashes and carried them across the hospital parking lot to my car, that the weight surprised me, and the size. I felt very acutely that I was holding your head. But your entire head, complete, including the part that you chose to slough off onto the walls and ceiling of that motel room.

Do you know that I think this way? I'm not sure if I want you to. In my head I write dead letters to you all the time. I re-speak conversations, changing them to hurt you more, or to hurt you less, depending.

Do you know that I still can't look at recent pictures of you? For nearly a year I fooled myself by carrying shots of you from the seventies, from before I was born, because you were so adorable back then, with that leather cord tied around your forehead. It took me so long to realize that I did this so I would not have to look into the face that I knew and meet your eyes and see there the blinding thirst for relief. If I look at the recent pictures I have to think about your thinning hair and the skull visible underneath it, the curve fragile and vulnerable as a newborn's. It seems so obvious, how easy it would be to ruin. So obvious to see that your unavoidable fate was not just an old powerless threat.

Did you know that I was divided down the middle so sharply there was no in between? I am two girls inhabiting one body. I am the girl who believed you every time, who crouched in a constant state of readiness and recoil, anticipating the shot with every breath. And I am the girl who was dead—asleep despite all your attempts to wake me. In your absence these two girls stretch between the terrible web of confusion inside of which I struggle.

Do you know that however hard I may struggle, I know that this is all there is left of you, so really I have no will to break free? I plan to live inside the protective caul of your shattered blood and bone and tissue forever. It may be hard to understand, that such violence could comfort rather than repel, but this was the nature of your relief, your deliverance from crippling pain, your life finally submitting to your will, your last seconds on this earth. So I will cradle your violence in the palm of my hand like memory, as precious as though it were my own.

Telling his dog goodbye—this is the hardest part. She loves him easily and it is easy to love her. He has never hurt her, until now, until the goodbye. She trusts him implicitly, and he knows this, and it is killing him.

He tapes the note to the refrigerator for his wife to find, reads one last time the short, vague lie about a fishing trip, and then kneels before his dog in the empty house. She is excited, she doesn't understand. He hugs her hard once, twice, and then drops onto the heels of his hands. He hangs his head, butts it against her, and she is squirming, anxious with happiness. She does not understand. She bows and snorts, her ears forward like a puppy; she thinks they are playing. He is crying and saying her name, a constant slurred indecipherable sound; he hugs her again and tells her he is sorry, he is sorry, he is *so sorry*. He stands quickly but unsteadily and goes to the door. She follows him, her stocky body wagging, trotting, as he steps out of the house. He shuts her in hard before he can see the hopeful tilt of her head, her paws on the screen, the beginnings of confusion. He walks rapidly, head ducked, to his motorcycle. He takes off fast, spraying gravel onto the grass like a rain of shrapnel, and does not look back.

Once he is on the motorcycle, spooling out more and more distance by the second, it is easy. His body is light with relief. Everything lifts. His eyes feel wider, and he takes in the air around him, the trees along the interstate, the stripes of white paint that mark the black asphalt lanes, heart beating past like some city pulse—he sucks it in, and the ruthless beauty of it all lies not in the actual seeing, but in how little time he has left to experience it.

In the motorcycle saddlebag by his left leg is the gun. He can feel it touching him like a hand, quietly insistent. Days ago, when no one was home, he sawed off most of the handle and barrel so that it would fit. He handled it with shaking fingers, anticipation, and reverence—rendering every move sacred. Temptation sunk into him like a fishhook, and pulled, but he waited. He stored it in a brown paper bag under his side of the bed, and he waited.

At the motel he stands in the open doorway of his room and looks out at his motorcycle for a moment. It has just rained and the pavement is wet, sending up the smell of summer like a ghost into the fresh December air. He thinks longingly of riding his motorcycle, the wind dividing sharply around him and closing up behind, the hectic speed, the fragile line between control and chaos. He looks at the motorcycle's cocked stance, and he has the idea that it is waiting for him, like a person. His heart turns on its axis, agonized. Softly, he shuts the door.

This is his space. He occupies it like a child. He takes off his shoes and lies down on the bed for a moment. He rises and goes to the mirror outside the bathroom and stares at himself. He turns on the television and flips through the channels without paying attention to what is on. He unfolds and refolds the few pamphlets about Texarkana, the nearest big town. He thinks about the two hours of distance from here to his home and he is momentarily giddy. Now that he is here, there is no turning back. The gun is dormant under the right side of the bed.

The people who work here are so nice. He wants to talk to them, he wants them to know his name. He wants to make them laugh. He pads around the grounds of the motel barefoot and says hello to people. He asks them if they want to see his motorcycle. He asks for extra stationary and envelopes at the front desk and they give him a complimentary pen. On the couches by the front window are the children of the girl who is working the front desk. They are bored, sprawled with coloring books and goldfish crackers. He bends at the waist and asks them their names and tells them how good they are at coloring. They smile half-smiles through shy, upturned eyes. When he leaves, the girl calls after him, saying he should let her know if he needs anything else. She says his name and smiles. He wells up inside until he can't breathe and thanks her and walks back to his room, the pavement cool against the soles of his feet.

On Saturday afternoon, after he has settled in, he writes letters. There is one for everyone. Sitting at the small round table, he opens a door in himself that closed when he left the house; he opens it for the last time and lets the anger rush out like bile and excoriate the inside of him. It pours down his arm and into his hand, into the last words he will ever say to them. When he is done he seals the envelopes and addresses each one, carefully. He stacks them on the round table. His hands are shaking. He turns on the television and lies down on the bed and breathes very evenly, very deliberately. The door inside him squeals as it shuts.

Later he takes pictures of his motorcycle, crouching, circling, planning each and every shot to show how perfect and powerful a machine it is. There is a connective energy between him and the motorcycle, and he wants to preserve it; he wants to be remembered through it. He likes the way it looks, slanted into the parking space in front of his room. No other cars are around so it stands alone in the pictures, as though he planned it that way. When he has reached the last few pictures on the roll he stands still for a moment and considers. Then he goes into his room and stands before the mirror outside the bathroom and looks at himself. He lifts the camera and holds it against his chest. The flash is on. He takes three pictures of himself this way, alone, lost in the liquid flower of light that blows open every time he presses the button. He does not know why he decided to do that, but after it is done, he feels calmer.

On Sunday he takes this film into the little town, to a Wal-Mart. He strolls the aisles and breathes the sterile air. It is cold, a manufactured cold. He thinks about the motorcycle ride to Wal-Mart, the way the sound of the engine tore those sleepy streets up the middle like cheap cloth. He thinks about his dangling cross and skull earring, his thick chain, the black crossbones bandana on his head, his boots and black clothes. He smiles to himself. He feels proud of the way he looks, the way people watch him. He may have been born in one of these nothing towns, but he was nothing like the people there, and he escaped. Now he is the kind of person that people watch and remember.

Later that night, he races his motorcycle up and down the highway in front of the motel. He swerves onto the exit ramp, the overpass, the access road, the highway, then onto the next exit ramp, the overpass, the access road, the highway, again and again in a circle as though he is on a racetrack. Beyond him the motel floats suspended in the glow of the parking-lot lights, waiting. On the highway he is free, laid flat over the handlebars with his teeth bared, the wind struggling to rip the helmet from his head. The volume of his own velocity is deafening. His entire body vibrates and his heart lifts, weightless, and soars towards the motel room, towards the gun in its brown paper wrapping, and his whole life beats with the precision of a clock working its way backwards towards one critical moment.

Afterwards he goes to the front desk of the motel and the same girl is working. Her children are jumbled together on the couch by the window, sleeping, their arms and legs flung out like starfish. The girl's eyes are tired but she greets him by name and smiles. He asks if she saw him riding up and down the highway and she says she did. He is flushed from the high of it. He launches into a little lecture about his motorcycle and she rests her elbow on the desk, her chin in her palm, and listens with a slight smile on her face. When he is done he asks if he can buy stamps. She rouses herself and gets some for him. As he pays, he says he is sending Christmas cards to his family, and she says how nice that is. She says she bets he is a good father, and he feels a glancing pain, but it is distant. It is easy to ignore because he knows it will all be over soon. She tells him to have a good night and he goes back to his room. He puts a stamp onto each sealed envelope, carefully, and then walks to the mailbox at the corner of the motel parking lot. He listens as they hit the bottom. Back in the room, he turns on the television but he watches the ceiling.

Monday morning he wakes early. His mind is moving in straight, logical lines. He sits at the small round table and writes another kind of letter, to his cousin in Washington. She is the only person who has ever understood him; she is the only one who loves him, except for his dog. He sends her the pictures of his motorcycle and asks that she put up several of them in her house, the best ones, to remember him by. He writes for a while about the motorcycle, about its history and its uniqueness, about why it is better than other motorcycles. Then he writes about his dog. It makes him cry. He wants her here so badly, the warm push of her body, her cold nose, her quick, hopeful breath, her solid, fat belly. He tells his cousin to make sure that she is OK; he talks about what a good dog she is, how she never goes to the bathroom in the house. The only problem is that sometimes she does get out, and she likes to run as hard and as fast as she can, but besides that she is so good—she is perfect. She is much more than just a dog. He pauses and holds his pen above the paper for a moment. Then he apologizes for killing himself, but he has to. He can't help it. He signs his name and seals the letter and the packet of pictures into a manila envelope and puts four stamps on it. He leaves his room and walks across the parking lot to the mailbox and drops it in. The last detail is taken care of. He watches the mailbox for a moment and then turns back to room 112.

It is quiet. The maid will come soon. He likes being in the room while she cleans. He speaks a little bit of Spanish and she speaks a little bit of English. He enjoys practicing with her. He imagines her changing the pillowcase while he sits on the chair, the sound of the coarse cotton material as she shakes it out, and it happens fast. His patience bottoms out and he can't stand it. He meant to wait until tonight, to have this last day, but the old agonies are pressing hard inside him like fists and the tug of memory is pulling sharply enough to yank open every closed door inside him. The weight of it is poised on a razor edge, tipping.

He takes the gun from under the bed and removes the brown paper. He sits at the round table and adjusts the chair so that he is facing the door. Inside he is very calm. He is sure. He cocks the gun and places it in his mouth resting the barrel on his bottom row of teeth. His mouth is open very wide; his jaw is so tense it hurts. He runs his left hand down the body of the gun, gently, until his finger finds the trigger. His right hand he rests in his lap.

He looks straight ahead and all at once allows every door to fly open inside him; every poison horror is released at once, coiling out like a torrent of snakes— two girls, his daughters, his babygirls crying as he screamed at them, their faces bulging as they screamed back, Devon rolling her eyes when she thought he wasn't looking, Chelsea checking her watch ten times during an hour-long visit, their distance, their hostility, their complete, cruel indifference, and the sound of his own snot-nosed crying as he fell to his knees on the front porch and begged the day his ex-wife kicked him out—all of this lived inside of him like a cruel and starving disease, and he couldn't take another second.

A sound comes from deep within him, from the scraping bottom of his stomach; it rockets up the length of his aching body and winds out of his mouth, strained and guttural and heavy with yearning, and his finger moves once, steadily, and the gun goes off.

The force of the shot opens his skull and destroys it from the nose to the base of his neck. The gun kicks from his hand, flips over the table where it leaves a distinct scratch, and wedges between the seat and the back of the chair opposite him. The barrel points straight at the ceiling. Everything falls to a ringing silence. The gun waits there, eerily upright from the headless man.

But he knows none of this. He is gone.

Dear Patricia

Alecia Savale

Dear Patricia,

It's me, Alecia, the receptionist at the 57th Street Salon next to your family's dry cleaning store. I don't know if you remember me or not, but that's OK. You will in a minute.

Apparently, your mother thought I was pretty. She thought I would fit the role in your boyfriend's movie nicely, seeing as how you were convinced enough to seek me out this summer. Sorry I forgot your boyfriend's name, but whatever.

When you came in around four that Wednesday, I thought you were another customer on a mission to interrupt me from counting up the drawer. It was right in the middle of a shift change, and I asked you to wait a second. You looked at the magazine rack and said, "No hurry." That was the first time I saw you smile, deceptively warm.

Yours is the type of beauty that must be clobbered out, I mean really pummeled out of you good. Don't take this the wrong way or anything, but sometimes I see people like you and I want to give them a good blow to the head so I won't have to stare so hard. Common folk like me have to work to look like you.

When you turned around, the other receptionist whispered that you weren't a customer, you were there earlier the same day looking for me. Imagine my excitement then! A gorgeous girl I've never seen before stopping by my work to find me . . . the mystery, the endless possibilities! It was a gruesomely lonely summer, Patricia. I needed something good to happen to me right about then.

My excitement quickly turned to embarrassment when I realized that my hair was not styled and it looked more like tumbleweeds, a blonde Afro. In addition, I was wearing a short-sleeved black turtleneck, my head seeming to sprout out of it like the eye of a potato. Perhaps you remember this as you recall the orange splotches on my face, the aftermath of self-tanner smeared liberally, drunkenly, all over my body the night before.

Enthusiastically, maybe a bit too eagerly, I said, "Hi, can I help you?"

You snapped around, face lighting up. "I think so, yes. Alecia, yes?"

I nodded and you extended your hand in introduction. Your mom owned the shop next door, and your boyfriend was a graduate student of film at UIC working on his final project. You were helping him look for an actress with a very specific phenotype. I watched your champagne-colored lips close firmly over the words "pretty" and "blonde."

Inexperienced though I was, my mind fueled rapid flashbacks from sophomore year of high school, when I was a chorus member in the spring musical, *Hello, Dolly!* Since then, I had been patiently awaiting my breakthrough role in the real world of acting, sure that it would come unexpectedly one day, a day like that day precisely.

I asked you to describe the part. You said first I'd have to be free on the following Monday and Tuesday to voyage out to Grand Beach, Michigan, with you and the crew.

Maybe my face contorted oddly when I heard the word Michigan, because you were quick to assure me that Grand Beach was only an hour away. Oh, Patricia! It wasn't about the distance that I made that face. It's because I'm a native resident of that place called Michigan, and for reasons you'd never guess, the very word sounds like hell to me! Poor Patricia, you couldn't have known.

The character I was to play would emerge from Lake Michigan with a golf ball in her hand and speak coyly to a stammering, drooling male. At this point, you laughed and scissored your hands away from your chest. "No porn," you clarified.

Continuing, there would be another brief scene of my silhouette, which worried me. I had been putting on weight because that's what happens when

I'm lonely. I grow jowls quicker than a Chia pet grows that green shit.

You said I would stay in my own room at a nice cabin with a hot tub. I can't forget the way you cocked your head in bribe when you said "hot tub." You regretted to tell me I wouldn't be compensated for my time, but I didn't care, Patricia.

I grinned like a fool and said I would do it. We exchanged phone numbers on yellow Post-its. You were going to call me.

After you left, the nosy stylists were already sniffing out the case; one named Ginge said, "Alecia, this might be your big debut."

I looked in the mirror to my right and saw my Chesire cat smile, the jowls. It wasn't going to happen.

You came back with your boyfriend half an hour later. I saw the two of you floating about outside the shop, gesturing at one another in a heated debate. He peeked inside and turned back to you, said something, then came in. You were following him but had to stop and give a homeless guy some change. I thought what a nice girl you must be.

Your boyfriend looked like the sort of guy I would expect a girl like you to date: "taken." He was Caucasian, with gelled hair, a honey golden tan, and perfectly straight, unnaturally white teeth. He had a Prada satchel . . . totally metrosexual.

Well, this is goofy. You know what he looks like. Probably the two of you have sex three times a week.

I'm sorry. That was rude. But Patricia, it was ruder for that bastard to shake my hand and tell me he'd call, then never call. That was rude. It was rude that when I called you and left a polite, soprano voice message, I never heard back.

Good thing I didn't take that time off work, that Monday and Tuesday. You almost screwed me out of over a hundred dollars, not like you know what that means. Probably your parents pay for everything.

But you know why I didn't take that time off work? You want to know why I called at all?

If you think I wanted to know whether or not to pack sunscreen in my overnight bag, you are so wrong. I had to tell you what you already knew: I wasn't what you were looking for.

I was sick, Patricia. Sick in ways your spoon-fed, bookish Asian mind never fathomed outside of biology class. I was just so lonely, living on my own for the first time with no one to talk to besides a West Side roommate who resembled Buckwheat. I needed friends badly.

Here's what would have happened if I went with you. First, I would have been nervous riding in the car so, feeling the need to make conversation, I would tell lousy anticlimactic stories and jokes to fill the dead silence. Your boyfriend would have driven in what I'm picturing to be a luxury sedan. He would have his hand on your knee, but each time you remembered I was in the back seat you would brush it away.

We would stare out our windows, suspended in private thoughts while we cruised outside of the city. Eventually, you would feign interest in my work and school life, and my responses would be mostly polite, meaningless bullshit. We would exchange fake smiles in the rearview mirror, where objects are closer than they appear.

Halfway there you would retrieve snacks out of a canvas Whole Foods Market tote. You would have an assortment of nuts, dried fruits, and bottled water: stuff that girls who have subscriptions to *Self* magazine eat. You would offer me some and I would graciously accept a handful of yogurt raisins. I would want more and be afraid to ask. I would surreptitiously wish we could eat Pop-Tarts and Mallomars and Gummi Worms like kids do on car trips.

I would silently launch into an elaborate fantasy of us as best friends or roommates, laughing freely together and meaning it. Our personalities would click like puzzle pieces. Patricia in conjunction with Alecia, our names ringing harmoniously together on our answering machine message. I would see us sprawled out on our bellies in pajamas on the living room floor of my apartment, watching TV. Hitting each other with pillows, lovingly calling each other "bitch."

Then I would say something witty out loud and watch it float by you like an unnoticed butterfly. You would be totally immune to my every word; I just know—completely unaffected. I would realize this and get sad. I would hate your boyfriend for whatever quality he possessed that kept you attracted to him.

Once in Grand Beach, upon my immediate suggestion we would stop at a convenience store to buy alcohol. I would persuade you to buy two cases of Jack Daniel's Cranberry Jack Country Cocktails, one of which I would finish on my own by sundown.

I would proceed to chain-smoke, possibly lighting up in the back seat of the car, only rolling my window down when your boyfriend grunted we were almost there.

Guaranteed I would fuck up the shoot, I wouldn't want to emerge from the lake with a golf ball because, unbeknownst to you, that lake is filth. Lake Michigan will forever remind me of a time when I was eight years old at my uncle's cabin in Muskegon. My family and I were in our suits and all ready to jump in, when my mother screamed, "Wait! Wait, everybody stop!"

Immediately, we saw why. The entire surface of the lake was blanketed in dead fish. It was horrifying, Patricia.

I'd down all four of my Country Cocktails and be too drunk to remember why I was there. I'd sit on the dock and chain-smoke while your boyfriend verbally unleashed his frustrations on you behind the cabin. You would end up crying and calling your mother to curse her out in your Mandarin tongue for suggesting me.

Meanwhile, I would schmooze with the geek I was supposed to hand the golf ball to and possibly, depending on the strength of my buzz, make out with him in my (picture me cocking my head here) hot tub.

The whole thing would be deliciously awful, and the movie would have to be reshot with someone else, maybe the someone else you ended up using instead of me.

Still, though, you should have called me back.

It hurt most when you came into the salon a month later and pretended we never met. Granted, I had changed my hair color, but still . . . still, fuck you. There's no way you didn't recognize me.

I'll have you know you got ripped off. Like your stick-straight Asian hair needed a clear prism deep-conditioning treatment. Please.

Patricia, maybe you think it's bizarre that I write to you now. After all, our exchange was short and trivial. But I'm writing to you because sometimes it's the smallest things in life that hurt the most. To get someone's hopes up, someone who never asked anything of you, and then just crush the person with no tact or grace . . . it's evil.

I pass by Grand Beach on the train home, and every time I see the sign marking it as such, I think of you. I think how if by some small grace I might grow to love this world, I can only expect it to hate me in return. It's not your fault, really. But in a way it is.

I hope the movie went well and you got the girl you were looking for. You can rest assured now more than ever that I wasn't her.

You, a stunning bright-eyed Asian beauty, were entirely fucking wrong. Just thought I'd grant myself the liberty of letting you know.

So maybe we'll pretend not to know each other again sometime, and I'll get to overcharge you once more.

Can't wait, Patricia. Really, I can't.

[In]sincerely yours,

Alecia

The Fire

Debra Ponczek

THINKING BACK, I BELIEVE OUR LADY OF THE ANGELS PARISH IN CHICAGO WAS a microcosm of America in the 1950s. While a specific tragedy changed the lives of the people in my parish, it seems now, in retrospect, to be just one of many seismic shocks that would shake America in the late 1950s and early 1960s, just one of many cataclysmic events—a war, assassinations, riots, serial murders—that would shape our lives in the decades ahead.

On a frigid December day in 1958, a fire started in a garbage can near a wooden stairway in the basement level of the two-story Our Lady of the Angels schoolhouse. The nuns and teachers and children on the first floor escaped, but the fire burned so quickly that many of those on the second floor were trapped by the blaze. When they found that the corridor was impassible and a door to the only fire escape was locked, the nuns and children stayed in the classrooms, sitting at their desks, praying for rescue, until the flames and the smoke and the innate thirst for life drove them to the windows. They shattered the glass with fists and chairs and jumped or fell to the concrete pavement two-and-a-half stories below, breaking their legs or their backs or their necks. Three nuns and ninety-two children died in the fire, and nearly one hundred were injured. Some families lost a child; some families lost several children.

On the day of the fire, I sat at my desk with the other first graders in a building nearly a block away from the main school. It was an old, brick, two-story apartment building that had been converted into classrooms that housed kindergarteners and first-grade students. My room was on the first floor.

I remember that the first whiff of trouble came on the wind. It wasn't a smell, but a sound. Sirens. The mournful wail of a fire engine, starting slow and low and building to a crescendo of alarm. Then another. And another. They raced by the little brick house toward the main school so fast that they sucked the air in after them, their throaty horns sending shock waves through the confines of the small side street. They were followed by the scream of ambulances, one after another, like a flock of birds in flight; the whooping of police cars, cutting through the chill afternoon air; the honking of car horns, their strident shrieks sounding the alarm.

Soon the air outside the little brick building filled with men's and women's screaming voices, sirens, and blaring car horns, the sounds of a buzzing, frightened swarm.

The young nun who taught our first-grade class tried to go on with her lesson, but the noise sent her to the bay window at the front of the room. She peered outside but could see only the commotion in the street. She told us to continue our lessons, then crossed the room and left for a short, whispered conference with the lay teacher who had come downstairs from the second-floor classroom. We could hear their quiet voices as they conferred in the kitchen.

Then the young nun returned and glided to the front of the room, her oversize rosary beads clicking a soft cadence against the voluminous skirts of her black habit. The childish hum of scratching crayons and wiggling feet settled into silence.

"I want you to be very still and to pray for the students in the big school," she said, her youthful face as serene as it had been at morning prayers. "Pray very hard." She closed her eyes and bowed her head, folding her hands in front of her.

I bowed my head along with the rest of the class and prayed for the big kids, thinking that there must be a fire or some kind of terrible accident. I didn't look to the right or left at my classmates. I kept my head down and repeated my prayers, asking God to help the kids in the big school.

The silence of the classroom was so overpowering it set up a buzz inside my head; outside, the air was filled with shouts and cries and sirens and horns. I don't remember how much time passed—a few minutes or an hour—while Sister had another quick conference at the back of the room with the teacher from upstairs, then took her place at the head of the desks again. We immediately sat face forward, hands folded in front of us.

She told us we were going to be dismissed early, but we couldn't leave until someone came to pick us up—a mother, a father, an older sister or brother.

This frightened me more than anything else. Something truly terrible was happening, and no one was going to come and get me. My dad was at work, and my mother was home with my two younger sisters, one of whom was only a few months old. I knew without being told that what was happening outside was no place for children. My mother would not come for me, and who else even knew I was here?

None of us asked any questions. No one ran to the window or started shouting. We did what we were told: we sat silently praying, worrying, occasionally exchanging a look with the girl or boy across the aisle. After a while, a few of the children started to cry softly to themselves, but they did not stir from their seats.

The news came when the first parent arrived. It was a fire. A fire in the big school.

I had never seen a fire, but I knew about the fires of hell. I knew that if you died with a mortal sin on your soul, the fires of hell would burn you forever and ever. I pictured hell as a dark place with big, thick flames of molten red, lashing out of the ground and engulfing you.

One by one, parents arrived to pick up their children. Mostly, it was women, crying or blank-faced with fear. Sometimes a mom would take her child and a neighbor's, too. I thought about our neighbors: Italian families—on both sides of our house—but they didn't speak English. They didn't have kids in my grade. No one would come for me.

I'm sure that as the seconds ticked away and the bedlam in the street grew in intensity, Sister must have thought about the other nuns in the big school, the women with whom she ate and prayed and talked in the cramped convent directly across the street from the school. She must have worried about the boys and girls she had taught in her first-grade classes, graduated now to the upper grades on the second floor of the school. But if her soul quaked in dread of what was happening a block away, she didn't show it. We took our cue from her and stayed hushed and obedient. And we prayed.

I was startled when the upstairs teacher tapped me on the shoulder. "Come with me," she said, "you're going home."

My savior was the man who rented the apartment upstairs from ours, a Chicago cop. He came for his daughter, who attended the kindergarten class in another building next door. He wasn't tall, but he had bright, friendly blue eyes and shiny black hair, and in his black-and-blue police uniform he looked like a friendly giant in the small classroom with its miniature desks and chairs. I remember he said, "Come on, honey, I'll take you home."

He held my hand on one side and his daughter's on the other. He guided us through the narrow, one-way streets choked with people, warning us to stay close and not to let go of his hand. I clung to him like a life preserver, cowed into speechlessness by the press of adult backs and legs and the choking atmosphere of fear and panic that made the good people of Our Lady of the Angels parish seem on the verge of becoming a riotous mob.

The man from upstairs led us right past the big school. He could have taken us the long way home, down a side street or around the block; but whatever small, internal voice that normally would have warned him that this was no sight for two little girls under seven must have been drowned out by the pull to get back to the fire, to see what was happening, to *do something*.

The crowd must have parted to let the policeman through. He led us to a spot across the street from the fire, and stopped. I remember he spoke to some firefighters who were wrestling with thick coils of black hose that curved in the wet street like huge worms on the sidewalk after a heavy rain. Small as I was, I could see only a forest of helmeted heads and beefy shoulders, and the ragged silhouette of fire trucks and ambulances and police cars that ringed the school.

Then the crowd parted, and I saw a vision worse than the hell of my imagining: the squat, two-story school was studded with ladders, like cloves on an orange, dozens and dozens of ladders of varying lengths, so many that I could not count them. Firemen with black coats and metal hats were perched here and there all over the ladders, some holding limp, dark bundles that did not resemble children except for their size. There were a few flashes of orange fire, at a window or in a corner of the building, but what overwhelmed me was the smell and the smoke—thick, oily, acrid black smoke that burst through the top of the building and the broken windows, and churned into the sky in large, round clouds. It carried the scent of charred wood and plaster, wool, and flesh.

I didn't see anyone jump from the second-story windows, which looked like empty black eye sockets against the dirty brick building. I didn't see any small, broken bodies on the hard pavement that ringed the school, although we learned later that many children broke the windows and jumped out in their frantic efforts to escape the smoke, to avoid the fire that licked at their hair and raced up their backs as they massed at the big windows, pounding and shouting for help. I didn't see the nuns breaking the glass and helping the children over the jagged threshold to jump two stories to the cement pavement below, breaking their arms and legs and landing on top of each other in their desperate attempts to outdistance the flames. I didn't hear any screams or shouts, just the muffled chorus of rage and sorrow around me.

I didn't cry. I didn't speak. I stood and looked and held onto the hand of the man from upstairs, and when he began to move, I moved with him, pushing slowly through the agonized crowds.

I don't remember what my mother said when I got home, but she hugged me hard, over and over. I recall that she had the radio on, the small plug-in she kept on top of the refrigerator, and that the men on the radio were talking about the fire on every radio station, talking about my school and my friends, the nuns and priests whose names I recognized. I didn't sit down at the kitchen table, as I usually did after school. I stood as if at attention and listened to them talk about the big kids in the big school, how many were dead, how many were injured, how many were missing.

The back door opened suddenly, letting in an icy gust. My mother's sister, who worked as a secretary at a local bank, whirled through the door, shut it and threw herself against it, her arms outstretched. "Thank God that you're all right," she breathed, staring at me with an intensity that scared me. Her appearance made no sense. Did her company let her get out of work early? All the rules of the normal world seemed to be changing.

I don't remember the rest of that day, or most of the days that followed. I was too young to attend funerals or visit friends who were hospitalized. Although I went to Mass every Sunday at the church that stood at the end of the same block as the big school, I never remember seeing the burnt-out shell. I think my parents must have taken me to the church a different way.

I kept asking my mother about the little girl who lived across the street from us, in a large, multifamily apartment building. She and I had played dolls together a few times, and we were becoming friends. She was in fourth grade, in the big school, and I was worried about her.

My mother kept assuring me that the little girl was all right; she said the girl was in the hospital. My mother didn't know when she was coming home. I asked and asked about her for weeks, and then I stopped asking. A long, long time passed. One day, I was sitting at the kitchen table; my mother was at the sink, washing dishes. I looked over at her back. "My friend is never coming home again, is she?" I asked.

My mother didn't turn around, but I remember that her hand paused in midair, so I knew she had heard me. Her shoulders sagged a little. I think, now, she must have been crying. She didn't want me to see her face. Or maybe she didn't want to see mine.

She went back to washing the dishes.

Depends

Richard Santiago

11/3

I'm not sure why I felt it important to mark the date. We found out about the miscarriage today. I realized I am a selfish son of a bitch today. Today I realized I was an addict. Today we found out about the miscarriage. The imminent miscarriage, waiting outside the window, watching us, no doubt pressed up against the glass making light vapor marks with its breath, just waiting for the perfect time to come in.

We know it's there, we've been informed by the nurse with the red plastic glasses and oblong hips, bringing us up to speed, she said, but it hasn't happened yet. She said between now and Tuesday. That's the torture.

We had to stop at Walgreens to get Depends diapers and baby wipes. She said last time it was really thick and chunky. Like slivers of raw beef soaked in blood, she said. I fake gagged when she told me, trying to make her smile.

She hopes it all comes out so that she wouldn't have to have her uterus scraped. She said it so plain. It fucked me up. The thought of scraping out a uterus (I imagine scraping out the last of the mayonnaise jar) sends a tingle from the crack of my ass to the base of my head, causing my shoulders to roll forward in a circle.

That's what happened last time. I wasn't here for the last one. By the time

I got here, she had already bought the Depends, used the baby wipes. I got here for the heavy sobbing on the couch, the baby hairs on the back of her neck wet with sweat. We just snuggled, it even sounds gay as I write it, but we did, nuzzling my head into the T of her neck, letting all my weight press against her backside, spooning. It was all you could do on that small-ass couch, so we did. And cry.

When it got hot we hooked up the cable in the bedroom and turned on the air conditioning. We ate ice cream (me, cookies and cream, her, raspberry) and watched movies. We laid on our backs in the dark and watched the lights from outside make crazy shadows on the ceiling. What do we do this time?

She's asleep right now. I always make sure my leg or foot or arm is touching her when she sleeps. I want to let her know I'm here.

She didn't want the Advil. She wanted something that would knock her out. She grabbed some Tylenol and it had the words "eight hour" and a clock on the box. The box was red, and I had never seen those before.

Her sister was on morphine today. She woke up this morning with a pain in her lower left abdomen. They took her to the hospital and found cysts attached to her ovaries. They were going to try to scrape them off. I couldn't believe this was happening. The nurse asked her if she had to go to the bathroom. The cysts were so big they mistook them for her bladder. The doctor told her that if they had to take out her ovaries, they would. Just like that. Cold.

She called while we were at the register at Walgreens. The reception on the cell phone was so bad (what do they make Walgreens out of?) that I told her to go outside and see if the signal got better. I'd pay for this stuff. Aspirin, baby wipes, and a ten-pack of Depends.

I was kind of an asshole when she picked out the Depends. She needed the Extra Absorbent ones, but the only ones we saw were a pack of fifty-two. I didn't want all those extras around after "it" happened.

Man, they don't have a smaller pack than that? When I said that I gave her this face like it was her fault these were packaged for geriatrics and not miscarrying mothers. She said, "We can donate the rest," through an uneasy smile. I am such an asshole.

So now I'm up at the register and she's walking out of the Walgreens saying, "Hold on, Claris," and waving her hand at me and then pointing outside. The young black guy behind the register looked up at me, and he had these big bottle-cap glasses that made his eyes look like eggs sunny side up.

I just gave him the card. He said, "Seventeen dollars, credit or debit?" And I couldn't look up anymore so I pretended like I was looking at my watch (which I wasn't wearing) and said, "Credit."

She's snoring now. Who knew angels snored?

Are You Sylvia? Autobiography and Voice in *The Bell Jar*

Tina M. Raffaele

DEAR MISS GREENWOOD,

I am writing to request that you cease representing yourself as my late wife, Sylvia Plath Hughes, immediately.

While it is well-known that Sylvia based her novel *The Bell Jar* upon some measure of her own personal experience, you are not the direct autobiographical representation of Sylvia. You are a fictional protagonist, and as such, do not reflect in whole my wife's intellectual, emotional, and physical life.

I am sure you are well aware that Plath scholarship has suffered greatly from what I consider an excessive fascination with the details of Sylvia's life. There is a lack of critical focus on her work, particularly as a novelist, as her writing is so frequently viewed through the narrow lens of biographical incident. I believe that if my wife had intended this novel to be direct autobiography, she would have dispensed with the conceit of calling the work a *novel* and simply submitted it as autobiography. Since that is not the case, it is clear that she intended the book to be a work of fiction and to stand on its own as such, separate from her personal experience.

Sincerely,

Mr. T. Hughes

Dear Mr. Hughes,

While I respect your views on this matter, I would submit that if you or any other reader perceives my characterization in the novel as a representation of Ms. Plath, then it is because Sylvia intended it that way.

My creator was certainly well aware of the implications of autobiography in her novel. She chose to have the book initially published in England under a pseudonym, Victoria Lucas, because she was concerned about the feelings of those real people whom she had only partially disguised as characters. The events of the novel and their parallels in Sylvia's life are well-documented. Sylvia gave me her internship at a ladies' magazine in New York, her experience of ptomaine poisoning, her memory of flinging her clothing from a rooftop in New York. My depression, suicide attempt, and shock treatment are all autobiographical incidents from Sylvia's life. It would be shortsighted to claim that this novel (and my subsequent characterization therein) is simply "some measure of her personal experience."

My voice is Sylvia's voice. She wrote in her journal of July 20, 1957, "that blond girl . . . Make her a statement of the generation. Which is you."

The resemblances between myself and Sylvia are marked. Again, while I understand your need to separate Sylvia's life (of which you were an integral part) from her work, I believe that in this case, it is not possible.

Respectfully,
Miss Esther Greenwood

Dear Miss Greenwood,

I resent your taking lines from Sylvia's personal journals out of context, as so many Plath "scholars" have done to support their own theories relating to her writing. While it is true that your physical descriptions of yourself in the novel ("five feet ten in my stocking feet," "skinny as a boy and barely rippled") resemble photographs of my wife from the period, the resemblances between yourself and Sylvia are not, as you say, "marked."

In the interest of setting the record straight on the matter of your voice as Sylvia's voice, I would remind you that Sylvia kept that particular journal as an exercise in what she called "the diary I". The passages in the journal, "the diary I," were written with an eye towards a novel that would eventually become *The Bell Jar.* Her intention was a first-person narrator based upon Salinger's *The Catcher in the Rye*, and in her journal of July 17, 1957, she wrote that your character must be, "in her way, limited, but only so she can grow to the vision I now have of life."

I belive it is apparent from this statement that you, Esther Greenwood, are not Sylvia Plath Hughes. There is a clear delineation between her recognition of herself as a person and her recognition of you as a character.

Sincerely,

Mr. T. Hughes

Dear Mr. Hughes,

I apologize for being so persistent in this matter. However, I feel there are one or two points that need addressing on the issue of autobiography in Sylvia's writing.

First, Sylvia was a poet. Having spent much of your own life at that avocation, you would certainly understand the extent to which a poet's life affects their work. Indeed, your own publication of *Birthday Letters*, a series of poems based almost in their entirety on your life with Sylvia, would seem to be a case in point. Sylvia was accustomed to filtering the moments of her life through her poetry; it is only natural that when her hand turned to fiction that she would draw most strongly on her own experience.

Second, when Sylvia was a young undergraduate at Smith College, she had tea with her sponsor, Olive Higgens Prouty (who is, in fact, the model for Philomena Guinea in *The Bell Jar*). During this afternoon, Sylvia related to Prouty that she wanted to write, but lamented that she had not had, in her eyes, enough exotic experiences to do so.

According to one of Miss Plath's many biographers, Paul Alexander, Ms. Prouty said, "Wait a minute. Is there any time in your life you've had a problem, a real conflict which seemed terribly important to you at the moment?"

Sylvia said yes, and detailed an incident from her high school years involving her sorority.

"Seems to me there's a story there," Prouty said. "An interesting one, too. Take life! Think of the material you have!"

Sylvia appears to have taken this comment to heart. *The Bell Jar* is not Sylvia's only work of fiction, although it is her only novel-length work. A number of her published short stories, including "And Summer Will Not Come Again" (based on her experiences as a babysitter for wealthy families), are clear fictionalizations of her own life.

During the fall of 1952, she wrote to her pen pal Eddie Cohen and asked him to return the letters she had written him. While Cohen did not return the letters, Sylvia's intention had been to write a short story based on their correspondence.

Cohen perceived Sylvia's disposition toward using her life in her fiction, and in a later letter to her wrote, "the two letters I have received from you since June indicate that I have ceased to be, as I once was, a real person . . . and have become instead, as have so many others of the males you have told me about, material for one of your future books . . ."

I mention these incidents because I believe they indicate a clear trend towards autobiography in Sylvia's fiction. In *The Bell Jar*, Sylvia addressed these issues by gifting me, her fictional counterpart, with her feelings and thoughts on the matter.

There is a scene in Chapter Ten of *The Bell Jar* in which I decide that my goal for the summer is to write a novel. As I contemplate what the topic of the novel will be, I think to myself, "A feeling of tenderness filled my heart. My heroine would be myself, only in disguise. She would be called Elaine. Elaine. I counted the letters on my fingers. There were six letters to Esther, too. It seemed a lucky thing."

As I'm sure you are well aware, there are six letters in Sylvia, too.

After a struggling attempt to start my novel I realize, "At that rate, I'd be lucky if I wrote a page a day. Then I knew what the trouble was. I needed experience. How could I write about life when I'd never had a love affair or a baby or even seen anybody die? A girl I knew had just won a prize for a short story about her adventures among the pygmies in Africa. How could I compete with that sort of thing?"

My belief that I needed experience to write a novel seems to indicate that Sylvia thought life experience was the best place to mine for fiction, in accordance with the advice she took from Ms. Prouty. Additionally, my worry that I did not have enough experience (and certainly none of the exotic sort) seems to directly parallel Sylvia's conversation with Ms. Prouty on the day of their tea.

I do hope that you will reconsider your position on this issue. The similarities between Sylvia and myself seem too pointed to ignore.

Respectfully,
Miss Esther Greenwood

Dear Miss Greenwood,

I will acknowledge that, based on the presentation of information in your last letter, it is easy to see how one could perceive your character in *The Bell Jar* as a fictional representation of Sylvia. However, as I have stated previously, I believe it is irresponsible to view the novel simply as Sylvia's life with some altered names and details.

Viewing *The Bell Jar* in such a light makes it too easy for critics of my wife's work to dismiss her considerable gifts as a writer. When one approaches her work with preconceptions of autobiography, it is a simple thing to say, "Well, she didn't seem to do any real writing here at all. She just copied things from her journals."

The truth, then, is that regardless of any similarities between Sylvia's experience and yours, she still had to treat the material as fiction—-meaning that she had to shape the events of her life in such a way that the work had a clear beginning, middle, and end. She also had to determine how much or how little to tell and what details and characters were most relevant and best served the story as she perceived it. For example, your Mr. Cohen does not appear in the story at all, despite the fact that he played a large role as my wife's correspondent during the period that led up to her breakdown.

In emphasizing the autobiographical nature of the novel, it is easy to forget the craft involved. In her journal entry of February 26, 1956, Sylvia wrote that her intentions for her novel's protagonist—shock treatment—would be written in "tight, blasting short descriptions with not one smudge of coy sentimentality."

These kinds of statements make it clear that while Sylvia was drawing upon her life, she was thinking as a writer, not a biographer. She had a specific intention with this novel, and as such she shaped the line of the book to suit those intentions.

It is also important to note that Sylvia did not simply choose to write the whole story of her life up to that point as fiction. There was a deliberateness involved, a choosing of a specific incident to draw upon. Once she made that decision, she related the story in a fictional manner, and the voice that she chose to tell it in—yours—was achieved through slow experimentation, culminating in her short story "Johnny Panic and the Bible of Dreams," which is a clear forerunner to the tone of *The Bell Jar*.

Continued emphasis on Sylvia's life makes it difficult to view her work with a clear eye. Her experience is filled with dramatic, emotional incidents—the death of her father, her emotional breakdown and subsequent hospitalization, her suicide at the age of thirty. Plath scholars want to empathize with her, as many of them view her as a tragic figure (and myself as the devil who drove her to her untimely end, I'm sorry to say). As such there is an overwhelming tendency to view both her fiction and her poetry as metaphors for her painful, difficult life.

Those who interpret her work want to find a straight line between Sylvia's experience and her writing, and tie it all up neatly as a package. I believe that such interpretations marginalize her work in general and the effort that she put into her writing of *The Bell Jar* in particular.

While it may be nearly impossible to do at this point, with the preponderance of biographies and scholarly critiques on every aspect of her life and work, I believe that readers should approach *The Bell Jar* as they would approach any other novel—that is, it should be viewed entirely as a work of fiction. Any analysis of the work should be straightforward, unvarnished by sentimentality or notions that biography affect interpretation.

Sincerely,

Ted Hughes

Dear Mr. Hughes,

It seems that despite my best efforts I am unable to convince you that any intelligent reading of *The Bell Jar* is dependent on a thorough grounding in Sylvia's life. The sheer quantity of biographical incident that Sylvia transferred to my character in the novel seems to indicate that this is so; however, the issue of biography is not one which I wish to discuss here. Our positions seem firmly fixed at opposite corners of the ring. In any case, the tendency of biographers to paint you as a devil, as you put it, would naturally put you off a discussion of Sylvia's work in that light.

What I wish to address is your notion that any analysis of Sylvia's work (or writing in general, as I perceive your statement) should be "straightforward, unvarnished by sentimentality." It seems to me that you are stating that a reader's emotional response to the novel is irrelevant, and that a recognition of craft issues such as voice or structure are the only legitimate concepts for discussion.

Mr. Hughes, if this indeed is your meaning, then I must disagree with you. You point out that Sylvia had specific intentions for *The Bell Jar*, and shaped her story to suit those intentions. The shaping of a story and all of the relevant craft that comes with it are part of an author's larger purpose—to glean an emotional response from the reader.

Sylvia Plath, in writing *The Bell Jar*, did not know what the future would hold. She did not know that she would commit suicide, or that her work would suffer, as you put it, from biographical interpretation. She only knew that she intended the reader to come away from the book having felt and experienced something. The reader's response has as much to do with content as design.

Analysis of this novel is meaningless without emotion. The emotion *The Bell Jar* evokes in the reader is both a testament to Sylvia's ability as a writer and the profundity of her autobiographical experience—in this case, her emotional breakdown.

I seem to find myself at the old biography issue again, despite my best efforts. But I believe that the emotional impact of this book is, at this point, impenetrably bound up in Sylvia's life. There are few authors who have had their life so meticulously categorized and analyzed, and it is naïve to think that a reader could separate their experience of her fiction from the events of her life.

In writing this book, Sylvia did not shy away from painful, humiliating moments, nor does she attempt to elucidate my moments of madness by clarifying them through the strain of the writer's intellect. She knew that trying to explain the breakdown my character experiences in the novel would only trivialize it.

But she knew this story—her story—was an important one, and she tells it as best she can, and as honestly as she can, and then she gets out of the way. Her emotional bravery is what drives this book, and to separate emotion from intellect in any analysis would be the worst kind of insult to Sylvia's work.

Respectfully,
Esther Greenwood.

Dear Miss Greenwood,

I must say that despite my unwillingness to acknowledge your similarities to my wife in any but the most insignificant of ways, she does seem to have gifted you with one of her strongest personality traits—an intense stubbornness and a fixation on an issue until that issue has been gnawed to the bone.

I do not believe that it is an insult to separate emotion from intellect in analyzing Sylvia's work, simply because it is my perception that much of that emotion has more to do with biography and less with her intended impact of the fiction.

You are correct in stating that we are firmly fixed at opposite corners of the ring on this issue. You are also correct in stating that when Sylvia wrote *The Bell Jar*, she did not know what the future would hold. It is that statement which I believe proves my point.

Were it not for Sylvia's suicide and the resultant fascination with the life of a writer whom the public perceived as having been taken from them tragically early, her life may not have been so completely analyzed and dissected. Indeed, many of the details which you seem to think have so much bearing on the reading of *The Bell Jar* probably would not have come to light after the publication of the book in the United States, particularly if Sylvia had published the book under a pseudonym as she had done in England.

I agree that her life is now, as you put it, impenetrably bound up in any reading of her work. But I would like it made clear that Sylvia did not intend it to be so. She wrote *The Bell Jar* as a novel, to be taken separately from her life.

You mentioned, in an earlier letter, Paul Alexander's biography of Sylvia. Mr. Alexander wrote me in an attempt to solicit my participation in the writing of his book. At that time, I wrote back to him the following, which should make clear, once and for all, my feelings on this matter:

"I don't suppose you will be surprised to hear that I have no interest, I'm afraid, in anything to do with biographical or critical writings about SP, beyond making some effort to protect myself from legal consequences. And I hope it doesn't sound too strange if I say that my home is the one place that I can keep reasonably clear of the agitations and foolishness of the public Plath debates, and that I wish to keep it so . . . Otherwise, I wish your research well."

What you, with your claims of being a perfect fictional representation of Sylvia, and scholars who want to view all of her work through autobiography have done is forget that Sylvia left people behind when she died. She had two children, a mother, a brother, a husband—however estranged we were. Sylvia did not, I think, want her life under a microscope, nor would she wish to have the lives that surrounded her to be treated like planets circling a star that has gone supernova.

If I seem to be putting too fine a point on the matter, it is only because this issue is one that has plagued me for most of my life. I am not an appendage of Sylvia's, nor were any of the other people that she knew and loved, and our actions should not be manipulated to suit critical interpretations of her work. So, too, should every effort be made to separate her own actions from her writing.

Sylvia did not want to be famous because she killed herself, or because she once wound up in a psychiatric hospital. She wanted to be a famous writer, and to that end she worked every day of her life. *The Bell Jar* is, in its final analysis, a testament to her abilities as a writer, not a jumping-off point for biographical analysis.

I am sorry if my unwillingness to be persuaded to your viewpoint is frustrating, but you must remember, after all, that she was my wife.

Sincerely,

Ted Hughes

But for the Grace

Excerpted from *The Blade Itself*, due out
January 2007 from St. Martin's Minotaur

Marcus Sakey

DANNY PEERED THROUGH THE PASSENGER WINDOW. THE ALLEY WASN'T AS DARK
as he would have liked, and Evan was driving him crazy, spinning the snub-
nose .38 like a cowboy in some Sunday matinee.

"Would you put that thing away?"

"Don't worry. It keeps me cool, like John Wayne." Evan smiled the bar-
fight grin that showed the missing tooth and side-cocked nose.

"I don't care if you're the guns of the fucking Navarrone. You shouldn't
have brought it."

"Yeah, OK, Mom." Evan sighed, tucked the pistol into the back of his belt.
"Happy?"

Danny shook his head. He always forgot that Evan got this way in the
midst of a job—didn't see it as work, more a thrill ride. Didn't realize that B&E
was one thing, a small-time fall where your term was measured in months. But
bring a weapons charge or, God forbid, assault, and shit got heavier.

Danny rapped his knuckles on the dashboard, counting down. Almost
time. Just shy of midnight, early enough that a car didn't draw attention, late
enough that no one should be inside. Terry had told them that everyone was
gone by seven at the latest. If they could trust him. By the white glow of one

streetlight—they'd broken the light beside the rear door yesterday—he scanned for warning signs, trusting his instincts. A few barred windows, but no lights on behind them. An hour ago they'd cut the phone line to kill the alarm, and no cops had come screaming, so there wasn't a cellular backup.

What was he doing here? So close to coming out. He could taste his new life, one where he didn't have to wake up with 3:00 A.M. panic. Things were going pretty well with Karen, three months and already talking about moving in together. He had to make this his last job, find something else, load trucks, work as a bouncer, anything, so long as he didn't have to worry about the cops knocking on his door or Evan fucking up.

A harsh whisper yanked him from his thoughts, "Check it out." Evan gestured through the windshield at a hunched man with greasy, clumped hair and a coat frayed at the edges staggering down the alley.

Danny slumped in his seat. "Shit."

The bum stepped over to the trash bin, gave a cursory look in either direction, eyes gliding right over them, and unzipped his fly. He leaned back as the piss splashed. Danny shook his head. What a fucking way to spend his Friday night.

The man finished and crossed to the other side of the road, where he leaned against the wall. Back to the bricks, he slid down to a sitting position, dropping his forehead against his knees.

"Christ," Danny said, "he's camping out."

Evan grunted, and Danny heard the whirr of the cylinder. He had the gun out again, spinning the chambers like he was prepping for a round of Russian roulette.

"I told you to put that fucking thing away."

Evan kept his gaze on the bum, eyes hard and more distant than Danny liked. "I could get rid of him."

"And pull cops out of every coffee shop for a mile? No." He paused, weighing the options. Every instinct told him it wasn't worth the risk. "Fuck it. We'll come back next Friday."

That got Evan's attention. His eyes snapped sideways to stare at Danny with an almost audible click. "Bullshit. We already cut the alarm, broke the light. The owner sees that, the job's over. This happens tonight."

"What, we kill the fucking guy for being in the wrong alley?"

"Happens all the time. I'll take care of it." He reached for the door handle.

"No!" It just got worse and worse. "I'll do it."

Evan stared at him, a little smile on his lips. "You?"

"Yeah."

Evan shrugged. "OK." He spun the pistol on one finger and held it out to Danny butt first.

Danny snorted, "Asshole." He stepped out of the car, leaving Evan offering the gun.

At the sound of the door, the bum looked up. His eyes had the tired panic of the street. He started to rise, a clumsy half-scramble up the wall.

"How you doing?" Danny asked, keeping his voice level. "You OK?"

"I got nothing." The edges of his words were rounded with drink. "Don't hurt me." He'd managed to stand up, his hands in front of him, palms out. The smell coming off him was unbelievable.

Danny shook his head. There but for the grace. "I won't."

The man looked at him suspiciously. He wore a ragged woolen cap faded to gray. A spotty beard clung to his cheeks. Danny moved closer.

"You got a cigarette?"

"I don't smoke. Now, my friend there," jerking a thumb towards the car, "he smokes. But," he paused, "he will hurt you."

The man stiffened, his eyes darting, frantic. "Listen, mister—"

"Shut up." Danny reached in his pocket, took out his wallet. "See this? This is fifty bucks."

The bum froze, paralyzed between fear and desire. "I—I don't do that stuff, the faggot stuff—"

Danny had to laugh. "You think I wanted to buy sex I'd talk to you? No, this is something else. You know what I want you to do?"

The man shook his head.

"You listening? You take this money and go up to Grand and LaSalle. There's a liquor store there. You go in, buy a bottle of whatever you like, take a seat in the parking lot."

"That's it?"

"No." Danny stepped closer, lowered his voice. "In about half an hour, a friend of mine will come by. I need to tell him something, but I don't want to say it on the phone, you know what I mean? My friend, he'll be wearing a tan raincoat. You tell him—you listening?—you tell him that the birds have flown the cage. You do that," Danny turned, mimed looking over his shoulder, whispered, "he'll give you a C-note."

"That's all?"

"Easiest money you ever made."

"Birds've flown."

"You've got it." He held the fifty out, trying to keep his expression straight.

The bum reached for it, hesitated, took the money. "Good man. Don't let me down."

The guy turned, started heading west down the alley, the wrong fucking direction. Danny almost called him back, figured what the hell, stood in the shadows until he was out of sight. The car door opened, Evan joining him.

"How much you give him?"

"Twenty."

Evan snorted. "You're too fucking soft, Danny-boy. A bullet don't cost but sixty cents."

Danny turned. "Let's go to work."

Evan opened the trunk, light flooding across his black T-shirt, dug around, and came up with a fistful of thick chain. Danny took one end and walked to the door, playing it out slow, the rattle loud in the close confines of the alley. The bum and Evan had gotten his blood up. It was on now, that tingling in the skin of his forearms, the steady acceleration of blood. He let the rush move him, keeping his head, the adrenaline working for him. Everything becoming clearer, sharper, his footsteps precise. The rear door of the pawn shop was sealed in a heavy steel cage, the metal old and discolored at the bottom from ten years of piss. Danny hooked the chain to the bars, thinking of movies, the way thieves were always tunneling up through the streets with high-tech explosives, or cracking safes with diamond-tipped drills. Eight bucks at Home Depot bought them all the supplies they needed.

Jesus, Danny, focus. There's enough wrong with this job as it is.

He thought of Terry, that weasely mustache that never quite grew in, the way his pupils expanded when he had the dope shakes. Not an ideal source for a tip, but he had a friend, guy who worked here, who told him the owner sold weed under the counter. Add to it that a pawn shop had to be ready to buy and sell any time, especially the weekend, and you were talking about cash on hand. And this friend of Terry's said the owner was old-school, a gun nut, so he didn't have a safe. Kept the money locked in a drawer. Easy money.

Yeah. Same thing you told the fucking wino.

No time. He had to keep his mind in the game, do the job and get out clean. Split the cash and walk away, no hard feelings in any direction. Evan may be a little crazy on the job, but he was a mate in real life. As long as all accounts balanced, Danny figured he'd understand.

Evan had climbed back in the driver's seat of his Mustang and inched it forward, the headlights off, the car a black shark. Danny checked the connection again, ducked under the chain to the other side of a rust-stained dumpster. As

Evan crept forward, the heavy links drew taut, twisting slightly as they settled. Danny kept to the shadows and waited.

Then it came, the Orange-line El, rattling overhead a block away, drowning out everything else. Evan gunned the engine quick and hard. For a second it seemed like nothing would happen, then with a screech the metal latch gave, the door flew open, the chain still attached, hinges straining as the car kept moving. For a second Danny thought Evan was going to keep going, tear the gate right off the wall, too amped to think about how much noise that would make. But brake lights washed red across him, then the white of reverse as Evan released the pressure on the chain, and finally the engine fell to silence. Danny's heart filled the gap, a roaring in his ears.

Now. Time leapt forward, things blurring around the edges. The chain felt hot as he detached it from the gate and bent to check the door the security cage had once covered. Piece of cake. He had it jimmied by the time Evan stowed the chain in the trunk.

The rattle of the El was fading as they stepped into the back office and closed the door behind them. Danny would have liked to take a moment in the dark, to listen to his instincts, but Evan already had the flashlight out. As it glared to life, Danny saw that he had the gun in his other hand. God damn it. Anger racked him, and he fought an urge to sock Evan. Danny's instincts began telling him this job was a risk from the beginning, and Evan seemed intent on making it worse. No point fighting about it now. Do the job and get out. Never do this shit again.

"There." A battered metal desk winked in the flashlight beams, below an automotive calendar with a bikini-clad woman on a beach. In the dim light, Danny could see a rumpled mattress on the floor beside it. "Terry said the bag would be in the manager's desk."

"Not for long." Danny knelt, taking the thin strip of metal from his jacket pocket. Some guys liked wire, some filed down coat hangers, but he found the bristles of a street sweeper worked best, hard but flexible.

"I'm going to look around."

"What?" His hands froze.

"It'll take you a minute to pop the lock, I'm going to check the front room. See if there's anything in the register."

"Evan, the flashlight—"

"Relax, Danny-boy. I'll be right back." Not waiting for an answer, he moved to the office door and slid into the pawn shop.

Shaking his head, Danny fumbled in the dark to find his own flashlight and set to work on the lock. It was a simple four-pin job, factory-issue. He had it in thirty seconds. He opened the top drawer, riffled through the junk, his gloves inky in the flashlight's white glow. Papers, pushpins, day-job junk. He found it in the bottom of the drawer. The lock-bag was under a newspaper. Next to it lay a sleek black pistol with an extra-large clip jutting out the bottom. Danny knew enough about guns to be able to tell that the safety was off. Definitely a gun nut.

Time to get Evan and go.

He stood up and slid through the door, his soft-soled gym shoes silent on the concrete floor. The pawn shop was a forest of dim shapes, electric guitars strung above what looked like power tools, a couple of racks of looming TVs. Danny couldn't see Evan, but a glow behind the counter marked his spot. All the cabinet doors were open, and there was a thumping sound, like Evan was pounding on something.

"Come on, man." His voice was low but urgent. "I found the bag. Let's go."

"Not yet. I want to find his weed stash." Evan's voice was muffled.

"Jesus, Evan, what for? We've got the money, let's go!"

Evan rose behind the counter, stretching, vertebrae popping as he flexed his broad shoulders. "Nah. We're not done yet."

Danny walked over to the counter. Evan dropped back down, reaching into a cabinet, his hands clumsy, knocking shit over, loud, always too damn loud. He was emptying the cabinets one at a time and tapping the sides, looking for a false bottom.

"Give me a hand, go through some of this shit, make sure it's not there."

Danny didn't move, just stood there at the edge of the counter, his heart pounding. Half the cons he knew—the smart ones, even—had landed inside because they changed the fucking plans midjob. He felt a trickle of sweat run down his side, the drop cold against his muscles. Adrenaline made his hands shake, and he clenched and released them, trying to think of a way to get moving, get out of here.

"Evan, man, you're making too much noise."

And then he heard the sound. A metal rattle, like—

"Evan!"

—a security gate. Suddenly the front door swung open, the night street glowing outside. A silhouette, big, stepped through the door, saying "Come on, little darlin', one hit before we do it won't make you lose control. I won't do nothing you don't want me to." The lights flickering on, everything slow motion. Evan scrambling to his feet, coming up fast, his shoulders tagging open the register drawer, the register tipping backwards at the feet of a middle-aged guy wearing one of those orange hunting vests, his face bearded, the expression blank, then the register hitting the ground, metal crashing, unbelievably loud, as Evan raised his arm, the guy's hand already inside his vest, a smooth, polished move, Danny yelling something, reaching. A ragged blast of orange fire spat from Evan's hand, and the man staggered back like he'd been gut-punched. The woman behind him, a scrawny chick with bad skin, eyes wide.

Adrenaline let Danny move. He jumped the counter, shoving the girl out of the way as he slammed the door. He almost fell, feet slipping in something, looked down to see a maroon pool spreading from where the guy lay, moving, a sort of crab-writhing, clutching at his stomach.

"Is he alive?" Evan, his voice calm, eerily level.

"Yeah."

"Check and see if he had a gun. You, little darlin'," gesturing with the pistol, "get over here." The woman moved to stand next to one of the racks.

The man at Danny's feet kept rocking back and forth. His hands were red, and Danny could see a stain creeping slowly up his chest. He'd heard being gut-shot was the worst, the most painful, and Jesus, was there a lot of blood. A kid from Bridgeport grew up knowing what blood looked like, broken noses and teeth knocked out, knuckles punched raw, but to see it pouring from someone's stomach . . .

"Danny!" Evan's voice jerked his head up, "ask him where the weed is."

Danny stared at him, the gun still in his hand, the knuckles easy on the grip and his voice calm. Evan seemed perfectly at home, almost sauntering around the counter to stand next to Danny.

"We need to get out of here."

"In a minute." Evan nudged the guy with his boot. "Where's your stash, old man?"

He groaned, a strange raspy sound. Danny saw blood on his face, little spatters of it, and wondered if he'd been hit in the lungs. His heart soared so loud it seemed to muffle the world, and his gut was turning in knots. They had to get out, Jesus, couldn't Evan see that?

"Evan—"

"Where is it?" This time he kicked the owner, his steel-toed boot driving hard into the man's stomach, near where his hands clenched the wound. The guy gasped for air, an agonized gulp.

"Evan!"

"Goddamnit, in a fucking minute!" Evan turned to stare at him, his arm half-raised. He didn't point the pistol at Danny, not quite. The air conditioning chilled the place as cold as January. For a long moment, they stared at one another, Danny wondering how he'd ended up here, calculating ways to get out. Then he saw motion, turned to look.

"Fuck!" Evan, yelling at the girl as she ran to the back room. "Stop!" For a moment she almost froze, but instead jumped a pile of junk Evan had dumped from one of the cabinets and leapt into the dark office, slamming the heavy door behind her. Danny heard the click of a lock.

The man on the floor groaned.

"Fuck!" Evan's face was bright red, that angry color he turned in a fight. He'd clenched his free hand into a fist. Turning, he kicked the owner, then again, and again, his feet lashing out, the guy trying to cover his head with one hand while the other held his bleeding stomach, a whimpering sound coming now, fast and hard, a sound Danny had never heard a human make. Danny stepped in front of Evan, hands to shoulders, shoving him back. Evan stumbled, almost went down, came up mad. His eyes narrowed, and he looked like he was about to bull rush Danny. The hand that held the gun was squeezed white.

"Stop! Stop, man!" Danny put his hands up, palms open, no threats. "Stay cool. Compadres."

For a moment, he wasn't sure it was going to work. But then Evan straightened, slowly, lowering the gun. He let out a breath, loudly, then took one in. Then he nodded. "All right, fuck the weed. Let's go."

Danny breathed again.

"We've got the money, after all. Let's go."

All of the good feeling dropped along with his stomach. "Shit. Oh shit, shit, shit."

Evan looked at him, then at the office door, closed and locked. "You left it inside."

"Evan, I—"

"You fucking left it inside!" That dangerous look was back, the gun was shaking again.

Danny kept his voice calm. "It's in the drawer."

"How much good is it going to do us in the fucking drawer, Danny?"

"Well, I wasn't planning on you shooting anybody! If we'd left when I said, we'd be driving home right now."

"You're fucking useless!" Evan raged back and forth, the gun swinging with his arm.

"Listen man, let's just go."

"No. No way." He straightened with decision.

"Evan, the cops are going to be here any second."

"We're not leaving empty-handed." Evan stepped towards the office door.

"What are you going to do?"

"I'm going to get my money."

Danny knew this mood. It was Evan at his most dangerous, ten drinks in and the stubbornest Mick at the bar.

Standing outside the office, Evan spoke loud and precise. "Lady, open the door or I break it fucking down."

Silence. Maybe the woman had been smart enough to leave, go out the back door. Jesus, he hoped so.

"Have it your way." Evan kicked hard, the door shivering in its frame. As he stepped back to wind up again, there was a sudden roar, and a chunk of wood exploded outwards, splinters flying in all directions. For a second everything was quiet. Then Evan exploded.

"Fucking cunt!" He aimed the gun at the door, pulled the trigger, the blast echoing off the wall. Evan shot again, punching another hole in the solid-wood door. "I'm going to fucking cut you open!" He threw himself at the door, then stepped back and shot again, not aiming at the lock but trying to hit her, trying to kill. At Danny's feet, the man groaned. Evan frothed and yelled, kicked the door again. The frame was cracking, and Danny thought he could hear a faint whimper behind it. Everything had gone crazy; he was standing in a pool of blood, Evan making enough noise to pull people for blocks, the lights on, the fucking lights on, for chrissake! Evan's face was scarlet as he beat at the door.

Danny had taken two falls, one county and one state, done the time like a man, but for this they'd get years.

No. No more.

Danny Carter opened the front door and slipped out into the night. His body screamed to run, just go, but he made himself walk. Not draw attention to himself. Just a guy headed for the El, nothing wrong with that.

When he was two blocks away, he heard the sirens.

Showers In the Attic

Jill Winski

AGAIN I AM IN THE SHOWER IN THE FAR CORNER OF THE ATTIC. IT'S THE SAME flimsy stall as last time, with the round, plastic, mildewed surface under my feet. The curtain, so excessively mildewed I can hardly bear to touch it, doesn't reach all the way around, and I am painfully aware of being naked. It's a good shower, however. Really good. The water is just the right temperature, just the way I like it—not hot but very warm.

As it pelts my face and runs down my body, I become aware of how crammed with *stuff* the attic is, to the extent that there are old, useless objects gathered around the perimeter of the tiny shower stall. A tall lamp with a yellowed, fringed shade is visible in the two-foot gap where the shower curtain is unable to meet itself. Next to this lamp, standing at its exact same height, is my mother. Her face is crossed with concern and a familiar weariness I can't stand seeing in her, like she's just too tired for life.

"Mom! I'm trying to take a shower!" I shout. I try to pull the slimy bathroom curtain closed, but my mother's hand clamps onto it.

"I have to ask you about something," she says, and I see her foot in its fluffy, yellow, faux-fur slipper moving as though she's going to walk right into the shower with me.

"Stop it!" I scream at her, trying to wrap the curtain around myself and realizing that either the curtain is way too small or my body is way too big. I don't know what makes me angrier—that I know the thing my mother just *has* to talk to me about is something trivial, something of great importance to her and of absolutely no consequence to me—or that in the back of my mind I have the queasying thought that she just wants to see me naked.

As my mother and I are pulling at the shower curtain—I can see her white knuckles against its brown slickness, and my bitten-down nails around her forearm—I realize that movers—moving *men*, that is—are stomping up the attic steps, one after the other after the other, bringing more boxes and old furniture. More and more stuff is piling up around my shower stall, and my chest clenches with the knowledge that not only am I being seen naked by my mother and the moving men, who glance at me first in surprise and then in a lazy sort of pleasure, but I will never get out of the attic because I will be boxed in.

My mother peers down suddenly and I think, great, Mom is staring at my chest. But my mother says quietly, with gravity, "Why are you wearing *that*? You're getting it all wet! You're ruining it!"

I glance down to see that I am not naked at all—I am wearing the dress I wore to the homecoming dance my senior year of high school, a strapless thing with a black velvet top and a white taffeta skirt that puffs out in three sections like the body of the Michelin Man. My breasts are hanging lower than they did when I was in high school, and I instinctively reach between my armpits and tug at the dress to keep it up. And then there is a rustling of plastic, and my mother pulls the shower curtain aside to reveal that my father, my sister, and Carlos, the Brazilian exchange student, are all watching me, along with the moving men, who wear identical white T-shirts with solid blue moving trucks on them and the words WE REALLY MOVE YOU. They stop midtask, boxes hoisted with flexed muscles, to leer at me. They are standing in the cluster to the left of my shower stall, in the midst of the brown-taped boxes that already nearly cover the creaky wood floor.

"At least I'm not naked," I think, the water pelting the velvet top of my 1989 Gunne Sax dress. I am suddenly aware that in the angled top of the attic's triangular roof, dead in the middle of it, some swallows, gray with black eyes and black beaks, are gracefully constructing an elaborate nest, slowly and with terrible precision. I know what they are doing without actually looking up at them, and their steady work feels to me like a ticking clock. The swallows are counting down, they are keeping time for me, and I must somehow get out of the attic before they are finished with their nest.

My eyes meet my father's—he stands next to my mother, who is still level with the fringed-shade lamp, which seems to me like a sort of bastard child, accepted gingerly into the family in the role of the fifth wheel. I am hit with shame when I see the expression on my father's face—his brown eyes are teary behind the lenses of his ever-present tortoiseshell glasses, and his forehead has a thick crease in the center, a deep worry line. His lips are pressed together so that they aren't lips at all but a sad little crack. He is deeply disappointed in me, and I am ashamed. And the shame bubbles up and spills out of me, and it is like water, so that I cannot tell the difference between the shame and the shower.

What have I done to be ashamed of?

Little Sister

Elizabeth Abruzzo

IT WAS A SPRING NIGHT, THE FIRST NIGHT OF WARMTH IN WHAT SEEMED LIKE forever. Mary rolled her windows down as she drove toward her house, braced herself as she crossed over bumpy railroad tracks, then settled down in her seat and steered with one hand as she passed what seemed like miles of cornfields and subdivisions and superstores before coming into downtown, which was really just a quiet street lined with a handful of steadily dying businesses, including the deli Mary's parents owned.

Mary lived in one of the houses that surrounded downtown—a big, old Victorian house her sister swore was haunted. All the downtown houses were like this, big and scary-looking at night, with ornate windows and spacious, open rooms, intricate woodwork, wrap-around porches and tiny yards. As she drove down her street and pulled her little red car into the driveway, she saw her neighbors out on their porches watching the sky get dark. She got out, slammed her car door the way her dad always told her not to, cut across the lawn, and climbed the steps to her back door.

The house was dark. It was Saturday night, and Mary was coming home from a performance of her high school's spring musical, *Brigadoon*. She had a tiny part in it, and she was still in full makeup and hair. Her hair was big, like

Texas beauty-pageant hair, and her eyes were dark and smoky. She hadn't been able to stop looking at herself in the mirror backstage. All around her, people were running around half-dressed, warming up their voices, chanting lines under their breath, and Mary was just staring at herself in the mirror. She couldn't believe the transformation. When she walked into the auditorium before the show, she was herself—plain-looking Mary with lifeless dirty blond hair, chubby, no makeup, worn-out jeans and T-shirt—nothing show-stopping. But now she was *Mary*—sexy Mary, confident Mary. She licked her lips, made coy, flirty faces, and saw for a second the woman she might someday grow up to be. After the show, she'd changed back into her boring clothes, but she'd kept the hair and makeup.

She walked into the dark house and dropped her keys on the kitchen counter. She slipped out of her sandals and headed toward the stairs that led up to her room, crossing through the living room with the old-fashioned fireplace and the piano, and the family room with its comfortable couches and the TV, and finally up the big wooden staircase, which creaked with age each time she took a step. She thought of peeling away her shirt as she walked, slipping it up and over her shoulders effortlessly the way grown-up women in movies always did, then unzipping her jeans and letting them fall gently off her hips into a perfect pile on the wood floor.

She wanted to leave a trail of clothing so that when Karl came in, he'd see it and he'd smile devilishly and know that she was in her room, waiting. But she didn't do it. Even with her new hair, her new face, she still lived with her parents, and she was only sixteen, and she was pretty sure Karl just thought of her as a friend. But maybe, she thought as she shook her head and felt her hair swish around her cheeks, maybe if he sees me like this he'll change his mind.

Up in her room, in her closet, Mary grabbed at T-shirts and jeans and corduroys, held them against her body and frowned at herself in the mirror. She wanted something that made her look thin, interesting, mysterious.

Even though she knew Gina, her older sister, wasn't home, Mary stopped for a second and listened for signs of her before tiptoeing down the dark hallway and into her bedroom. She flipped on the overhead light and scanned Gina's room before heading for her closet. Their rooms were different. Mary's walls were covered in magazine cut-outs and she had bunk beds, a rickety pink desk, and stuffed toys lying around. Gina's room was more adult, somehow. She had an old-fashioned wood-frame bed with a pristine, white bedspread. Her dresser and nightstand were made of shining mahogany and littered with jewelry boxes and bottles of perfume. It was a real girl's room—it even smelled girly, like soap and cinnamon.

She slipped into Gina's closet and began running her hands over her clothes, her funky, stretchy shirts, her soft, bright sweaters and silky dresses. Mary slowly pulled one of Gina's sleek black shirts over her head and looked at herself in the mirror. She twisted this way and that, torturing herself by looking at her body at every possible angle. She pulled the shirt up and looked at her belly button, grabbed at the fat that hung around her midsection, and jumped up and down to make it jiggle.

Mary knew deep down that Gina's clothes wouldn't fit her or look right on her, so she settled for a few dabs of her perfume on her wrists and neck. Before she left, she stopped to look at the pictures Gina had set up on her bedside table. She felt a little panicky doing it, knowing that at any minute Gina could burst in and start yelling the way she always did when she found Mary in her room without permission.

But it didn't stop Mary from snooping around. Gina was thin, with light blond hair and big blue eyes. She had a slightly bigger nose than Mary, which people always said gave her character. She was taller, more athletic, and braver, tougher, cooler. She was like a lot of pretty girls. She had a hint of meanness in her, in the way she drove her beat-up gray Ford Escort like it was the fastest, coolest sports car. She was three years older, and she hung out with the cool kids at their high school—not the stupid football jocks and homecoming queens, but the *cool* kids—the kids that hung around the art room all day and snuck out at lunch to drive to Taco Bell even though they weren't supposed to. Gina smoked, not once in while with friends—she was a real smoker. She'd leave the house in the evenings, telling their parents she was going to run an errand, but Mary knew she was really going to drive around and smoke. She'd seen her doing it a couple times, and she wouldn't tell. She wanted Gina to take her along, and turn up the music and smoke and drive around and around some random subdivision where nobody knew them. She wanted Gina to tell her about guys, about how to be mysterious. But that's not the way it was. Gina didn't want to be friends with Mary. She just wanted her out of her room.

Mary knelt down and looked at a picture of Gina locked in a hug with her boyfriend Chris, her sexy boyfriend Chris with the blond hair and the rosy cheeks and the good taste in music, who'd once told Mary he thought she'd grow up to be prettier than Gina. "You've got a cuter nose," he'd whispered to her while Gina was out of earshot, and then he'd winked and leaned across the table and tweaked her nose the way an uncle or a grandfather does sometimes.

She perked up when she heard the faint sound of knocking at the back door. She ran back to her room and threw on the first shirt she saw, a light green button-down shirt she'd bought at a thrift shop. Karl would like it. He liked thrift shops. He'd driven her to one once a few towns over, and helped her pick out cool things for her room, like an old exit sign that didn't light up anymore.

"Hey," he said when she opened the door. He was standing in a shadow and she could barely see him, so she turned on the back porch light. When she did, she noticed he had a yellow carnation in his hand. Karl was lanky with spiky funny-guy hair, wire-rimmed glasses, a big nose, and a wide, toothy smile. He was older than Mary, a senior at their high school, like Gina. He drove her home from school a lot and hung around with her while she worked at the deli. She'd helped him fill out his college applications, and sometimes they talked on the phone about things like how many birds the average cat kills a year. Gina had asked her once, "Why do you hang out with that guy? Don't you think it's kind of weird that you're practically his only friend?" But Mary had just shrugged. She liked him, even if he didn't have a lot of friends. Karl was the kind of guy who could easily go unnoticed and not mind it at all.

"Why's it so dark in there?" he asked, leaning around Mary to look inside.

"Oh…I don't know…I just got here. I just set my stuff down, and I guess I haven't had time to, uh, turn the lights on yet…I guess." She opened the door wider and stepped aside so he could come in, and then she went around turning on lamps and flicking light switches.

"Well, you were great tonight." He walked behind her as she bent over, pulling cords and twisting knobs. She turned and looked at the carnation he was holding. She watched to see if his hand was shaking, because maybe he was nervous to give it to her, because maybe a carnation was his way of saying that tonight was the night he was going to kiss her. "This is for you. I stopped at CVS to get it. You know, they've got a pretty good selection there . . . but the flowers are all floating around in this bright blue stuff that kinda looks like that stuff they put combs in at the hair salon . . ." He held it out to her. "Anyway, you were so good. Uh . . . I could never do that, be in a play."

Mary put the flower to her nose and breathed in while she looked up at him. "Thanks . . . I just had a tiny part. I was no good, really. Let me just go find something to put this in." She'd always wanted to be able to say that, to leave a guy waiting in the other room while she went to put flowers in a vase, even if it was just one carnation. He started to follow her, but she put a hand on his shoulder and one on his back and redirected him toward the living room. "Stay here," she said. "I'll only be a minute. You can . . . look for something to watch on TV."

She made a big production of rustling around in the kitchen, looking for a vase in the high-up cupboards where her mom kept them.

"I saw your parents!" Karl called over the noise of the TV. She imagined him sitting there, his long legs crossed at his feet and resting on the coffee table, his arms stretched out behind him, eyes focused on the TV screen.

"Oh yeah?" she called back. "Where?"

"What do ya mean, *where*? They were at the play."

"Oh," she said quietly. She set the vase with the carnation in the middle of the dining room table, where it stood out, where Gina and her parents would notice it right away when they came in. Then she walked back toward the living room, paying attention to the *way* she walked, to the way she smoothed her shirt out and ran her hand through her hair—her big, beautiful stage hair.

She sat down next to Karl, just close enough that he would notice she was close to him, close enough that he could smell the perfume on her neck. "They must've left right after," she said slowly, taking a deep breath and looking up at him sadly.

Karl lowered his voice to almost a whisper. "*Rocky's* on," he said. "The *Rocky* marathon on TBS . . . uh, 'Movies for Guys who like Movies' . . . it's part of that whole thing." She nodded and looked at the TV, racking her brain for something interesting to say, maybe some sort of Sylvester Stallone trivia. She settled in on the couch and wondered if at this angle, with him sitting taller than her, he could see down her shirt a little, into the dark shadow between her breasts. She laid her head back against the couch and leaned it to one side, so it was almost resting on his shoulder. Every so often Karl would put his hands to his face and adjust his glasses by rocking them from side to side, settling them deeper into the grooves on the sides of his nose.

She wondered if he'd kiss her if she just leaned in a little closer. And she'd kiss him back and then they'd become a couple like Gina and Chris were a couple and they'd go to prom together and they'd lie around in each other's bedrooms listening to music and Karl's mom would yell at him to keep the door open a little, and they'd go to family barbeques and Karl would be overly-polite to Mary's aunts and uncles and he would shoot her looks from across the room, looks that only *she* understood, and she'd wink at him and he'd wink back and later they'd go for a drive and they'd stop at the grocery store and wander around for an hour just talking and picking up weirdly-shaped fruits and inspecting the donut cases and laughing at nothing and falling in love.

Karl looked down and caught Mary staring up at him. "I've never seen *Rocky*," she said, blushing. "It's *awesome*."

He smirked. "*Yeah*, it is." He laughed a little. "Watch the movie…this is a good part."

Just then, they heard muffled voices and the sound of someone turning a key in the back door lock. The door swung open and hit the wall with a loud wooden smack, and then Gina started screaming.

"Lindsay McKinley?! Lindsay McKinley?! She's a *slut*, Chris. She's horrible…I can't believe… How…*how* could you do this?" Her voice got louder and louder, then broke into a sob. Mary heard her slamming around the kitchen, throwing her keys down, kicking her shoes off. In a house as big and open as theirs was, Mary and Karl could hear everything they were saying and doing as clearly as if it were coming through speakers. Mary turned to him and put her finger to her lips, motioned for him to stay put. She got up off the couch and crept through the living room and dining room and perched herself just outside the doorway to the kitchen, where Gina and Chris couldn't see her but she could see them. Chris was backed up against the counter. His cheeks were red and he looked kind of all-American, Mary thought, in his baseball cap and worn-soft jeans and light plaid shirt with the sleeves rolled up. Gina was standing with her back to Mary. She was shorter than Chris, but not by much, and right now she seemed to tower over him. Her thick, blond hair hung down her back and shook as she spoke. Her jeans fit her just right, made her look tough and pretty, and her plain black T-shirt was loose and worn-in and hung lifelessly at her sides.

Mary got that panicky feeling in her stomach again, like at any second Gina was going to feel her watching and turn around and just go wild—beat her up or scream at her to get out, pounding her little fists on the kitchen counter and stomping her bare feet on the wood floor like an angry horse. Gina was scary when she got mad, but in an exciting way. Her face got red and her eyes lit up and her hair floated goddess-like around her.

"*Gina*," Chris said in a loud whisper. "*Shut. Up. There are people in the other room.*"

"Oh, big deal," Gina said, her voice rising again. "It's just my stupid sister and Karl. I don't goddamn care if they hear me!! I don't *care*, Chris!!" She stopped to take a breath.

Chris was leaning on the counter, gripping it as if it was holding him up. His face was flushed and he'd pulled his baseball cap down over his eyes, but he wasn't crying. He looked more nervous than sad. He looked pale, like he was about to be sick, and it only seemed to be making Gina madder. She stepped closer to him, pushed her chest out at him like she was some guy in a bar asking did he want to take it outside? "You are such…a *dick*, Chris. I'm glad you're so fine with everything. I'm glad this is so easy for you."

He didn't say anything, just stood there and took it, wouldn't even look at her. He bent over, hung his head and gripped the counter. Mary could see that the back of his neck was bright red. There was silence for a few seconds and then Gina said, slowly and pretty calmly, "I hate you, Chris. I really hate you."

He didn't move, didn't try to hug her or anything. Mary got up and quietly ran back into the living room. "Oh my God," she whispered as she sat back down on the couch, reached for the remote and lowered the volume. They leaned forward, waiting for a sound from the kitchen. But the only sound came from the TV, the low hum of a shampoo commercial.

Karl sat back and ran his hands through his hair, widened his eyes. "What do you think he did?" he whispered, concerned. For the most part, Karl was a funny guy, a goofy guy, the kind of guy who's always joking and doing tricks, like tying cherry stems into knots with his tongue. But he could be serious too. Maybe, Mary thought, this was the kind of moment where Karl would feel the need to comfort her, to put an arm around her shoulder, to hug her even, and stroke her hair and tell her everything was going to be OK.

"I don't know," she said, scooting closer to him and wringing her hands together worriedly. "I'm worried about her."

There was a back staircase in their house, like there was in a lot of the old houses around downtown, and it led from the kitchen to the upstairs, where Gina and Mary's bedrooms were. Mary and Karl heard Gina and Chris pound up that back staircase, down the hallway, and into her bedroom. They heard Gina's door slam shut, and then there was more yelling, but they couldn't make out the words. "Do you…think he's beating her up or anything?" Karl asked, wiping a hand on his jeans.

"*No* . . . God, of course not." Karl looked anxious, anxious enough to maybe hold her hand like they were at the Pix watching a scary movie. "I mean . . . it *does* sound pretty bad . . . but I don't think Chris would do that." She put her head on Karl's shoulder and looked up at him sadly. "Do you?"

"She sounds pretty upset." They heard a loud wail and then the hiccup and wheeze of Gina's stuttered breathing. "Well maybe…should we call your mom and dad?"

"*No*. We *cannot* call my mom and dad. She'd kill me!" Mary pulled her legs to her chest, put her hands over her ears and shut her eyes.

"All right . . . well maybe we should just put the movie back on. I mean, it's their business, you know?" Mary didn't say anything, so he picked up the remote and turned the sound back up, way up. He spread his legs out wide, set the remote on his thigh, and sighed happily.

Karl watched the movie intently, like he was in his own bedroom tucked snugly into bed and slurping up a bowl of chocolate chip ice cream, but Mary couldn't concentrate. She rested her head on the top of the couch and looked out the window at the headlights of cars passing by. Her house was on a corner next to a stop sign, and she watched car after car roll up to it and barely pause before driving on. She wondered what it would be like if Gina and Chris broke up. They were a great couple, in love, in love like when you make each other mixed tapes and have nicknames for each other and inside jokes. They loved each other enough to scream and cry and make scenes—and that's a lot. Mary looked over at Karl, who was picking lint off his T-shirt, and wondered if he'd ever find a reason to scream at her.

Mary heard the door to Gina's room fly open and smack thickly against the wall. Footsteps pounded down the hallway toward the creaky old front stairway that would lead whoever it was right into the living room where they were sitting.

Chris appeared on the stairs holding the black Blind Melon T-shirt that Mary knew Gina had bought him for his birthday last summer. She was there when he opened it, when he squealed with excitement the way she hadn't known guys could squeal. Later, Mary had gone out and bought all the Blind Melon CDs, had spent days listening to them, jumping and dancing around to "No Rain" in her room, feeling like she'd been let in on a secret.

He stopped halfway down and froze as he looked into the living room at Mary. He looked down at his feet, then back up, and she thought he might start crying right there on the staircase. He waited a split second, then kept going, moving quickly down the stairs, one foot in front of the other, so fast Mary thought he might tumble right down them. He had the T-shirt in one hand, his car keys in the other, and as he passed Mary and Karl he just nodded and mumbled that he had to go. A few seconds later they heard the door click shut behind him.

Before they could say anything, Gina came flying down the stairs after him. She was barefoot and wearing pajamas and her silky white robe, which billowed out behind her like a bed sheet. Her hair was down and wild-looking. She ran by, still sobbing, her back heaving, fists clenched, legs churning, feet pounding against the wood floor. She looked athletic, determined. They heard the door fly open again and then they heard Gina screaming after Chris in the street.

Mary got up and ran to the kitchen, out the back door, and into the driveway, where she crouched behind her car and watched what was going on. It was darker now, but people were still out on their porches, smoking, talking, drinking beer, just like it was the Fourth of July. Everybody noticed Gina and Chris, but they didn't pay too much attention. The downtown area wasn't like the outlying subdivisions, where everybody was best friends and took turns mowing each other's lawns and doing neighborhood watch. Downtown, people pretty much minded their own business even though the houses were close together, almost right on top of each other. The people downtown wore their problems on their sleeves. They were used to hearing screaming around here.

Karl was behind Mary now, tapping on her back. He kept whispering, "Come *on*, Mary . . . please just come back inside. It's really none of our business . . . OK?"

"Be quiet," she said, waving him off and turning back to watch the action. Gina was standing in the middle of the street, crying, silhouetted by buzzing white streetlights. There were cars parked on one side of the street, and Chris was walking toward his old-fashioned white Ford truck. A cowboy's car, Mary thought.

"I'm not crazy!" Gina screamed as he reached his car and moved to unlock the door. Mary couldn't help but smirk, because saying that always makes you look even crazier.

Chris was half in and half out of his car when Gina ran up and tried to stop him. His door was open, his lights were on, and his car was running, exhaust spilling out into the air. He pulled halfway into the street, and Gina clutched the side of his open window and let him drag her a little. He waved her away and started to drive off, the driver's side door still swinging open, one leg still hanging out, but Gina grabbed his arm and held on like the little fighter she was. Mary could make out one word she said between sobs, the word "please." Chris finally pushed her off him, and she fell to the ground.

He drove off quickly, barely pausing at the stop sign on the corner, not caring that he was leaving Gina crumpled and crying in the middle of the street. Her silky robe lifted slightly in the wind and the world went quiet. She lifted her head and watched until his truck disappeared around the corner, then covered her face with her hands, picked herself up, and started to walk back toward the house.

Karl and Mary inched around the other side of Mary's car and hunkered down even lower so Gina wouldn't see them as she walked past. When they heard the back door slam, Mary turned, grabbed his shirt and looked up at him desperately. "You've got to *do* something! Go talk to her. *Please* go talk to her."

She knew Karl could do it. He could fix anything. He had a way with people, could make them laugh. He was charming, the kind of guy that puts his suit coat over a rain puddle so a girl doesn't have to get her feet wet. This was the moment in the night when Karl would work his magic and Gina would come watch *Rocky* with them and they'd all share a bowl of buttered popcorn and when Karl was out of the room Gina would whisper to Mary that she'd really hooked a good one and Mary would smirk and say, "I know." Then she and Karl would get in his car and he'd drive her to the highest point in the county, turn on the radio, and there'd be a guy on with a thick, smooth voice talking about love and playing something slow by Van Morrison. Karl would look at Mary, say something clever, and she'd laugh, and before she could think about it, he'd be kissing her.

He backed away. "What? Why me? *You're* her sister."

"*Because,* she'll listen to you. You guys are in the same class. She won't listen to me." Mary sat down on the scratchy concrete of the driveway, crossed her arms over her chest so she was hugging herself, and made her best damsel-in-distress face. "Please?"

Karl sat back against the car, cracked his knuckles, and looked at Mary without saying anything. She knew he was going to do it. He couldn't resist her, not with her stage hair and her smoky eyes, not with everything he knew she'd been through tonight. He was going to do it. She knew he was. "You know..." he said slowly, his voice whiny, "I think I'm just gonna go." He put a hand on her shoulder, squeezed lightly.

"Don't go," Mary said. "Don't go. She'll be OK. Or . . . we could both go somewhere. We could go somewhere in your car." She saw him for a second the way she'd seen him on the day they met. He'd been standing on the sidewalk outside their high school, kicking at broken pieces of cement and milling around the way all the kids do after school. She thought he looked like the kind of guy who names his car Suzie and washes it every Saturday afternoon in his driveway with a hose and sponge and a big bucket of soapy water. *He likes horror movies,* she'd thought as she watched him. *He goes to double features and buys popcorn and candy—Gummi Worms or licorice sticks, and he'll shush you if you talk, and if you cover your eyes during the gory parts, he'll shake his head and call you a lost cause. He listens to Led Zeppelin and has a leather jacket hanging in his closet that he's never had the guts to wear.* None of it was true, she thought now. He was just a guy, a guy who takes his car through the car wash and doesn't give a damn about scary movies and thinks leather jackets make people look skeezy.

"Nah, I'm just gonna go. I mean . . . sorry," he said as he stood up and brushed himself off. He held out his hand and helped Mary up. "Wanna walk me to my car?"

"Sure."

They walked out into the street, until they were standing next to his car, and he didn't try to hold her hand like she thought he might. They could hear highway traffic from far off.

"Well, goodnight," he said as he turned to unlock his car door. "You really were good in that play. You're . . . you looked good up there." He adjusted his glasses and swung his car door open, bent his head down and ducked inside. He closed the door and rolled the window down. Mary watched him turn the engine on and search for a good radio station, twisting the knobs with his long, skinny fingers.

"Thanks," she said. "Thanks for coming. And, thanks for coming over, too. Thanks for the carnation. It's really pretty. I'm sorry about everything."

He nodded. "It's OK . . . I understand." He put a hand over her hand, which was gripping his halfway rolled-down window. "I'll see ya at school, OK? Tell your sister I hope she feels better."

Mary nodded, and then Karl waved and drove off. She watched him stop at the stop sign at the end of her street and lean forward to look both ways before driving on. She watched his car until she couldn't see it anymore.

Back inside, Mary walked down the dark hallway toward her sister's room. She reached her door, turned the knob slowly so it wouldn't make too much noise, and pushed it open. She stood half in and half out of the doorway and watched Gina, who was curled up on her bed. She watched the line of her back as it rose and fell, and thought that she looked beautiful even when she was crying. She looked beautiful, but she also looked small, helpless, like a little kid. Mary had never seen her sister look so ruined, and it gave her that panicky feeling in her stomach again. She wondered if Gina would let her stay.

"Go away," Gina said without turning to see Mary standing there.

"Are you all right?" Mary whispered.

"No." She grabbed a pillow and hugged it to her chest, as tightly, Mary remembered, as she used to hug her teddy bears. "I'm not all right. Just get out of here, OK? And turn off the light when you go."

Mary nodded. She walked over and flicked off the lamp on Gina's bedside table. The room was suddenly aglow with glow-in-the-dark stars, the ones Gina had pressed onto her walls when she was in seventh grade and determined to grow up and become an astronomer. There was also the glow of streetlights outside and the occasional pair of car headlights that cast huge shadows on the walls for a second or two before they passed. Mary sat down on the edge of the bed and put a hand on Gina's back, and Gina let her.

"He's just . . . he's a jerk, OK? He's so *wrong*. I can't believe . . ."

"Yeah," Gina said. She kept crying and Mary kept her hand on Gina's back, kept telling her everything was going to be OK, even pulled her hair away from her eyes, and Gina didn't tell her to leave.

Mary sat still and practically held her breath, looked at the moon out the window and the way its light fell across the white bedspread. She sat in silence listening to the cars on the street below and Gina's softening sobs. Pretty soon, Mary knew, she'd cry herself to sleep.

Eve

Keesha Johnson

SO, DAVID AND I ARE SUPPOSED TO FUCK BECAUSE WE ARE THE ONLY TWO BLACK people at the party. It's New Year's Eve, 1999, and I guess it doesn't have to be a full-on fuck as there are other people in the room, but I should at least let him lick my neck or squeeze a nipple, because it will be the new millennium, and although I promised myself I'd smoke or swallow but never snort, I've just tried coke for the first time, and we are the only two black people at the party, so we've got to stick together, right? Here's the problem with all that: 1) It's not officially the new millennium until 2001, so that a "Hey, let me fuck you, it's a new millennium!" come-on isn't valid. 2) Good luck trying to penetrate. I may prance around like a little vixen, but while my mind and my mouth have been raunchy since puberty, the body has remained sexually clean. The steel of my chastity belt was molded by eight years of Lutheran school, a Catholic baptism, the fear of getting naked that comes with being overweight, and a high standard developed by the lessons of my mother. On top of everything, the intense new cocktail of Ecstasy, weed, and cocaine coursing through my veins makes me tighter than a strained rubber band. 3) I cannot stand David. While I'm supposed to find comfort in his matching skin tone, his personality, or lack thereof, kills any interest. His dryness makes Tiger Woods seem like Tupac Shakur, and that doesn't work for me. More importantly, he is just not a very nice person. Arrogant does not begin to scratch the surface. Black, white, red, or green, David is an asshole, and that overshadows everything else.

We're on the sofa, and most of the room has emptied out. Like most of these kinds of parties, those who do snort have staked out their own area of the condo, and everyone else has moved upstairs. I pray that the new day will somehow begin in the next five minutes, as opposed to the next couple of hours. I don't know what the hell I'm doing at this party in the first place, and that's what I want to ask David as his knee brushes against mine. Why are we here? Why do we associate with these people? Why are we doing drugs and faking happiness? Shouldn't we be off somewhere changing the world? My conversations with David in the past have lasted fifteen minutes at the most. This night, his loose posture, the cocky smile, and the narrow slit of his eyes solidify that his intentions are beyond verbal. He reminds me of a horny marionette.

"Hey," he says softly.

He doesn't even bother to come up with anything else, simply concentrating on the placement of his hand on my knee. After all of my resistance, am I really going to give it up in this random condo, at this random party, amongst these random people, with David, simply because he is the only other Black person in the room?

"I don't feel good," I think. Did I say it out loud? David continues to touch. Obviously not. "I need to go home." Again, no response. I chew my lower lip in frustration. All the other times I have been high, most of my thoughts have come out of my mouth. But tonight, when I need my words the most, they stay stuck in a bubble above my head. I feel the bitter acid from the coke rise up in the back of my throat. It is a night of firsts; maybe I should just give in and continue the trend.

"Simone," David says. And my mind races to the time sophomore year in high school when Janet Anderson told me about having sex, or juicin', which is what we called it back then, with her boyfriend Derrick. "I put it on him so good that the muthafucka called my name!" she said. Ever since then, I had made up my mind that any sexual experience I have will be defined by this litmus test—can I make him call my name? And not just call it, but scream it, gasp it, even croak it—just make him feel the uncontrollable urge to have the word come out of his mouth—*Simone.*

David's effort is futile at best. As his hands hover towards me, my hundred-mile-per-hour brain begins to flash multiple instances when I might be able to hear my name called the right way. Suddenly, sexual circumstances post like a row of photographs. My mind becomes a raunchy opening to a *Brady Bunch* episode.

I think of all the types that I have been attracted to. My Thug Boy with his fearless swagger will push me against a wall, grab my face, wrap my long legs around his waist, get deep on the first try, tell me to shut the fuck up, and when I lift my hips to let him get even deeper, spit out—"*Simone!*" David squeezes my thighs.

My Hippie Boy will get me so high that we won't really fuck as much as purr and giggle. While he takes a deep hit from his glass bong, I will outline his nipple with my tongue and through a smoky exhale he'll murmur—"*Simone.*" David runs his hands along my waist.

My Business Boy will let me ride him on one-thousand-thread-count sheets, with the Chicago skyline sparkling on the other side of the sliding doors to his penthouse balcony. He'll lift his torso to meet mine, and grab an open bottle of Cristal. He'll take a sip and we'll ride each other, laughing the laughter of not having a care in the world. He'll pour the champagne over my tits as they bounce in his face, and between licks I'll let him get out a muffled— "mmph-*Simone*-mmph." David puts his hands under my shirt.

My Artsy Boy will trace my face with his finger, gaze into my eyes, and wrap his mouth over mine. We'll come up for air and he'll smile, blink slowly, and our faces will meet again, but before our lips touch, he'll whisper— "*Simone.*" David's hands grip my breasts.

My Athletic Boy will fuck me in his car. We'll know that the logical thing would be to do it in his truck, but he'll be really strong and I'm flexible, so we'll choose the challenge of squeezing our long bodies into his Pontiac Firebird. We'll stay in the driver's seat; me on top, the seat reclined as far back as it will go. We'll find a rhythm and he'll call me his little cheerleader. I'll play along, telling him to "Give me a S—give me an I—" and so on until I'll finally shout, "What does it spell?" And he will scream, "*SIMONE!*" David's hands pull on my nipples.

My Funny Boy will jerk at my waist and we'll share a chuckle. I'll kiss his cheeks and his forehead and his chin. He'll run his hands across my breasts, and smiling again, say "Damn . . ." He'll move his hands across my ass and I'll lower my body down. I'll unzip him and our smiles will almost break our faces. I won't lick or tease, I'll go straight for it all at once. After I fit his entire dick inside my mouth, he'll say a surprised, "Oh!" followed by an elated—"*S-S-Simone!*" David's hands squeeze my shoulders.

My Shy Boy will be sitting across the couch from me. I'll inch toward him and wrap my legs over his lap in a tight straddle. I'll ride him a couple of times, then let go. I'll extend my entire torso up, leaning on my knees, putting my pussy right in front of his face. He'll smile, shrug his shoulders, and say sheepishly, "*Sim-one.*" David's hands caress my neck.

My Sexy Boy will make me get naked first. He'll keep his clothes on, and lay me down on the bed. He'll stand there staring at me and licking his lips. I'll get wet before he even touches me. He'll climb on top and go down. He'll taste me, look up, eye me passionately, and coo, "Mm, mm, mm *Simone!*" David's hands reach inside my pants.

My Revolutionary Boy will tell me about all the injustices in the world and at the climax of his lecture I'll scream, "Hell, yeah!" When I raise my fist, he'll tackle me to the floor and fuck me missionary style. We'll talk dirty and after a minute-long monologue about all the nasty things we're going to do to each other, he'll throw my legs over his shoulders and yell, "Simone! Simone! *SIMONE!*" David's lips sloppily touch mine.

A fuck for every personality, and he doesn't fit one. My shoulders drop with disappointment. I pull away, and I say his name.

"*David.*"

Strangeland

Suzie Sorenson

ONE-NIGHT STAND, TWO-MONTH RELATIONSHIP (THAT ENDS IN A SHRUG), bridesmaid in best friends' wedding; one-night stand, bridesmaid in wedding, two-month relationship (that ends with a quick message on a machine); head usher in wedding, personal attendant in wedding, one-night stand, two-month relationship (that ends with realization he was once a one-night stand). This was the way Molly's life was moving, being pulled forward by the hope that the next guy would be *the* guy—but there were too many guys to count, Molly was thinking one day, weaving down a city street when the strap of her purse, strained from the constant bulk in her bag, broke. Her purse dropped to the ground, its contents pouring out and littering the street around her. Marcus was the only one from the stream of people that split around her to stop, stoop, and help her. The conversation between them as they picked things up and stuffed them back into her bag was too trivial to mention, but it led to Marcus taking Molly to a nice restaurant she would typically never go to, which led to Marcus standing on her back porch looking through all her paintings haphazardly stacked in piles, saying, "Wow, Moll . . . these are incredible!" What was incredible was that Marcus had a job that he liked, which was more than she could say for past boyfriends. And when she eventually took him to parties to meet her friends, her friends would pull her aside and whisper, "Wow, Marcus is an *attorney!*" And then screech, "God, you're so *lucky* to be dating an *attorney!*" To which Molly would respond by smiling and nodding, not quite sure why Marcus being an attorney and her choice to date him was so *lucky*, but knowing that two months with him had come and gone now, and her life hadn't moved away from him even a little.

So, one day when Marcus is standing naked and yawning in her kitchen, waiting for the toast to pop, Molly looks at him from the kitchen table where she sits, staring at his bare ass jiggle as he jams a knife into the toaster and swears. Molly doesn't think about electrocution, even when Marcus starts slamming the toaster against the counter over and over again, and little sparks start flying out against his bare stomach. She can only think that Marcus treats her like he thinks she needs to be treated; when he goes in search of a plate for his burnt toast, opening Molly's overstuffed pantry to all its contents and the Tupperware, the cake pans, the blender, all go crashing to the floor around him, and he just looks up at Molly and sighs instead of screaming at her, which he could have done and past boyfriends have done when constantly confronted with her clutter, but Marcus just sighs and nudges everything back in with his foot. Molly pulls a dish from the dishwater and hands it to him smiling, and he looks at her, wagging his head, but grinning slightly, and within that look Molly thinks, *Whoa, this is love.* Months later, Molly justifies her love for Marcus by agreeing to move with him to the West Coast, to a coast she's never been to, but Marcus is so excited by the idea that one day he comes into her apartment with these big, brand new coffee table books—*California Living*, *California View*, and *California* scrawled across their covers, and tosses them down next to her on her ratty old sofa, causing dust to billow up around her as he says, "Molly, you'll love it there! Really!"

Molly nods dutifully while paging through the books, but all the pictures are the same in every book; a woman with a giant smile, grinning like she couldn't be happier, walking down a deserted beach in her modest one-piece bathing suit, one arm clamped down on her big flimsy hat so it won't blow away, her long brown hair whipping around her tanned wrist, while the other arm wraps around some guy's waist, who's always smiling, all white-toothed and tan. Marcus moves dozens of old magazines from the seat next to Molly to make room to sit down amidst her clutter. Marcus, tapping his finger on one of the glossy photos of the man and woman on the beach says, "See? See how much fun they're having, babe?"

★ ★ ★

Molly researches California on the Internet, but the pictures of Rodeo Drive and the Beverly Hills sign scroll through her head endlessly, so much so that it starts to keep her up at night. One night sitting up in bed in the soft, peach light of a city night, with Marcus a snoring lump beside her, she asks herself, *Can I live there? I mean, REALLY live there?* She pictures her dirty dishes piled high in a sink below a window with a view of a palm tree outside, when in reality, a cop car has just gone screaming by, rattling the bars over her window. She pictures her paintings no longer stacked up on her dirty porch, but leaned against nice white walls, and she pictures Marcus with a tan. Snapping on the lamp on the nightstand, she holds her pale arm out to see her blue veins pumping through her translucent skin and thinks about owning a big, flimsy hat, and how her ratty old sofa would look in direct sunlight, and the bus outside that has just pulled up at its stop, chimes, "Next stop, Fullerton. Next stop, Fullerton," before groaning away.

So they move to a town in California, and Molly can never remember the name of it, because it sounds like all the surrounding towns: *Beach Town, Beachville, Beachington*, and Marcus will cock his head and look down at Molly's attempt, asking, "Are you serious? You can't remember the name?" Molly shrugs her shoulders, and rolls her eyes like, *whatever*, but Marcus says, "Beach City, Molly. Beach . . . *Cit-y*, can you remember *that*?"

Marcus starts working immediately at a law firm, the reason for their move, and he'd been referring to this job as his *once-in-a-lifetime opportunity* for what already feels like a lifetime. The first Monday morning he is there, Marcus stands in front of the full-length mirror adjusting his tie, Molly sitting on the edge of the bed with a T-shirt stretched out and pulled over her legs, watching as Marcus runs his hands through his black hair, pulls his shirt cuffs out a little more from beneath his suit sleeves, and quickly turns his whole body to view his backside in the mirror.

"Marcus, are you checking out your ass?" Molly asks. Marcus's reflection whips around to roll his eyes and sneer at her. He leaves his reflection and comes to the bed, digging into his briefcase that sits propped open next to Molly. "So what are you going to do today?" he asks. It takes Molly a minute to realize he's talking to her and not to his briefcase, so she rocks forward and her bare legs shoot out from beneath her T-shirt, planting themselves on the floor as she says, "Oh, ahhh...I'm gonna ahh . . ." and she tucks her hair behind her ears. "I'm going tooooo . . ." and she can't think of anything to say, so Marcus bends down in front of her face and points at her, "You're going to maybe get some boxes unpacked," and Molly nods. "You're going to maybe start cleaning and straightening this place up. You're going to maybe start looking for work, see if any galleries are hiring, maybe call the cable guy," and his finger is cutting up and down in front of her face. "Maybe call the landlord about the air, make a grocery list, maybe these *boxes*, Molly," he says, throwing a thumb over his shoulder to the stack of boxes in their room. "Maybe you'll do that?" Marcus stands up and runs his hand down his tie, as a grin snaps on his face, "OK, I'm going, wish me luck," and bends back over to quickly kiss Molly on her head. And as he slips out the door, Molly can hear him utter, "God, I can't believe I'm *here*, I'm finally here."

Here isn't anything that can't be believed. *Here* is a peach-walled apartment with bamboo cabinets and light blue carpeted floors. Here is a place where Molly spends her days sitting amongst the packed boxes in their empty apartment, considering finding the sheets, considering making a fort, but just coming to the conclusion that the box marked *tools* makes a better chair than the box marked *kitchen*.

Molly stared out the window for days, occasionally getting close enough to press her nose to the glass as she thought about the cable guy, getting a job, and the groceries, the glass steaming up beneath her nostrils, as she felt, for the first time in her life, homesick. She wondered what the city was doing right now, as she watched an old man across the street cut his grass in white shorts and white socks that were pulled up to his knees.

Molly found her cell phone and called a friend back home.

"Hello?"

"Hi, Marge, it's Molly."

"Molly! Hey, how's California?"

"It's OK."

"Great, how's Marcus?

"Oh, you know, this is *his* opportunity."

"Yeah," Margo snorts, "once in a lifetime, right?"

"Hey, can you do me a favor? Can you look out your window and tell me what you see?" Margo was never one to ask too many questions, or tell Molly how lucky her life had become, so she said, "OK, let's go see. Well, it's about to rain." Molly looked out her own windows at the sun brightly shining through, reflecting off anything that would let it, so she closed her eyes and pictured the brick buildings rising up from the busy streets, darkening with the rain. She pictured people huddled in doorways staring at the sky, and Margo cut in, "And there's an old woman sitting in her window across the street from me, she's like a floor down and in a rocking chair." Molly opened her eyes a tiny bit and saw the man across the street between her eyelashes, his lawn mower, his socks. "Ha! Jimmy, the guy that runs the newspaper stand, you know the one that always calls me Margo-*rita*? He's peeing in the alley across the way!" Molly smiled, but sadly. "I've never thought about that, ya' know," Margo continues. "When do those guys get to go to the bathroom when they're working in those booths all day?"

"I guess we know now," Molly says.

Marcus comes home every evening all smiles and kisses her on the head, talking about his day, every day, without ever being asked. He does all the talking while rummaging through the bamboo cabinets, which Molly has barely begun to fill because she can't remember where things should go, or where Marcus would want them to go, or where a crock pot should be placed.

"Mr. Stein said the funniest thing today after our meeting," Marcus says while Molly wonders what things can be so funny after a meeting. Marcus ecstatically moves around the kitchen pulling out a strainer, boxed pasta, sauce in a jar. "So I don't know, I think this Morris case might be a tough one to crack," and Marcus will crack his knuckles and then punch one hand into the other, which Molly assumes is a gesture that shows he's up for the task, and then Marcus says, "but I'm up for the task." The wicker chair creaks beneath Molly, the only sign that she's alive, and Marcus drones on while uncorking a wine bottle, and while grating fresh cheese, on and on he talks, saying, ". . . I'm thinking a two-seater," staring up at the stucco ceiling, grinning like there's a sports car there, floating beneath the light fixture, ". . . something we can put the top down on, something small and zippy." Marcus dips his finger into the red sauce on the stove, and Molly watches his licked finger move from the red sauce, to his mouth, to the sink drain to dislodge the food that has stuck there, and then slide across the counters she's been considering cleaning. It's the same finger he jabbed at her that morning while saying, "You (jab, jab) should try to get these boxes unpacked." It was the finger that always seemed to be pointing out the direction she needed to take, "Why don't you call some art galleries here? Here. *And* here." And always popping up in her dreams saying, "Look (jab, jab), look how much fun everyone is having *here*."

The first time Molly sets foot out of the house, she goes cautiously, like she's never stepped outside anything before. But this outside has palm trees towering over her, mopeds whizzing by, and the temperature is the same day after day after day, the only variation being in the shape of the clouds that float by. Convertibles drive by with their bass turned up and booming, and Molly mumbles *zippy* to herself, *something small and zippy*. People walk by grinning and hand holding, and everyone is tan and toned, and the constant sun only accentuates that. And the grass grows immediately back behind lawn mowers but even more lush, and dogs are lying in the shade with their bellies to the sky, and kids are running between their houses giggling, and Molly knows this should be relaxing, the heat making everything seem like liquid, but all she can picture is Marcus's finger sticking into this world, and how it would cling to him, for a second, before rippling away.

The outside and the constant sunlight wear on Molly, like it's a big spotlight shining down on what her life is not, as she stakes out art galleries and even applies for waitress positions. Eventually, with no idea of what else to do, she goes into a movie theater she's been passing by for days. The theater looks so old and decrepit from the outside; it was probably once, a VERY long time ago, referred to as a "movie house," but Molly goes in one day and finds solace in the darkness of the theater, which leads to her seeing everything that's playing. And after she's seen everything that's playing, she starts hanging out in the movie-theater bathrooms, which have begun to feel more like home then her peach-walled apartment. Slipping through the swinging bathroom door that says *WOMEN* on it feels right, as do the overflowing trashcans, the leaky faucets, the broken stall doors. Stepping across the cracked concrete floor, and over stray pieces of popcorn, and the gummy candy Molly has to pick off the soles of her shoes, she'll throw her purse and keys on the counter, like it's the table by their door. The bathrooms are always littered with paper towels, paper cups, toilet paper, and wrappers, like the gutter of a city street. And the walls are covered with graffiti, all the *For a good time call*, and the *So-and-so was here,* and there's always the urine stink of unflushed toilets and sewage standing in pipes, that stink that makes her lean against the crumbling, cream-tiled walls and breathe with big gasping gulps, as if she were in the city again.

No one notices her in the theater bathrooms at first; it's just a three-screen joint with a staff of two: the old man who works the concession line, and when there is no concession line he'll be shuffling around with the broom; and there's also the old lady who's squeezed securely into her ticket booth out front, with only enough room to slide the ticket under the window to Molly, day after day after day.

But during the day the theater will be virtually empty, and it will be like stepping back in time, eerily quiet with its seventies shag carpet and the peeling wallpaper, and even the selection at the concession counter will seem old and outdated, everything veiled in dust. And Molly can hear the muffled sound of movies playing as she sits on the toilet in the middle stall, reading a magazine left behind about movies soon to come. And she starts to accumulate a small collection of things, things that she carries around with her when she's not there perched in the bathroom stall, kind of like little reminders: a ticket stub with a lipstick mark on it, a broken pocketknife, a pair of sunglasses, a pen, a key, coins (she'll constantly find coins).

She starts bringing a plastic bag with her to carry all her found objects in and to have something to add to if she finds more. And at night when she's back at the apartment with Marcus, and while he's talking and talking, and pointing and talking, she'll hide her bag in the darkest corner of the biggest closet, but she'll never stop thinking about it, the ticket stub with the lipstick mark on it, the broken pocketknife, and the sunglasses. Marcus will say, "Honey, are you *ever* going to get these boxes unpacked?" And, "Jesus, we've been here for three months now, three months!" And, "You know I'm at work all day, and dammit I have so much more to do when I get home," which leads to, "Are you going to get a job or not? Are you going to paint?" and then looking over her attempt on a canvas in a corner, which looks more like an accident then a painting, Marcus will look back to her and say, "Something decent? Are you going to paint something you can actually sell? You're not just lying around here on the sofa all day, are you? Are you, Molly? Are you just lying around all day on the sofa? Shit, I don't know what to do with you, I really don't." And his finger will come out wagging, "I'm tired, Molly," he'll say, rubbing his eyes with his fists, and Molly stares blankly, playing this dialogue out in her head like a movie she's seen a million times, before she thinks, *What's wrong with you, Moll?* and then Marcus says, "What's wrong with you, Moll?" And then Molly thinks, *We can't keep living like this*, and Marcus says, "Because we can't keep living like this!"

Marcus spends his evenings at the dining room table amidst a pile of books and stacks of papers, notebooks, his open briefcase, and his cell phone, which rings and rings and rings, and Molly learns just to loathe the weekends, because it means that Marcus will be home all day, barking into his cell phone until he sees her perspiring from the way she's nervously picking things out of boxes and stuffing them into drawers randomly, and he'll feel remorse, sort of, and say, "Maybe we can just go to the beach again?" Or, "Hon, let's just spend some alone time together, we never spend time together. I think we're growing apart, do you think we're growing apart? Do you even still love me? Do you? Do

you? Do you?" Molly pictures them on the beach, in a glossy photo, Marcus
leaning into her, talking, and her arms wrapped around his waist as she tries to
smile through her clenched teeth, the ringing in her ears, the hot sand beneath
her feet, as his finger grazes her back, and she knows all that will lead to is him
whining about the burn on his back and all the sand in the bed.

Eventually Marcus starts working weekends too, and Molly gets her plastic
bag and goes to the theater, which will be busier then, but she can still sit in the
bathroom stall and just breathe, and no one hassles her or acts like she's even
there, so she continues to acquire things, too many things for just one bag so she
has to have two bags, which will lead to four, which will lead to more for the
movie flyers, and for the leftover popcorn, and for the half-empty box of
gummy candy, and for the magazines, and for the cigarette butts, and the ticket
stub with the lipstick mark on it, and the sunglasses, the hair extension, the
hooded sweatshirt, the broken pocketknife, the matches, the diaper, the pen, the
key, the stuffed animal, the tampon, the lip gloss, the date book, the Kleenex, the
leftover popcorn, the hat, the water bottle, the apple rind, and the artificial nail.

And she has to find bigger hiding spaces in the apartment, and it's hard to
hide anything in such an empty place. But in the night when Marcus is asleep,
Molly digs through the bags, spreading the stuff out around her on the wood
floor as she crouches down to touch the half-empty box of gummy candy,
while mumbling to herself, *half-empty box of gummy candy*, and the coins (she'll
constantly find coins), and the little vial of perfume, and she'll say, *little vial of
perfume* as she sets it on the floor, and the aspirin, and the brush, and the cracked
mirror, and the business card, the library card, the leftover popcorn, the water
bottle, the artificial nail, the half-empty box of gummy candy, the stuffed
animal, the coins (she'll constantly find coins), the movie flyers, the ticket stub
with the lipstick mark on it, the pen, the key, the leftover popcorn, so many
pieces of stale popcorn are spread around her that they start to dip into the bag
devoted to paper, and the bag devoted to changes, and the bag devoted to
devotion, and Molly wakes up as the sun comes up, and Marcus is towering
over her with hands on his hips saying, "Honey, where the hell did all this
garbage come from?" Molly rubs her eyes and picks the little kernels of popcorn off her face that stuck there when she fell asleep on them. "Oh, I just
found all this stuff . . . in this closet," she says. "The previous tenant must have . . ."
and looking at the pile around her, "must have left it," and she begins to sweep
her hand through the pile around her and pushes everything back into the
bags, while Marcus continues to loom above her, staring down at her with

complete contempt, and shifting from foot to foot not knowing what to say until he just grunts while turning on his toes, "Throw that shit out, will ya?"

Sitting in the bathroom stall, her bags at her feet, Molly wonders where she'll stash them in the apartment, or if she can even stash them anymore, or maybe she should rent a locker or a storage spot. The leaky faucet drips and drips and drips, and the echoes of it fill her ears and she thinks about the gummy candy that always sticks to her shoes, and the Chapstick, and she'll picture the lady in the travel book sitting on a toilet, in her modest one-piece, clinging to her flimsy hat and smiling as the graffitied stall walls rise up around her, and the paper wrappers, and the cookie crumbs, and the coins (she'll constantly find coins), and the green grass growing back behind lawn mowers, and the wicker furniture creaking, and the unflushed toilets, and the broken pocketknife, and the matches, and the leftover popcorn, and she'll mumble to herself *leftover popcorn*, and the movie flyers, and the ticket stub with the lipstick mark, and the mopeds, and the Kleenex, and the pens, and the empty coffee cups, and she mumbles *zippy . . . a two seater that's small and zippy*, and the hair extension, and the battery, and the artificial nail, the lip gloss, the gummy candy, the peach pit, the key, the swinging door that says *Women* creaking open, the ticket stub with the lipstick mark, the photographs, all white-toothed and tan, the aspirin, the library card, the jiggling lock on her bathroom stall, and someone shouting, "Hey, who's in here?" And the stuffed animal, the paper wrappers, Marcus's finger digging in the sink drain, the police banging the stall door open 'til it swings open hard against her knees, and the cop's hand on her shoulder pulling her out as she stumbles through her bags, past the leaky faucets, the tampon, the key, the brush, the cracked mirror, the stuffed animal, the lip gloss, the old man sneering at her as he grips the broom by the concession counter, the hat, the coins (she'll constantly find coins), and the leftover popcorn, the cop saying as he drags her, "Hey . . . you can't be living in here, you know, lady," the peeling wallpaper, the Chapstick, the gummy candy on her shoe, the shag carpet, Molly saying to the cop over her shoulder, "But, but Marcus . . ." the tampon, the apple rind, the little, old ticket lady not even looking at her or the cops or the way her bags are gripped in his hand, the peach pit, the ticket stub, the hooded sweatshirt, the movie flyer, the glass doors pushed open as they all go tumbling out onto the sidewalk, "Ma'am we're going to need you to leave the premises," the coins (she'll constantly find coins), the mirror, the travel book, the notebook, the aspirin, the blinding sun spotlighting down on her, the artificial nail, her hand shading her squinting eyes, the people who've stopped to stare in the street, the ticket stub with the lipstick mark, her bent over in the street scrambling to gather her bags that the cops just tossed out in the gutter, the gummy candy, the brush, the movie flyers, the empty coffee cups splayed out under the marquee, the pink stucco walls and bamboo cabinets, the popcorn, the peach pit, the cop that plants a hand on her back and pushes, saying with a grunt, saying, "Ma'am. Leave. Now." The way his finger points out onto the street, the water bottle, the key, the pen, the gummy candy, the talking, and the pointing and the talking, and all that sand in the bed.

Molly crashes into the apartment's front hall, and Marcus rounds the corner in boxers, his jaw dropping to the floor when he realizes it's Molly in that big flimsy hat, trying to smile from amongst the dozens of bags that surround her. Marcus has his hand over his nose and steps cautiously up to her, mumbling, "Molly, where have you been? And what's that smell?" Tears are streaming down Molly's face, rolling over her grin. Marcus starts to back up and Molly notices how tan he is as she tries to stand up, and that's when she realizes she's been kneeling in sand, and that the whole hallway is covered in sand. And she looks past Marcus into the living room, which is covered in sand, and the boxes are gone, and her paints are gone, and she can see a couch that was never there before stuck in the sand, and she gets to her feet while looking down at the modest one-piece bathing suit she's now wearing. Molly turns when she hears waves breaking against the beach. She turns to look out the doorway she just came in, but it's no longer there. Now it's just sand and ocean stretching out to the horizon line, the sun set low in the sky. Molly turns back to see the house is gone, the new couch is gone, just Marcus backing away down the beach, grinning all white-toothed and tan, and the waves crash again, and the wind picks up, causing Molly's brown hair to whip around her wrist as she extends towards Marcus who's backpedaling to where the sand meets grass, and all she can manage to say is, "Marcus, wait."

Close to Good

Meredith Grahl

HAVE YOU EVER TRIED TO HOLD YOUR FRIEND'S DRUG-ADDLED BOXER IN YOUR lap in the passenger seat of the friend's car, because the backseat is jammed with stolen computer parts so the dog has nowhere else to go? And this is the car that you rode in way back in high school, and it's still got the busted passenger-side window that's permanently down, and the fucking dog doesn't even have a collar that you can grab onto, but this dog knows in its peanut brain that it wants to get away, claw the hell out of your lap and bark and shake and even try to jump out the window, because the dog knows the only time it ever has to get in the car is when it has to go to the vet, and it's your job to make sure the dog doesn't jump out kamikaze and splatter its dumb ass all the fuck over I-75 at ninety miles an hour because your friend is a swerving lunatic thief who doesn't have the sense to stick to the speed limit with a car full of panicky dog and hot Hewlett-Packard.

I was in Michigan for just a couple of days for my stepmother Kim's funeral, and that thing with the dog happened to me when I was hanging out with Holly, the one friend I have left, and it was fucking pie compared to everything else that was going on. That ride with the dog was a stroll through the park; that dog was an all-expense-paid trip to whatever place seems nice and easy to you. That dog was a no-strings lover in just underpants bringing you hot buttered croissants stuffed with bacon and jam, if you compared it to the funeral.

Let me breathe a little now. The Detroit Zoo opens at ten. I was waiting in the parking lot in Kim's flashy truck; it wasn't like she needed it, she'd been buried for almost two days. Nobody was around. It was raining and windy, and the thing on the dashboard said it was forty-eight degrees out. It felt good out, though, clean—opposite the way I felt.

I'd come home to Michigan for my stepmother's funeral. I didn't like her when she was alive, and I won't pretend I liked her any better after she died. She was only forty, fifteen years older than me, fifteen years younger than my mother. That's if you assume that my mother is still alive. Nothing can surprise me anymore about these women that my father picked out.

Anyway, the services were on a Saturday. I tried to keep Dad company during the day on Sunday and then went out with my brother and some of his friends that night. Next morning Dad went to work, forfeiting his grievance days because he had some project to wrap up. The hospice people were supposed to come by and collect the hospital bed and some other things, and I didn't want to have to deal with it so I decided to take my hangover to the zoo. I'd thought about the zoo on the plane ride back home, thought it would be fun to go. Throughout the trip, through going with Dad to help pick out the coffin, through the service and the reception with my brother and his friend, every time I pulled on the same old pair of black tights, I thought of the zoo, and my desire to visit had increased a little each time I thought of it.

There were only a few cars in the parking lot. Abandoned souvenir cups rattled in the puddles, and the wind stirred a bunch of plastic bags to start mating in the turn lane. Nobody was parked in the spot that said, "Congratulations! Employee of the Month" so I pulled in, wrestled an umbrella out of the backseat, and made my way to the front gates.

I have good memories of the Detroit Zoo. No, that's a lie. In the photos, though, the photos from when I was little, I look happy, my posture is loose and my smile is wide. My mother has the same tight-lipped mouth that she has in all the pictures, but Dad grins like an idiot. He insists that we went to the zoo every year, and that we always had a good time. There's one snapshot of us going up in a hot air balloon; my dad said that the thing was tethered on a tight leash, that they'd let you up just high enough so that you could see Woodward Avenue and then they'd pull you back down again. Still, Dad assures me that I went up in that balloon and that I had a great time.

If I tease him and say, "Are you sure that you didn't do that with your other family?" he doesn't think that's funny at all.

There was a bus at the front turnaround, and a group of little kids in ponchos were filing off of it and standing around shivering. I had on a red coat, the kind of big, long coat that looks like a sleeping bag, the kind of coat that makes you feel conspicuous at a funeral, but it's the only warm coat I had anymore.

The umbrella I found in Kim's backseat was red, too. I would look like some coordination-crazed idiot, like a blind person who had someone else pick out my clothes for me so that I'd always match. One of those moods, you know. I didn't care what people would think about the sort of person who would walk around the zoo in a cold rain, but I didn't want them to think I was fussy about matching my clothes while doing it.

I paid my $15.50 for admission and parked the car. I stumbled through the turnstile. My coat made an already-wet squish against the metal rod as I pushed past it. The kid in the booth had handed me a map, but it was soaked just from making the trip to my hand; I pitched it into a garbage can that had a frog's head on the top of it, so that the trash went into the frog's big mouth. I wasn't concerned with knowing where I was going, anyway. The plan was to follow the big, raised elephant prints that had been painted in white on the sidewalk since I was tiny. I thought for years that they had really painted an elephant's feet and made it walk around the zoo to make that trail. For a couple of years there was even another trail, little bird claws that led to the Penguinarium.

Now I wanted to try to feel something good about Detroit or Michigan or the fucking animal kingdom including my family and myself, so it didn't matter how fucking wet I got; I was going to do it. I didn't invent the concept of coming back where you came from in the first place and then wanting to die once you got there. I hadn't invited anyone with me because the mission I was on was a private one. I wanted to be happy, and I thought the zoo could give me that.

The only thing keeping me alive was knowing that my heartbeat was one more thing that made me different from that evil Kim. But knowing that you're not the first person to feel shitty makes it all feel even shittier, sad just like everybody else, and then I finally found some of the elephant tracks that were all chipped and faded like everything else in Detroit. Not enough of 'em left even to fit my feet on.

When I went into the wood, cabin-looking building that had a silhouette of an otter over the door, I expected something good, some crazy rain-loving otter action, but all I found was a drained pool surrounded by cement logs.

My father had told me that once when I was little, even before Mikey was born, he and my Mom had taken me to the zoo and my mother had got pissed that they'd paid the admission; this was back when my Dad wasn't making any money and if he did Mom would snort it. Those were the good old days. He said that the little me didn't care about any animals except for the squirrels that would bully right up to the blanket we sat on and try to grab my sandwich, that all day my mother had been complaining that she thought I was turning out autistic because I didn't care about any of the animals that were standing thirty feet away behind ropes. Of course I reacted to the squirrel—it was right in front of me and movin' around.

My father has displayed a thing for ridiculous women. My fear is that someday my mother will reappear, horribly covered in dust and sores, and she'll try to take him over again. And that he'll let her. He'll buy her a new black Escalade, 'cause she wouldn't want to drive Kim's black Escalade. Even though I haven't seen her since I was nine, I can't imagine that my mother would drive a dead person's car.

I got the hell out of the otter house, and the rain didn't, couldn't, soothe me. I guess I didn't even want to feel good, just final. I needed something big to put the final seal on the Kim years, and fake logs were not big at all.

Dad had gone and shut himself up in his room. I went through the house and threw all of the framed photos of Kim into a cardboard box. That woman had been house-proud even on her deathbed, which she had insisted they roll into the living room probably because she wanted to make sure that Dad wouldn't be able to escape her and her yowling for even a second. I was not around for her last words, but I'd bet that they included "gimme" or "I want." On Saturday, when we came back from lunch after the cemetery, there was a Post-it on the door that said we'd just missed a Fed-Ex delivery from Pottery Barn, so that viperous woman had been express-ordering shit out of catalogs with Dad's Platinum card right up to her very last, stupid second.

Looking around the house I found nine different pictures of Kim, always alone, in expensive-looking frames. In a lot of them she had a tight-lipped smile, and there's a reason for that. She made Dad buy her braces when they got engaged, and then she'd delayed their wedding because she was bound and determined to have a "perfect smile" on her "special day." For their first anniversary she made him buy her a boob job. Thankfully, I had gone away to school by that time.

Now I feel bad, having abandoned Dad with her, but he was the one who exchanged vows with her, not me. My visits home got shorter and shorter;

whenever I had friends over, Kim would follow them around as if they were stealing. And she put my father on a diet, and she made him put my dog Shelly to sleep when he was still perfectly healthy. How do you act at the funeral of someone you hated? I didn't wish death on the bitch, but I can't say I minded that she was gone.

I got back on the fucked-up elephant trail and pushed on. The field-trip kids had been split up into groups with a couple of moms and a red-ponchoed zoo guide in each group, and the kids were all panting and wagging their tails and freaking out, slapping at each other, displaying all the outward symptoms of excitement that I wished I could have at least on the inside of me for even a minute.

On Sunday night I went to the bar. My brother and his friends, who are all men now—or not even men but dudes—were playing darts. I ended up sitting at the bar, talking to a waitress for a long time.

She already knew my brother well enough to know what had happened with Kim. She asked me what I was going to do the next day, and I said, "I'm gonna go to the zoo." I was still just thinking about the zoo; I hadn't told anybody I wanted to go yet, but once I said it aloud, it sounded final.

So then the girl told me about how she had just taken her friend's baby to the zoo, and that it had been so frustrating because the only animal the baby was interested in was this seagull that kept coming up to their picnic table.

I have resolved never again to think something is special just because I've lived through it or have been able to remember it for a long time.

Anyway, there I was, and there were these camels. They looked like they'd been jacked. They stood around and didn't look like they noticed much of anything, let alone the rain that was pissing onto their ratty, balding, busted-down humps and snouts.

A voice came out from a docent's poncho: "Does anybody know if these camels are Dromedary or Brahman?"

The kids shot several of their puffy arms into the air, but the poncho must have obstructed the docent's view, so she went on, in a voice as sweet, thick, and synthetic as fruit cocktail.

"Because I'm going to tell you children a trick so that you'll never forget the difference—A 'D,' D as in Dromedary, has only one hump, and then a 'B', as in Brahman has two humps—so how many humps do we have here?"

The camels had two fucking humps, one, two, and they were balding and busted over, flopped over, drooping like Benjamin Franklin's tits. The kids didn't answer the woman; the canny things had already begun to ignore her.

"Two!" She yelled. "One, two!" The idiot woman thought the kids couldn't count to two. Hell, even in my state I could count two. "Two humps, just like the letter 'B'—so these camels are . . . ?"

She waited for the resounding chorus. It didn't happen. This was Detroit, bitch, at least the nice northern fringe of Detroit where people mowed their lawns and had decent cars, bitch, but anyway those kids weren't there to look at another condescending human. They saw those every day; they were there to eyeball some beasts if that poncho would ever flap itself on out of their way.

Far behind me I heard her say "Brahmans" in a very flat voice. But I'd been walking for a while, I'd managed to fit my feet into a few elephant prints, and the woman and her poncho and the plight of our nation's under-respected children were already a ways behind me.

My shoes stopped squishing when I walked. Now they were just as wet as everything else so they sloshed, instead, and I wasn't worried anymore about water. The animals didn't seem to mind it. I was walking really fast without looking where I was going; I'd gone to the back of the zoo and come back around, walking without noticing anything that was going on around me, except that I'd lost my umbrella. Once I almost bumped into a peacock that was wandering around like a hoodlum and scared the shit out of me.

At the funeral it had been my Dad and brother. There was a real crowd of people, but I didn't know many of them, and I don't think they knew each other either. A few of Dad's co-workers showed up and they all looked stiff, and Mikey's stoner friends had tried to scrape suits together but they all looked like hell, just really dumpy, and their ties were all as crooked as their teeth.

Kim's own mother hadn't even bothered to show up. Dad said he had called her and she had hung up on him. None of Kim's relatives were there. It was as if she had turned them all to stone when she was still alive, maybe because they didn't pay her enough attention or something, and so they couldn't make it to the funeral because they were all sitting petrified like statues in their trailers.

Dad had gone through her whole damn phone book letting people know she had finally, in his quiet euphmism, passed. Most of the time, when he dialed a number to reach a Bree or a Cyndie or a Dawnelle, he would reach the automated answering service of Thomasville Furniture or some fucking spa or salon. So it turned out that she didn't have any friends at all, only stylists and manicurists and decorators and personal shoppers and women who ran tanning salons—people she paid to do things for her on such a regular basis that they had started, in her stupid world, at least, to resemble friends.

It was a hell of a wake. Dad had rented chairs, and most of them were empty. One of the people from Kim's phone book had agreed to cater the event—to over-cater it, since they brought food for 200 but there were only thirty people, mostly Mikey's friends who stayed for the food. Mikey's friends would stand together and bullshit until one of them said something that another one would guffaw at and then shut up real fast, remembering where they were. And the caterer hadn't even given Dad a discount or deigned to throw on a suit or anything. He showed up late in a ratty T-shirt and Chuck Taylors, with his folding tables and trays of lasagna and wilty salad and white bread. It was absolutely what Kim wouldn't have wanted, but strangely it wasn't what I wanted either. When I found out I had to come home, I cleared it at work but I didn't tell anybody I was going. I have friends, but I couldn't think of anyone I would want to talk with about my situation. I don't want to die and leave behind a phone book full of nothing but acquaintances.

The wolverines were in a small enclosure, and they were running around it in circles, chasing each other, nipping at each other when they caught up, and then running around in the opposite direction, like they were playing tag. And I found myself in front of the thing that almost did it for me, that made me feel almost sweet and almost happy, and hell, I'll say it: almost pure. I guess it's called Rackham Fountain. Thank you, Mr. Rackham, thank you for your fountain that made me feel so almost good. You got me the closest I'd been to OK in a long time.

Two huge grizzlies hold the fountain up; they're posed so that they look away from each other. No matter what side of the pool you view the thing from, you can spy one of the bears' faces, but they look away from each other. They are turning green in the middle of the long pool, and at each end of the pool there's a seal serving as a smaller fountain. Of course the fountain was drained and the pool was covered over in tarp and it looked so crazy and so still and so crazy. Honestly, what sort of artist would condemn a pair of bears to hold up a bowl spurting water for all eternity? Without even giving them each other's company, since they were posed so that they would have to converse at the backs of each others' heads? I mean, that's if they were living things instead of sculptures and if they were humans instead of bears. But it was beautiful anyway, the whole thing—it was.

I stood looking at it for a long time, breathing deep, damp breaths that got trapped under the umbrella and kept me warm. I stood there thinking that even though the bears are pointed away from each other, at least they're together. Kim was a bitch, but I hated to think of my Dad alone. All Sunday he and I walked around the house, walking right past each other without looking at each other, sitting on the same couch without talking, even though I hadn't seen the guy in like eight months and I would like to think we'd have something to talk about. We had been like the fountain, next to each other but frozen away from each other.

I was thinking that I hadn't cried at all yet and that I shouldn't start.

Then I stopped thinking at all and started pretending that I was part of the fountain until I could hear voices coming up behind me, and I took off to keep anybody from coming up and spoiling what had come so close to happening for me. I decided to leave.

I had come home for my Dad, to show him that I support him and I'd hoped maybe to talk some sense into him, discourage him from women, but I hadn't even talked to him yet, not really. I'd talked to Mikey as much as anyone can, but he didn't need me. My brother just needs beer and gasoline to be happy—maybe some hot wings and a hot date once in awhile. I wasn't sure if my Dad needed me, either, but I wanted him to know that his life hasn't been wasted and that I want him to be happy. I guess that's just something you can't force on someone else, not any more than you can force it on yourself.

On the way out of the zoo I walked past a huge island of an exhibit with nothing in it except some trees; at least they were real trees, and a wooden structure that had one tiny, soaking-wet ball of fur curled up on top of it. It had gray fur, and I stopped for a second to look at it and shiver. I didn't stop for long, though; I wanted to get into Kim's truck and take off my soaked shoes and socks and coat and blast the heater and drive the hell away barefoot and thawing, into a life that would be rich with friends and bursting with love and people to confide in, a life that wouldn't resemble Kim's life at all. Whatever that little gray thing was on the top of that little fort, it didn't have anything to show me that I didn't already feel, but at least I knew in what direction I wanted to drive.

Arlene's Song

Cynthium Johnson-Woodfolk

THE SETTING IS 1940s LaGRANGE, GEORGIA, SITE OF THE DUDLEY HOME, IT IS an old plantation house that sits in front of a flourishing, green field. The porch is wide and rectangular, with railings that encase the porch like a picket fence. Attached to the railings are two wooden pillars that support the roof on either side of the porch, and in the middle is a screen door. On opposite sides are two windows. One has a long bench swing swaying in front of it, the other, a chair. To the side of the house is a clothesline filled with clothes. Underneath it is a wicker laundry basket. A large tree stands in the center of the yard. A small wire fence surrounds it.

CHARACTERS

MAVEL—Strong-willed, attractive woman of statuesque build in her sixties, who speaks her mind. She is the family matriarch. She talks little but says much.

ARLENE—Mavel's daughter

JAKE—Mavel's son-in-law

KOOTER—Jake's friend

Act 1, Scene 1
Lights Up

KOOTER

You sure got a lot of heart, Jake, talking to Mr. Randall like that. I never would've done it, no, siree!

JAKE

Well, that's the difference between me and you. Some niggers just happy being where they are, and hell, Kooter, talking to Mr. Randall whatn't no big thing. You just got to know what to say, that's all.

KOOTER

And you sure knew what to say the way you softened up to him. I like to kissed you myself but I didn't know how you was gonna take it. So tell me, how'd you get him to tell you about the job? What he say when you asked him?

JAKE

Well, see, Kooter, I didn't ask him nothing. He brought it up to me and he say, Jake, 'cause you know he call me Jake—all white men like to call you by your first name when they think they know you. He say, Jake, and I say, Yeah? I got myself a new place I'm building across town, I guess you heard. And I say, Naw, suh. Then I look at him real funny, like I don't know what he talking 'bout, not letting on, you see, playing it real smooth. And he say, Well, I gots myself this place and it's gonna take a mighty big man to help me run it. Then he put his hands on his hips and got to rocking back and forth. A mighty big man. You reckon you know any?

KOOTER

And what you say?

JAKE

I say, well . . . Then I take my hat off and gets to scratching my head like I'm thinking, 'cause I don't want him to know that it's me, you understand, 'cause I wanna ease into it. See, Kooter, you cain't jes run into things, you got to easssseeee into it, like I was doing with ol' Randall. And he just thinking, cross his big ol' arms across that 'sociation of his . . .

KOOTER
His what?

JAKE
'Sociation, rich man's gut. All the rich ones got it, Rockefeller, Kennedy, all of 'em.

KOOTER
A 'sociation.

JAKE
Right. So he folds his arms across that big ol' 'sociation of his and gets to wondering, tapping his finger on his chin. "Now who can I get?" Now at that point I was thinking he was playing with me 'cause he kept cutting his eyes over at me like he was suspecting me, but I played it cool and shook my head. "Naw, sir, but if I thinks of any I'll let you know." And I tell you, Kooter, he darn near died! He laughed so hard he like to busted my ears. I kept standing there. "Boy," he says to me, "you sure got some guts." Then he wipes his eyes and goes on, "But I'll tell you what I'm gonna do. You come on over to the office in the morning and we'll talk about it." I tell you, Kooter, opportunity's a knocking and I'm standing at the door waiting.

KOOTER
What you gon' tell Mavel? She's not gonna like you picking up and running off with Arlene. That new hotel way 'cross town in Rawly. She gonna have a hard time with that.

JAKE
Ain't got to tell her nothing. Arlene's my wife, Mavel just her mama, and what I do ain't got nothing to do with nobody but me. See?

KOOTER
I hear you, Jake, but what you gon' tell Mavel?

JAKE
Kooter! Why you . . .

[*He chases him and they run around the yard. Arlene enters from the house car-*

rying a basket of clothes in her hand. She is the same age as Jake. Her love for him stems from dedication and responsibility.]

ARLENE
Who's that running in my yard? Y'all know better than playing.

JAKE
Aw, girl, please, me and Kooter just having a little fun. Besides, I'd rather be chasing you!

ARLENE
G'on now, Jake. You know I'm not going to play with you.

JAKE
I say you will!

ARLENE
Don't start, Jake.

JAKE
I say you will!

[*He chases her around the tree. Kooter watches. Jake catches her, and the two wrestle.*]

ARLENE
Let go of me, Jake! Let go!

JAKE
What for? Can't I hold you?

ARLENE
Not like that. Not in front of company!

JAKE
Kooter ain't no company! He's here to see Mavel, ain't you, Kooter?

KOOTER

I got some dirt for her. Thought I'd help her with that tree.

ARLENE

She ain't gonna let you. Nobody's touched that tree but her since my daddy died.

JAKE

I told you, Koot. She don't even let her touch it. Ain't that right, baby?

[*He kisses her. She shies away.*]

Why, the tree is like a god.

ARLENE

He don't wanna hear that, Jake.

JAKE

Yes, he do. He wanna hear all about Mavel.

ARLENE

Kooter's just being nice.

JAKE

Nice as the weather. Kooter know he wanna talk to her, don't you? Look at him. Say her name and the nigger get shy. But you forget I know you. That dirt ain't for no tree. Kooter be down there at Bailey's reeling them women in all the time. He's a real ladies' man. Instead of him dishing out the money, they be buying him drinks. He got everybody fooled. I bet the money he spent on that dirt probably wasn't even his.

KOOTER

Don't listen to him, Ms. Arlene. Jake just a lot of talk. Ain't nothing but good intentions behind that dirt.

JAKE

Um hmmm. Sure it is.

ARLENE

Don't nobody pay any attention to him. He's like this all the time.

JAKE

He don't need you to tell him about me. He know how I am, just like you know how your mama is with that tree. There it is, Kooter, just like I told you. Strange looking, ain't it?

[*He points to the tree.*]

Boy, if that tree could talk.

ARLENE

Well, it cain't and it don't need nobody to speak for it.

JAKE

Woman, I don't need you to control my mouth! You ain't my tongue! Kooter, look here, you see that branch up there? Mavel's great grandma hung from that tree and the story is that she died for this land. Wouldn't give up. Now, that's some kinda stubborn. You? I can see you selling it lock, stock, and barrel 'cause that's the kind of nigger you are—give up too easy, wouldn't have to ask you twice. But me? I would'a played like Mavel's grandmamma and held on. Now that's just the way things are.

ARLENE

Jake! What's the matter with you? You know she didn't have no choice!

JAKE

What? I cain't say what I want to?

ARLENE

Not what you said to Kooter.

JAKE

He can speak for himself.

KOOTER

Ms. Lene, it don't bother me. Jake always talking like that.

ARLENE

That still don't make it right.

JAKE

Don't make it wrong, either. A man ought to be able to say what he want to intead of swallowing it in, holding it in like it's vomit in his mouth, scared to spit it out. I ain't no holding man. I say what I want when I want.

[*He tries to kiss Arlene but she pulls away.*]

See that, Kooter? She mad. She don't want me to talk about that tree.

ARLENE

He speaking foolishness. Whatever come out of his mouth, don't pay no attention to it.

JAKE

Every year her mama come out here and sit out there in them fields. She be holding hands with something that can't nobody but her see. And she be singing and dancing. Lord, Kooter, you'd swear she was chanting.

ARLENE

Don't say it like that, Jake. Don't make her sound like that.

JAKE

It's true.

ARLENE

You ain't got to say it!

KOOTER

What she do it for?

JAKE

Don't know. Don't nobody know but her.

KOOTER

Ms. Lene?

JAKE

She cain't tell you. She don't know herself. But as for me, I watch. I come sit out here on this porch and I watch her move back and forth, swaying from side to side, lifting her arms, letting them rise and fall. And I wonder what it's like. Then I get this twinge in my stomach when they're on their way back down. And I say to myself that I don't wanna be like that. I don't wanna go up just to fall back down. Come here, girl, and give me a kiss.

ARLENE

I ain't doing no such thing, standing up there lying like that! You oughta be ashamed of yourself!

JAKE

Shame for what? Telling the truth? Hell, girl, I ain't got no liar in my blood!

KOOTER

That's right! Them's called stories.

ARLENE

Yeah, well, they're called lies in my book.

JAKE

Call them what you want, but get on over here and give me my kiss.

ARLENE

I got chores to do.

JAKE

You ain't got to do 'em now! Why you pulling away, 'cause I talked about the ol' tree?

[*She doesn't answer.*]

Shoot, girl! You ain't got to act like that in front of Kooter. He seen grown folks kiss before.

KOOTER

Kiss people all the time.

JAKE

And you my woman. I talk any way I want.

[*He kisses her. She hits him.*]

ARLENE

Don't know what done got into you today, but I hope you go in there and sleep it off.

JAKE

Sleep off what? I ain't drunk! Not with wine, anyway. Tell her, Koot. I ain't been drinking, have I?

KOOTER

Naw, we ain't had a thing.

ARLENE

Well, something wrong with you! Telling Kooter stuff like that!

JAKE

Kooter know what I'm saying and, besides, cain't a man just be happy that he home?

ARLENE

Not when he come here everday.

JAKE

So tell her, Koot, what done get into me?

KOOTER

His new job.

ARLENE

Job?

KOOTER

He ask Mr. Randall for one today, and I'll be damned if he ain't get it!

ARLENE

What kind of job, Jake? Well, don't just stand there looking, tell me!

JAKE

Now you want me to talk. Woman, I tell you, you ought to make up your mind! One minute you say stop playing and the next you telling me to talk. Now which one you want me to do?

ARLENE

Stop playing, Jake, and tell me, what kinda job you got?

JAKE

A new one.

KOOTER

His interview tomorrow with Mr. Randall. And don't just anybody get a job with Mr. Randall.

JAKE

You should've seen me, Lene, you would've been proud, and Kooter wrong. I ain't ask nobody for nothing. I got it 'cause I know how to talk. I'm a talking man!

ARLENE

Must've been if Mr. Randall give it to you. What are you gonna be doing?

JAKE

Don't know yet. Got to go see him tomorrow. It ain't promised to me, but I know I'm gonna get it. Got to be good 'cause everybody talking 'bout it. Niggers everywhere wanted it and I'm the one that's got it! I'm the one that's gonna talk tomorrow. Kooter was gonna go for it hisself but didn't know what to say.

ARLENE

You all right with that, Kooter?

KOOTER

Don't bother me none, Jake the one with the words. I probably wasn't gonna get it 'cause I don't talk as much as Jake, and besides, I like what I do.

JAKE

Now see that's where you wrong, Kooter. You lying. There's lots more to life than carrying other folks' bags.

ARLENE

Jake!

JAKE

It is and ol Kooter know it too. That nigger don't like being no porter! He just scared of trying.

KOOTER

I ain't scared of nothing. I just don't want to.

ARLENE

Ain't nothing wrong with doing what you wanna do. Don't listen to Jake. People do it all the time. He just messing with you.

JAKE

No, I ain't.

ARLENE

Stop saying that!

[*She picks up the basket of clothes and goes over to the line.*]

JAKE

Kooter know he's fooling you! That nigger's got dreams just like the rest of us. Be daydreaming all the time and most of them be about Mavel. Tell her. Tell her one of them dreams.

ARLENE

Jake, you need to go in the house!

KOOTER

Oh, it's all right, Ms. Lene. I ain't worried 'bout no Jake.

JAKE
Yeah, well you better be.

[*He pushes Kooter playfully on the head.*]

So what's for dinner? You got something on the table for me in there?

ARLENE
You know I ain't no piece of wife. Everything you need is there on that table.

JAKE
You wanna stay for some dinner, Koot?

KOOTER
Naw, I best be going but I sure appreciate it. I know Ms. Lene is a good cook. Where you say you want this?

ARLENE
By the stairs. She'll be out after a while 'cause it's getting late in the day, and I know she wants to tend to that tree. I'll let her know you brought it—unless you wanna wait for her?

JAKE
Naw, ol Koots got somewhere to be. Ain't that right, Kooter? Ain't you say you had somewhere to be?

[*Kooter doesn't answer but stares off.*]

Kooter?

KOOTER
Hungh? Oh, he's right Ms. Lene. I should be going.

[*Waving as he walks off.*]

I'll see you bright and early in the morning, Jake, walk with you to your new job.

ARLENE

It ain't good to count eggs before they hatch. He ain't got it yet.

KOOTER

But I know he will.

[*To Jake.*]

See you in the morning.

JAKE

Yeah, see you in the morning.

[*Kooter leaves. Jake talks to Arlene across the line.*]

JAKE

What you go and tell him that for?

ARLENE

Tell him what?

JAKE

'Bout them chickens, not to count them before they hatch?

ARLENE

That's just a phrase. It means don't get your hopes so high.

JAKE

Woman, I know what it means.

ARLENE

Then why you ask me?

JAKE

'Cause I wanna know why you said it? Lots of men would die for a chance at that job, and he give it to me.

ARLENE

And I'm real proud of you.

JAKE

Don't sound like it.

ARLENE

Well, I am. Jake, you know how you are. You dream so big, and I just don't want you to . . .

JAKE

What's the matter with you? I keep telling you how hard it is to get an offer like that, and yet you keep questioning me.

ARLENE

I'm sorry Jake, it's just that . . .

JAKE

What?

ARLENE

I don't know, maybe . . .

JAKE

Maybe what? Damn it, it don't sound to me like you're happy!

ARLENE

I am. Jake, baby, I'm proud of you, but . . .

JAKE

But what?

ARLENE

Jake, what if you don't get it?

JAKE

He came to me. Did you hear me, Lene? He came to me.

ARLENE

He came to you last time and . . .

[*Pointing to a small section of the field.*]

We can build a little house over there, and . . . maybe put a garden over there.

JAKE

And we can do the same thing in Rawly. Now what you go and bring up the past for? You don't trust me?

ARLENE

I didn't say that. Don't go feeding words into my mouth.

JAKE

Cain't feed what's already there. Now I got a chance to leave these fields, and if you think I'm gonna stick around . . .

ARLENE

How'd you get it, Jake? What you have to do?

JAKE

What difference does it make?

ARLENE

[*Walking away.*]

I'm just asking you a question.

JAKE

Well, what you asking it for? I'm the one that did the talking!

ARLENE

I know, Jake, but...if Kooter didn't go for it...

JAKE

Who gives a damn about Kooter? What Kooter got to do with us?

ARLENE

Nothing. I'm just saying...

JAKE

He ain't as smart as me! Kooter don't know how to talk! That nigger happy being here. He love these fields. Mavel love these fields. But me? I ain't got no place here!

ARLENE

Maybe if we give it a little time?

JAKE

Time? Woman what you talking about, time? How much time you need?

ARLENE

I don't know, Jake, maybe a week or two, a month, three . . . baby, I don't know. It sounds good. I, I'm just scared...

JAKE

Scared of what? I'm the one that's got to talk to the man! Woman, I swear I don't understand you. I tell you I got a chance for a job and you fighting me! I tell you I got a chance to leave and . . .

ARLENE

Jake, baby, wait!

[*He storms towards the house, almost knocking Mavel over as he enters the door.*]

Jake!

MAVEL

What the . . .

JAKE

Excuse me!

MAVEL
What's going on?

JAKE
Nothing!

MAVEL
Nothing? You darn near knock my shoulder out of place and you tell me nothing? Naw, you gonna have to do better than that!

JAKE
Ask Arlene. I'm going to get something to eat.

MAVEL
Lene?

ARLENE

[*Turning from her.*]

It's between me and him, Mama. Me and him.

MAVEL
Then let him knock your damn shoulder out of place!

[*Mumbling.*]

Me and him!

ARLENE
Keep out of it, Mama.

MAVEL
Keep out of it? He darn hear knocked me down and you tell me to keep out of it? Even a fool can see that he mad!

ARLENE
Mama, you remember how Daddy used to stand here and look out at the

fields when he got tired of talking?

MAVEL
Yeah, so?

[*Arlene turns to the field.*]

Very funny, miss smarty-pants, but don't try to change the subject.

ARLENE
He used to stand out here for hours just looking at it. Sometimes he looked so long that it seemed like he was asking something from it.

MAVEL
Talk or don't talk. That's your business, but maybe I'll just get up and go in there and ask Jake myself.

ARLENE
Mama, please! Just this one time could you let me have some peace?

[*She sits at the bottom of the stairs; a moment of silence passes between them. Mavel mumbles.*]

MAVEL
If you wanted peace you wouldn't have been talking so loud.

ARLENE

[*Covering her ears.*]

Aw, Mama!

MAVEL
Well, you wouldn't have! I heard y'all all the way in there! Now where's this so-called job at?

ARLENE

[*Throwing her hands in the air.*]

In Rawly.

MAVEL
Rawly?

ARLENE
Um hmm. He was probably gonna wait and tell you tomorrow because that's when he'll know more about it. Says he's got to talk to Mr. Randall, first but since you know already . . .

MAVEL
Came to him, hungh? Walked right up to him and said, "Go to Rawly." You ought to have more sense than that.

ARLENE
Now, Mama, he said Mr. Randall saw something in him.

MAVEL
Oh, he saw something all right.

ARLENE
Don't start that again.

MAVEL
Don't start what? Talking about the truth? Now, you know just as well as I do that Jake is a dreaming man. He spends all of his time on dreams, thinking that one day he gonna be like them, one day if he works extra hard and carries more bags and bows and bends more than any man, that he gonna be like them

[*Imitating.*]

"Oh, yes sir, Mr. Randall. I'll do anything you say, Mr. Randall. I'm just like you, Mr. Randall."

ARLENE

Jake's a good man! He's worked hard for what he's got!

MAVEL

And what has he got, Arlene? He's a porter, a goddamn porter! And whether you want to admit it or not, I remember what brought him back here. When Jake first left here and went to that school, they could hardly function without him, "Oh, Jake" this and "Oh, Jake" that. Smartest man they ever had, right on top till they needed somebody in that office and Jake applied, then it became "training." We can't give it to him because he need more training, and Jake knew that job better than any man, could out-count them under a rock! But they made him waste all that time, and for what? To be a porter? Now if they didn't respect him then, what makes you think they're gonna respect him now? No matter where he go, he still gonna be a black man.

ARLENE

Mama, I don't wanna hear this! Everbody ain't prejudiced like you.

MAVEL

Prejudice or no prejudice, it's the truth, but if you don't wanna talk about it, we won't! Don't make me no difference.

[*Pause, stepping into the yard, noticing the bag.*]

What's this?

ARLENE

Kooter left it for you.

MAVEL

Who?

ARLENE

Koot-Lonny, Mama. Lonny left it for you.

MAVEL

[*Inspecting the bag.*]

What he want me to do with it? I ain't ask him for nothing.

ARLENE

Mama, he just trying to be nice.

MAVEL

Yeah, well I don't need no nice. You can give it back to him in the morning.

ARLENE

Mama, don't do that.

MAVEL

Do what?

ARLENE

Push him away. He's just a nice man who wants to do something nice for you.

MAVEL

I do fine by myself.

ARLENE

Fine? Daddy been gone for six years and you still holding onto him, holding onto me, and putting your everything into that tree! You cain't see what's in front of you 'cause you're too busy looking behind.

MAVEL

Oh, I see. Now you full of wisdom. So tell me, since you so smart, why is it that your husband's in there eating alone while you out here?

ARLENE

You just cain't leave it alone, can you, Mama?

MAVEL

Naw, naw. You started with me. All I did was ask about that dirt and you started in on me.

ARLENE
Mama, please! All I did was say that Kooter…

MAVEL
Who?

ARLENE
Lonny, Mama, you know who I'm talking about.

MAVEL
No, I don't. I don't know a damn Kooter. That's an animal ain't it? One that come round peeking all the time?

ARLENE
It's just his name, Mama. He likes to be called that.

MAVEL
He likes to be called an animal.

ARLENE
Naw. He likes to be called Kooter.

MAVEL
Well if the man wants to be called an animal then that's his business, but if he wants to leave dirt in my yard then that's mine, and I ain't accepting no dirt from no animal!

ARLENE
OK, then, Mama, Lonny left it. Is that better?

MAVEL
Much.

[*Inspecting the bag, twisting and turning it.*]

Now what he leave it for?

ARLENE

I didn't ask him.

MAVEL

You let some strange man named after a damn animal walk up and leave dirt in my yard and you didn't ask him?

ARLENE

Mama, Kooter ain't strange. He's just a nice man who wants to help, that's all. And for somebody that ain't interested . . .

MAVEL

Never said I was or wasn't, just trying to figure out what kinda help dirt is supposed to be? He want me to eat it? Cause you know I will. Red dirt is supposed to be good for you. Hell, as a girl I ate it all the time, even fed you some.

ARLENE

Mama, naw! You know it's for the tree!

MAVEL

Then I don't want it!

ARLENE

All he wants to do is help, Mama!

MAVEL

And I don't need his help!

[*Picks up the bag of dirt and carries it into the yard, leaving it by the fence.*]

You give that back to him tomorrow and tell him to take it somewhere else. There's plenty of trees out there. He don't need to be wasting his time with this one.

ARLENE

Mama!

MAVEL

[*Cutting her off.*]

I spoke, Lene! And that's all I'm gonna say!

ARLENE
I hear what you saying, Mama. You just won't say it to me.

MAVEL
What, that I think you oughta be helping me?

ARLENE
Mama, I told you. I ain't ready.

MAVEL
What's to get ready? Look! Look at it!

[*She points to the tree.*]

What do you see?

ARLENE
Mama . . .

MAVEL
Don't Mama me! Look at it! What do you see?

ARLENE
I see a tree.

MAVEL
You ain't trying!

ARLENE
I see a tree!

MAVEL
Look harder, Lene!

ARLENE
Mama . . .

MAVEL
Look beyond it!

ARLENE
It's not for me, OK? It's just not for me!

MAVEL
And that job in Rawly ain't for Jake, either.

[*Arlene storms into the house.*]

Lights Down.

After Hours

Brian Parenti

Players
  Mario and Vinny, brothers in their early twenties.
  Jamie and Carisa, friends in their early twenties.

Action takes place in a club. A sign hangs which says: THE V.I.P. There is a bar at one end; couches and tables are on the other. The couches and chairs should look very hip and colorful. There is an empty space, which is a dance floor. A female bartender BARBARA behind the bar. (The song "I Don't Give a Fuck" by Lil Jon & The East Side Boyz blares loudly like it's coming from another room.) VINNY, 24, enters dressed in a tight shirt.

VINNY

[*Yelling back.*]

No. THAT'S MY BROTHER. HE'S NOT FUCKIN' PAYING. Fuck you.

[*He exits.*]

[*Pause.*]

[*Vinny enters with Mario laughing.*]

VINNY
See the fuckin' pull I have in this mother fucker.

[*He puts his arm around Mario.*]

Do you hear me? I fuckin' go up to the guy, I'm like, Big Brian and I have known each other for two years, I mean, and he's, like, "I know, I know." I'm, like, that guy's my brother, I'm here every fuckin' weekend. I mean, he would care, you can call him up here, I says. Fuckin' Brian comes up there and he's, like, to the bouncer, "Whatever Vinny wants!" I mean, dude, who's the fuckin' man? I own this fuckin' club.

[*Pause.*]

Dude. The fuckin' stunna, Jenna, gonna be here. What a piece of ass, dude. I mean you see that fuckin' billboard, that ass, dude? Shit. She's bangin', dude. I mean, I know they airbrush, but shit. A ten. She's a fuckin' ten! All calling me, like asking me if I'm coming tonight. She wants my dick so bad, dude. Tonight. I'm gonna close her prissy ass fuckin' tonight, baby! Take her to the crib and give her the nine in the crack, ohhhhh!

[*He grabs Mario and hugs him and gets in his face.*]

MARIO
Get off me, dude.

VINNY
What?

[*Mario moves over to the couch. Vinny follows.*]

VINNY
Mario!

[*Vinny goes next to him.*]

MARIO
I'm just invisible, right?

VINNY
What? What the fu...the schoolgirl? [*Pause.*] No. Come on, let's get a drink.

MARIO
No.

VINNY
Come on. I'm buying, come on. What do you want?

MARIO
I'm not drinking with you.

VINNY
Don't be a bitch. Come on. You want a Jäeger bomb, Bacardi and Seven? Fuckin' whatever, I got it.

MARIO
I'll buy my own drink.

VINNY
No. I'm buying, come on . . .

[*Vinny grabs Mario and pulls him toward the bar.*]

MARIO
Don't...

VINNY
Come on!

[*Mario shoves him off.*]

MARIO
Don't fuckin' pull me.

VINNY
All right. [*Pause.*] Dude, I didn't know. OK, I was hammered.

MARIO
Yeah. what else is new, right? I wasn't even there.

VINNY
Dude, don't. You know I wouldn't fuckin', like, do that on purpose.

MARIO
Yeah, that's why you, like waited, for me to, like, go to the bathroom. I come back and you're all fuckin' tonguin' the chick. Fuck you, Vin!

VINNY
I didn't know you liked her, dude.

MARIO
I was talking to her all night.

VINNY
So what, fuckin' talkin'? I mean how the fuck am I suppose to . . . ?

MARIO
We were making out and shit.

VINNY

[*laughs*]

Hold on. You mean to tell me that you're all pissed because of some slut that—excuse me—was all tonsil-hockeyin' it on you. And just, like, as soon as you walk away to fuckin' piss she fuckin' grabs me and just starts going to town.

MARIO

That's not the point, Vin.

VINNY

She obviously didn't give a shit about you.

MARIO

I go to school with her. We always kinda, you know, like, fucked around and shit. I mean she told me she was gonna be there.

VINNY

Mar, she was a slut, OK? That schoolgirl outfit, I mean, her skirt was all up her ass and shit. I mean those pigtails with the fuckin', like, little school glasses. Come on. She's lookin' to get stuck. I mean look at her dance, what you think?

MARIO

That's what I'm . . . I dunno, maybe if you didn't like . . . whatever, man.

VINNY

Fuck that bitch. You don't want some fuckin' skeezer rat who's like waiting for a cock, OK? Seriously, Mar. I did you a favor.

MARIO

Whatever.

VINNY

Besides, man, I mean it, like, didn't mean shit. I mean you could still nail her, I don't give a shit . . .

MARIO

Stop being a moron, dude.

VINNY

Let's have a drink.

[*Vinny guides Mario to the bar. They each do a shot and then get a regular mixed drink.*]

I'm just saying don't get all roided over some skank, you don't want some average hoochie who's flashing her ass all over town and shit . . . I mean . . .

MARIO
Yeah.

VINNY
I don't . . . I mean, dude, I don't even remember the chick's name . . . Like what? Lisa . . . or fuckin' . . . I don't know. What was her name? You know the chick. Wha . . . ?

MARIO
Her name is Olga.

VINNY
Her name is Olga?

MARIO
Yeah.

VINNY
That's a terrible fuckin' name. That wasn't her fuckin' name.

MARIO
Yes, it was.

VINNY
No, it wasn't.

MARIO
OK. Fine.

VINNY
You must have been drunk as fuck, dude; you're supposed to remember this shit.

MARIO
I ain't your fuckin' errand boy.

VINNY
Olga?

MARIO
Who gives a fuck? You had like nine Jack and Cokes. Makin' me all drive you guys home like a damn chaperone.

[*Vinny laughs.*]

You're all in the backseat tonguin' her like death and the maiden. Every time I check the fuckin' rearview I gotta see you two . . . it got to the point I stopped checking.

VINNY

[*Laughing.*]

I didn't know.

MARIO
Fuck off!

[*Mario goes toward the couch.*]

VINNY
Come on, man.

MARIO
Vin . . .

VINNY
No, seriously. You know if I knew you liked some chick I wouldn't have fuckin' [*Laughs*] been all in the back seat like pre-gamin' it.

[*Vinny laughs.*]

MARIO

[*Mario laughs.*]

You're a prick.

VINNY

[*Laughing.*]

I . . . that chick was hot.

MARIO

[*Laughs.*]

Shut up, Vin.

[*Mario sits down on the couch.*]

VINNY
No offense, dude, but she was smoking! Her legs in that skirt. Damn!

MARIO
She was all right. Her face was ugly.

VINNY
She was not fuckin' ugly.

MARIO
She was cool and shit, but, dude, I mean her face looked like a meat grinder went to town on that shit.

VINNY
She had a bangin' fuckin' body, man, tight ass, nice perky—I mean her titties were all right, they weren't like huge fuckin' knockers, but they were perky and shit.

MARIO
You're the tit-man. Her face was still ugly, though, dude.

VINNY
Fuck you. Thought you like the chick?

MARIO

I'm just sayin' she wasn't like smokin', OK? Her face was ugly. Face it.

VINNY

It wasn't that bad.

MARIO

Vin, it doesn't matter. You were so fuckin' drunk, Vin, you woulda banged any two-legged rat that walked by.

VINNY

Didn't fuckin' matter.

[*Pause.*]

[*Vinny sits down.*]

She fucked like, unbelievable, she was twenty-six, dude, her ass is the shit; I mean I've fucked my share of bitches in my time but this chick. Dude. This broad didn't give a fuck, she was like a fuckin' porn star. I fucked her in the ass, and she must like shove a dill up there and shit because I didn't use no lube, I mean I used lube but she didn't need it.

MARIO

Yeah. You're a nice guy.

VINNY

Well, dude, I don't wanna fuck up her shit.

MARIO

Literally.

VINNY

She put her legs behind her head like "Oh, sure, no problem." Makes it easy for . . . you know, so you can . . .

MARIO

Yeah, I know.

VINNY

Dude. The best part, I used a condom like the first two times but the third I didn't, you know, so I pulled out and dude she turns toward me and starts suckin' my dick and shit, until I come and shit, I mean, if I had a camera, I could sell this shit on fuckin' eBay and shit. I mean this bitch was un-fuckin' real.

MARIO

Did you paint her face?

VINNY

Dude. I got some kind of respect, I mean, but dude, you don't understand that was probably the best fuck, I mean I'd let, I mean I know you haven't been with a whole bunch of chicks, you know, I mean I'd let you fuck her just so you can experience what she does.

MARIO

Well, I'm honored.

VINNY

I'm gonna keep that chick around. I gotta fuck her a few more times, I mean, ass like that, shit. Fuckin' JLo booty, right, I mean you seen her. Like apple ass and shit.

MARIO

I don't care.

VINNY

Dude, what? You don't care, what? What the fuck does that mean?

MARIO

[*Simultaneous with mean.*]

It means, Vin, shut up. I don't give a shit, OK? So you plowed her . . . Whatever.

VINNY

Fuck you.

MARIO

No, it's just, I don't need to listen to all this shit, OK? So you pleasured the pussy, I mean, so what? I'm just sick of hearing this. I don't care. I mean you fucked her, I get it.

[*Pause.*]

VINNY

You gotta fuckin' chill out, man, you were all, like, walkin' around all pissed and shit.

MARIO

How the fuck was I pissed?

VINNY

You didn't even hit on any chicks, man, I mean.

MARIO

Well, I wonder why?

VINNY

Like that was the only chick there or somethin', dude.

MARIO

There was all these ugly skanky-ass hoes who couldn't even dance, I mean, what the fuck? Am I just gonna hit on some chick for the fuck of it?

VINNY

You better fuckin' find some chick tonight.

MARIO

Well, whatever.

VINNY

All these chicks in the city are hoes, and there'll definitely be a ton of fuckin' hot-ass chicks at this club.

MARIO

They're all stuck up.

VINNY

You got no fuckin' confidence.

MARIO

I got more confidence than you.

VINNY

[*Laughing.*]

Yeah, OK. Yeah, you're a confident guy; you enter a room and people are shunned to the floor. In fact, when you walk into a club people's self-esteem tends to lower, because you feed off the self-esteem of others.

MARIO

Fuck you.

VINNY

No, I've seen them actually stop being confident.

MARIO

That makes a lot of sense. Go look at yourself in the mirror, go pamper yourself for a few more hours. Put on some cover-up.

VINNY

You know you tell me all of these fuckin' tales about you at the Roach Coach and how you fucked' this stripper, and you banged these two dykes . . .

MARIO

Wait . . . I never said . . .

VINNY

 . . . How you fucked this short chick in your car four times, this one chick from the Holidays . . .

MARIO

I said those chicks gave me head—the lesbians. I didn't fuck them.

VINNY

Well, you're king-swinging around the land of suburbia on fuckin' Thursdays, but on Saturday when you come out with me, you barely pick up on the fact that you rarely even hit on any chicks.

MARIO

It's fuckin' different on Thursdays, man—the chicks are all sluts.

VINNY

How is that different?

MARIO

It's different, the chicks in the city are all these high-class hoes who aren't even that hot but who think that they're the shit, and they're only interested in like these prototypical fuckin' model-type mothafuckers.

VINNY

That's the fuckin' stupidest thing I've ever heard. Fuckin' Jaime, OK, probably the hottest chick in the surrounding suburbs wanted you; fuck that, she still wants you. Look at fuckin' Jenna, the so-called hottest chick in the city, you fuckin' know her. I mean, OK, she wants my dick, but you know her. You talk to her; does she, like, shun you?

MARIO

That's not the fuckin' point.

VINNY

That is the fuckin' point, man, and don't give me this height shit, man. You may be, like, five feet three or whatever the fuck, but you got the mind of, like, a six-foot motherfucker. Man, these other dudes ain't got shit on you.

MARIO

I know that shit, but it's just different and shit. I don't know.

VINNY

You gotta walk in the club like you own the motherfucker, like nobody can fuck with you. You are the baddest dude in the place, and you can't hide that shit, *flaunt* that shit, unbutton your shit a little. You gotta fuck around with these chicks, man; you see how they dress. You don't think they wanna get fucked?

MARIO
No, I know. I don't need them.

VINNY
They all want cock.

MARIO
They all think they're the shit with their fuckin' tight skirts and shit, acting like they can't fuckin' talk to you. Like these fuckin' chicks that dance with each other. Like last week there were two chicks like that, and I was dancing with one shorty, really fuckin' cute and my height, but her fuckin' friend comes in and is all, like, "No, no sorry," like pulling her away and shit. What a fuckin' jealous cunt, get your own fuckin' dude. No, but she can't be alone. What a bitch.

VINNY
No shit, man. Stuck up.

MARIO
That's the fuckin' problem with all these fuckin' high-class hoes? They got the lowest self-esteem in the world. They are so fuckin' insecure with themselves it's pathetic. Fake titties, fake fingernails, fake personalities. It's like if you compliment them they keep walking, but if you tell them to fuck off they come back and want to know why.

VINNY
It's drama, dude.

MARIO
Makes them feel so fuckin' important.

VINNY
Don't give a fuck 'bout them, just fuck 'em.

MARIO
All they want is cock.

VINNY
Fuckin' A.

Nice Cars

Bahiyyih Davis

WHEN I WAS SIXTEEN NOTHING REALLY MATTERED EXCEPT FOR BOYS WITH nice cars. And it didn't matter to me if he was particularly attractive, or nice, or possessed any admirable qualities at all, as long as he had rims. I didn't even limit myself to young boys. He could be a grown man close to thirty—I didn't care. I would choose a Quasimodo with a flashy SUV over a Johnny Depp look-alike in an Omni. The cars were all that counted, and all the money it took to buy them.

I had myself a "friend." That's what I called him in quotation marks with a little sly smile, because he wasn't my boyfriend. I had one of those—his name was Donald, and he was the sweetest boy I knew. We'd met in the hallway of Auburn High School during my first week as a nervous freshman. He was short and skinny, but when you touched him all you felt was tight muscle and, when you hugged him, a ripply stomach. And he had braids that dangled off of his head like live bait. When he laughed he always bounced up and down and the worms would shake. We called him Tigger. He covered his mouth when he smiled because of bad teeth, he said, but none of the freshman girls noticed something wrong with his teeth or anything else about him. Everyone was jealous when he led me with his finger in the waist of my jeans back into a corner of the busy hall where I could write down my number. And the rest was high-school history. But in the middle of my sophomore year he had to move all the way to Tulsa, Oklahoma, with his mom. He still called me on an AT&T card that always ran out on him in midsentence, and he wrote long love letters and rode a bus eighteen hours when he could to visit me in the summers, but he did not own a car with leather seats or chrome detailing, and my new friend, Dewayne, had three: a Viper, a short-body Cadillac, and a black Expedition, my personal favorite.

"Someday you can drive my cars. Any one of them you want," he told me with his hand settled snuggly in my back pocket. He leaned in to whisper, "Maybe I'll even buy you your very own . . ." and winked at me as he squeezed my left ass cheek. It sent waves from the bottom of my spine to the top, where it began to numb my brain.

Dewayne was always selling his cars and buying new ones, going on shopping sprees in Chicago, and traveling to Vegas to gamble away thousands of dollars that wouldn't be missed. There was always more coming in. He never told me what he did for a living, but I didn't have to guess. He stored big blocks of weed the size of a suitcase in his grandmother's basement; his pager went off every few minutes, and he stayed out at all hours, roaming the city, working. If I wanted to find him I just had to get in my car and take a drive, going by certain spots—the liquor store on Auburn Street, the liquor store on West State. It made him both scary and fascinating. He had a two-story blue house all to himself in a quiet neighborhood on the northwest side of the city, still around black people but far from any of the projects. He wore new shoes every day and kept thick wads of cash that permanently clogged both pockets of his jeans. He was always breaking dates, but before I could even get mad he was making it up. "Here, babygirl," he'd say, reaching in the window of my sputtering Honda and stuffing a roll of bills into my open palm. "I can't kick it with you right now; I gotta go handle some business. But you and your friends go out to eat on me. Somewhere nice."

After he walked back inside I'd speed to my girl's house and honk for her to come out. I'd unroll the green tube and count it while she shook her head and said things like, "You're so lucky." He would give me a hundred dollars for breakfast, so we'd go to McDonald's and spend as little as possible, then head to T.J. Maxx or Old Navy to splurge on discount designer jeans and flip-flops.

"Get whatever you want," I liked saying. "It's on me."

Dewayne and I had not met by accident. My friend Jean had known him for a while because he was the older half-brother of a boyfriend she'd had.

Even after Jean and the brother split up, Dewayne was always stopping her in traffic, seeing if she was OK, did she need anything? If she said yeah, he gave her what she needed—money for her nails, or gas money, whatever. And if she said she was fine he insisted on giving her even more, calling her his little sister. I thought it was kind of weird but nice, I guessed. I wouldn't have minded it. And for more than a year I had listened to how sweet he was and how he resembled Tupac, how much money he had, and how much he would like me.

"I want you guys to meet," Jean said. "Next time I see him I'm setting it up."

One day we were in the drive-through line at Taco Bell, and Jean spotted his black Cadillac pulling out of the car wash across the street. "There he goes!" she screamed, leaping from the back seat into the front. "Catch him!"

We abandoned our order and tore out of the parking lot laughing. He was at a red light just ahead. As we eased up I noticed the glint of white sun on the silver rims; the wetness of the black paint, no chips and no scratches; the sleekness of the curves, the mystery in the black-tinted windows all around, and how the other cars in front and behind it looked dull in comparison. It was love at first sight, and then I took a glimpse inside the car and it got even worse.

Jean reached over me to lay her hand on my horn. The Cadillac's driver-side window rolled down slowly. "Oh, my God," I whispered. Jean squeezed my arm excitedly, squealing quietly in my ear, "I know, I know, I know, he's *so* fine." She was pleased with herself. "Dewayne!" she yelled. "Pull over!"

We parked on the shoulder of a bare street behind Taco Bell and got out of our cars. He was like a mirage; my knees wobbled as I walked toward him. I had thought I was pretty but not anymore. It was the wrong time to realize that my face was too round, I looked like a big baby, my outfit was all wrong, I wasn't sexy. Why hadn't I at least thought to put on some mascara before being introduced to the spitting image of the most beautiful man in the world, only Dewayne was beefier? I could have collapsed from the way he was already looking at me.

Jean introduced us and then had to pinch her own cheeks trying to contain her smile, but it didn't work. I saw it and caught the giggles like I used to do during prayers. I tried to cough them away and tell myself, *This is not funny.*

We shook hands. He held on longer than a standard first shake and I could feel the warmth of the creases in his palm. He had his eyes fixed on me, grinning like he knew what he was doing to me inside, how he was twisting me up. He tasted his lips.

"Very nice to meet you," he said softly, and he didn't let me go.

I was blushing way down deep into the fleshy insides of my cheeks. "Yeah, you too," I said, darting my eyes from him to the pavement and back, as if staring at him for more than a few uninterrupted seconds would turn me to stone. I started to take my hand back, not because I ever wanted it back but because I didn't know anything else to say or do—but Dewayne gripped tighter and pulled me to him.

"Can I have a hug?" he asked, but we were already touching chests. This wasn't a normal hug. It was warmer and more intense than I imagined sex would be. He rubbed his hand inside the back of my shirt and swayed with me like there was music. I didn't know men could smell so damn good. "Awwww," he whispered, like I had given him something I shouldn't have, "thank you." And reluctantly I allowed him to let me go.

"I'll be callin' you, sis," he said to Jean with a nod, a smile, and a wink as he slid back behind the leather wheel of the Cadillac.

"OK!" she exploded after staying quiet the whole time.

He licked his lips again and I thought there must be something on them that tasted delicious. He turned up his bass and thundered away.

Oh god, there was no rattle in that trunk, I thought in a blissful daze. *And what were those on his tires—nineteens? Twenties, maybe?*

"So?" Jean asked, skipping to catch up to me as I stumbled back to the car. I couldn't answer, only shake my head like I'd just witnessed a bloody accident and might die from the shock.

"See," she laughed, "I told ya."

Usually Dewayne and I would just ride around in his cars. He made stops at almost every other corner, it seemed, getting out to have a quick exchange with someone, letting young boys stick their heads inside the car to see what I looked like. Dewayne was always keeping close watch, though, and would only allow them a glimpse before he'd slide back into his seat, laughing and saying, "Take y'all nosy asses on somewhere. Leave us alone." Everyone on the West Side of the city knew him. They gave him icy beers out of their coolers for no reason or bought something from the inside of his palm that he never let me see. I sat and observed and smiled when I needed to. If people thought I looked out of place they never said anything. They were always nice, inviting me into their houses with him, giving me pieces of chicken and offering me seats. We never stayed long anywhere. We were always right back in his car, driving to the next spot, answering calls like people depended on him. "I got this," he'd say, leaning back, biting his juicy bottom lip. He was so fucking fine.

"Where you been at?" my boyfriend asked in a small voice one night.

"You're never at home anymore; you never return my calls."

I was on my way out the door right then. I could hear Dewayne's car waiting outside in my driveway. "Baby, it's summer," I whined. "I'm just out. I'll call you tonight, I swear."

Dewayne had a reputation, especially with guys my age. "That nigga's a killer," one of them told me. "I heard he killed like five people."

"Whatever," I said.

"All right! Don't listen. Just don't make him mad."

But I wasn't scared of Dewayne. I'd never known anyone who gave away so much money to little kids waiting outside of gas stations, telling them to go crazy on candy. He wasn't a killer. We watched *Turner & Hooch* on the screen built into his dashboard, and he got teary-eyed when the dog died.

My mother did not approve of Dewayne, nor appreciate how he addressed her as "Baby" when he called her house to ask for me. "How old is he?" she questioned me with narrow eyes and hands on her hips.

"I don't know!" I lashed back defensively, sticking out my chin at her, narrowing my own eyes. "Like, in his twenties. Who cares? We're friends. He's like a big brother."

She rolled her eyes and stomped away sighing, and the panic that had begun to rise inside me momentarily calmed again. Upstairs, she slammed her door. Somehow she always seemed to know too much.

In August, going into my senior year of high school, Dewayne had his twenty-ninth birthday and wanted the two of us to celebrate with a private party. I thought he'd go to a club or out of town, but he said he was tired of that, he just wanted it to be him and his baby. Over the phone he told me to wear my sexiest panties. The thought made the blood rush to my head.

"What for?" I asked, taking a seat.

"You know, you're seventeen years old now," he said impatiently. "When are you going to stop acting like a little girl and be a woman?"

But I didn't own any sexy panties, or anything that I thought would qualify as panties at all. My mother had just bought me a new package of day-of-the-week underwear, each pair picturing a different fruit like the ones the hungry caterpillar ate. I thought they were funny and they'd been suiting me just fine until now. Now I had to rethink everything.

I got off the phone and felt strange. It was a queasy feeling like I'd eaten bad chicken again, but I thought that it was probably just nerves and that he was right, it was time to grow up. Staying a virgin was completely nineteenth century. But it was also safe, and all that I was really good at being. I was a great virgin, nobody else I knew could say that, and I wasn't sure I wanted to give up my title. I called Tulsa.

"I was just thinking about you, baby," Donald said. And as usual, I sat quietly for a few minutes to let him get out all his giggles, just like we used to do when I'd run into him in the hallway at school and he'd have an excited fit. "I wish I didn't have to work!" he shouted like he was cursing the world. I pictured him balling up his fists. "But call me at eleven, right when I get off," he made me promise. "OK, OK!" I said, but I was laughing. We went through the hundred good-bye-I-love-yous before I felt OK hanging up, and I sat on the steps looking at the phone and feeling horrible for what I was thinking about doing. I went into my closet and dug out a letter Donald had written me months before. At the end of it he'd added:

P.S. Don't let one of these imaginary players come and sweep you off your feet and steal the "apple pie" and beat it like Mike. You know when 1999/2000 rolls around I'll be back, and I'll have some money and be able to stay and marry your sweet little ass. So just keep shit real as always, baby.

And I read it three times over and felt a sting in my nose, and I decided, "OK, OK, I won't do it. I will NOT do it. Even though he looks a lot like Tupac and just got new twenties put on the Escalade, I won't do it."

Dewayne picked me up after eight. I hadn't planned on letting my parents know where I was going and definitely not who was taking me. I told them some lie, like I was going to get dessert at Cheddar's with Jean and Camille. I was watching out the window for his car, sweating. My stomach turned over every time my mom passed through the room. I knew he was close because I heard the booms; he had the loudest speakers in the whole city. I watched as he rounded the corner and then jumped up, calling "Bye!" into the kitchen. He parked hastily on the wrong side of the street and before I could get out the door he was walking up onto my front porch. My father was in the doorway behind me now. They shook hands and Dewayne said it was nice to meet him. My father gave a stony face to Dewayne's smiles and barely said a word. We cut across the lawn and he opened the door to the burgundy Viper for me, waited until I slid into one of the two seats, and then gently shut me in. My parents stood observing from the brightly lit doorway of our tall brick house. I wondered why they were letting me go.

As we sped along quiet side streets, Dewayne played Tupac so loudly that it vibrated the leather seats. He always played Tupac, and it was almost creepy, like he wanted to fill the empty role of the dead rapper just because he had that same skin, dark and flawless as black marble, and that trap of brown eyes lined in long curly lashes, the whites of them always tinted pink. But I decided, looking at him now, that he didn't look so much like him, really. He had a much larger head, and fuller lips. The top of his hair was turning gray if you looked close. "I've always had gray hair," he said, "since I was little." But I couldn't picture it.

He sipped from a square bottle of dark liquor; at a light he rolled up the windows and asked me to hand him a lighter that had fallen on the floor, then lit the end of a blunt. He reached under his seat and pulled out a bright orange knit hat and pulled it over his head with one hand, down to his ears. *Trying to cover up that gray,* I thought. The sweet smoke wafted over to my side of the car and canceled out the spicy scent of Dewayne's cologne. It snuck into my lungs and made me feel dizzy, under water.

I watched him, his fluorescent head bobbing to the music as I felt the tickle of the bass in my back. I examined him in his heavily starched jeans and silky white shirt so thin it was nearly see-through, and I knew it might be the weed, but I thought he looked ridiculous. And suddenly he seemed so close to thirty to me, and strange, and wrong for having me in his car, an underage birthday present to himself.

"What ya thinkin' about, pancake?" he asked, pausing the music on the stereo, kneading the inner part of my thigh like bread dough in his dry hands.

"Nothing," I said. I turned to the window. I wanted to throw up.

He had said that we would go to dinner but we had passed all the restaurants now. At a light near the Interstate he turned to me and grinned, running his glossy eyes over me, licking his lips like he was mentally eating me up. The smell of Hennessy was overwhelming. I wanted to ask where we were going, but my throat was too tight for me to say anything. All I could do was gulp.

I stayed in the car in the hotel parking lot while he ran inside to get a room. It was called the Comfort Inn. My friends had all lost their virginity in crummy places, like the backseat of a car or someone else's parents' bed at a party. They told me if I was going to do it I should do it with Dewayne. He wasn't some clumsy high school quarterback. He was a grown man, experienced and smooth. They said he would take me somewhere nice and probably fill a room with roses and run me a bubble bath, take everything real slow. They told me not to be scared and to remember everything—they wanted details.

I pulled down the visor mirror and checked my hair. I'd straightened it, trying to look older, but I wasn't fooling anyone. My hands were shaking. I looked at my face, my fat cheeks, a pimple on my chin. I still looked seventeen, maybe younger. I didn't look like a woman. Maybe I would in the morning. Maybe I'd look skinnier, more serious. I hoped my mom wouldn't notice a change.

He surprised me when he opened my door. He pulled me out by my clammy hand, his hand rough and hot. He motioned for me to follow him. Suddenly he lost all his sexiness. He was short and old, and he rushed me along up the stairs. He was so anxious to get to the room; I felt like a prostitute. I wanted to run. There was nothing around us but highway and a cluster of more hotels.

The room was nothing better than any room I had stayed in with my parents on family vacations. It had a single bed draped in a generic flower spread, and a nightstand with a phone. I sat down and looked up at him.

"Can I get a 'Happy Birthday'?" he asked, lying on his back next to me.

"Happy birthday," I choked.

"Are you nervous?" he teased.

"No."

We sat silently as he broke up his weed and put it into a cigar. He looked at me as he licked it shut and I knew he was trying to entice me with the movement of his tongue, but I just felt impatient. I sighed.

"All right," he said, laughing. "Get undressed."

He disappeared into the tiny bathroom and I thought to myself that I should be the one in there, changing into something more comfortable, like they said in movies. I pulled off my jeans but nothing else, then sat there under the covers and waited. I wanted to cry. I wanted to call my real boyfriend and have him talk me out of this.

A month ago Donald had been in town, in middle of July. I hadn't expected him. He'd called me in the morning and I'd asked why he wasn't at work. He'd giggled more than usual and I kept asking, "What?" He wasn't very good at lying. "I'm in yo' city, shorty!" he'd finally yelled.

I'd picked him up from a house behind the community center where I worked with kids after school, helping them with homework. When I pulled up and got out, a chubby guy in an old car with a fresh paint job had stepped on his brakes in the middle of the street. He'd leaned out the window calling, "Eh, eh!" and I'd paused halfway up to the house. Before a word could get out of my mouth, Donald erupted from the front door like a racehorse from a starting gate, dancing down the steps.

"Hey, man. Move around!" he'd said, jogging up to me, wrapping me up like he was going to carry me inside. "This my wife, man."

"My bad," said the chubby guy, and pulled away.

I'd looked at Donald. He was wearing army fatigue pants, white shoes, and a red shirt that I knew he'd taken hours to iron; he had his hair in the braids I liked, the worm braids. I didn't like him in cornrows, they made him look like a dinosaur. He wore barrettes at the end of each worm, little-girl barrettes that were red and white to match his clothes, and somehow they looked adorable on him. I was wearing a green sundress made of cotton with flip-flops on my feet; my hair was past my shoulders now, longer than he remembered, and curly out of control. I knew he liked it better straight, but he didn't say anything. I think the hug lasted five minutes.

We'd gotten into my car. He'd moved around in his seat like it was hot. He could never sit still. I kept looking over and caught him staring at me. He had the biggest eyes in the whole city. "You have almond eyes," I'd said. He'd liked that. He loved it when he got a compliment. "And you're the most beautiful girl I've ever seen in my life, on TV and everything." He was lying, but it was OK. Guys might have called me pretty before, but nobody meant it like Donald.

We'd passed a group of young girls on the sidewalk. He had stuck half of his small body out the window and yelled, "Y'all bitches don't got shit on my girl, she fine as hell!" My cheeks flamed up. "Stop it, that's mean!" I'd said, pulling his shirt. We'd laughed the whole way to Arby's.

"What do you want?" I'd asked.

"Just a drink," he'd said, "whatever." He didn't want to talk, he was concentrating on staring at me again.

"Stop it," I'd said, pushing his cheek. His face popped right back around like it was on a spring. "Stop it," I'd whined, covering my face with a hand. "Look at something else."

We'd driven around, turning here and there, trying not to run into Dewayne, going past my high school that used to be both of ours. "I miss the shit outta you, babygirl," he'd said.

When it started getting dark he had to meet some of his friends, so I'd dropped him off at one of their houses. He didn't want to go inside, but I said, "You have to, you haven't seen them in a year." He'd looked at me for a long time in the shadowy car and I'd noticed a thin line running from his eye to his lip. "Are you crying?" I'd said.

He hadn't broken down or anything, but another tear fell and he sniffled.

He hadn't turned away. He was brave and looked right in my eyes and said, "Charles and them . . . they say you messin' with some older cat. Someone named Dewayne."

I'd looked hard at the dashboard, burning a hole into it. I'd felt like crying, too, but instead I'd rolled my eyes. "Your friends are so fucking stupid," I'd snapped. It wasn't a lie or the truth either.

"So you're not?" he'd asked, releasing a breath. But I'd sworn that really he knew.

"No," I'd said. "Don't listen to them."

Dewayne emerged from the bathroom in a pair of tight blue briefs that resembled cheerleading shorts, the least attractive thing anyone has ever worn. I wanted to snap my fingers and turn him into an eighteen-year-old, because eighteen-year-olds wore boxers and at least they kissed you, but this old man just climbed on top and was annoyed to discover that I hadn't taken off my Friday underwear.

"Are you keeping your shirt on, too?"

I nodded.

It was just dry skin on dry skin. His was warm, the only thing that felt good about him. My friends told me that it was like a shot, the first time. The second time, too, they had laughed, and maybe even the third. Then after that it would get better. So I had to go through with this. It was insignificant, really, just a means to an end. He was rubbing and thrusting at me but I wouldn't open my legs any wider; it had already started to burn and felt like something was going to pop. He wasn't gentle or sweet, just bothered by my shyness. There was no kissing or whispering anything comforting. I'd thought guys usually asked, "Are you all right?" when they knew it was your first time. He kissed my forehead once in the beginning, but that was the end of the show. After that it was just rough, stiff jerking, and pushing. It felt like we were wrestling. I didn't mean to, but I was being difficult. He stopped and wiped his forehead. Then tried again.

At first he ignored the wetness on his shoulders, creeping into the folds of his neck. He sighed but kept going. They started to fall heavier and faster, and I couldn't help it. The mascara felt like wet paint on my face, all the way down to my chin. He had to stop now. He sat up. I was crossing my arms over my chest and melting into the sheets.

"Awww, boo-boo," he said softly, pulling me up to his sticky chest for a hot hug. I cried even harder. "Don't cry, don't cry," he begged, petting from the top of my head down. I sniffed it up, relieved that it was done. I took a breath, eying my jeans that lay crumpled on the floor like a discarded wrapper. I started to reach for them. "You OK?" Dewayne asked in a fatherly tone. His eyes were shiny. I nodded and laughed at myself. "Good," he said, sternly guiding my body back down, "it's almost over."

On the ride home I didn't say anything. He touched my cheek once and my knee. But he couldn't think of anything to say either, so we just listened to Tupac.

It wasn't even midnight when I walked sorely through my back door and collapsed on the couch before anyone could see how strangely I was walking. I picked up the phone and called Tulsa. I woke him up, but he was glad I called him. I hardly ever did anymore.

"I miss you," he said in a deep voice.

"I miss you, too," I squeaked, and the tears gushed.

"What's wrong, boo-boo?" he asked, and I could hear him sit up in bed.

I wanted to tell him what a mistake I had just made, about the unflattering blue briefs, and how badly I was still burning. I wanted to apologize, but I never would.

"Ohhh, you miss me, huh?" he asked, touched, and I nodded and made sounds. "I miss you too. You been holdin' this in for a long time. You don't *never* cry over me!" We both laughed. "Let it out, baby," he coaxed. "It's all right, Don-don's here."

"You're so stupid," I told him, meaning everything opposite. I waddled to the freezer and grabbed an icepack to sit on, and I swaddled myself in a blanket and just cried until the feeling ran out. And then I let him make me laugh, and we talked until we stopped making sense. And I fell asleep on the couch with the TV on and Donald snoring loudly in my ear all night until the next morning when I gently put the phone back into the cradle and went upstairs to shower before school.

Dear Jovan

Leah Ignacio

TONIGHT AFTER DINNER WE WAS LINED UP TO GO BACK ON SECTION WHEN MS. Hollister came by and pulled me outta line. "I'm a need Wilson," was all she said to Q. But Q wouldn'a noticed no way. He was too busy lickin' the orange offa his fat fingers from his hot flamins. He so greedy. He wouldn't give none a us some, 'cept for that Rena, but we all think that 'cause she a white girl and cry all the time. Anyway, I was followin' Ms. Hollister down the hall, and I realized she was takin' me back to the school. Then I started hearin' this click. Click. Click. I don't even know when it started, probably been happenin' the whole time but I just now noticed it. So I closed my eyes, I swear I did—I didn't bump into no one 'cause ain't nothin' up in these halls after dinner, 'cept for maybe the boys exercizin', but I was too late to see that—and just listened to that click. Click. Click. Sound so pretty. Yup, and it sho reminded me of Neicy's barrettes, you know, the ones she forever be losin' but sho nuff Mama forever be sendin' me to the dollar store to buy that child some mo. I swear when I closed my eyes I saw that crazy way Neicy used ta run, her being bow-legged and all. You know how we used ta talk about her. Her big head swingin' side ta side, side ta side, makin' all them fat braids bang into each other like click. Click. Click. Yup, so I closed my eyes and I wrapped myself in that clickin' sound, wrapped myself up real tight, like Mama used ta do for me back before you was even born, when I real little. She used ta wrap me up real tight in that big yellow blanket, before it got all fuzzy and full a holes, kiss my forehead, then head out to work. Yup, I just let that clickin' sound wrap all around me, and I swear it lifted me up outta this nasty place. Out past these doors that be locked all the time, past these tall, brown brick walls—everywhere you look, brown brick walls—past all these back-biting tricks up on section, past all the whistles and yellin' that let you know when it time to sit, eat, stand, or wipe you own butt. Yup, I was sho outta here, that click. Click. Click. Sound takin' me right on home. And before I knowed it I was back on the block. You, and the twins from next door—Ricky and Man Man—runnin' up ahead a me laughin' and fightin'. Me havin' ta walk real slow 'cause I had to walk with Neicy or get a whuppin'. Yeah . . . and I saw that gas station on 123rd, the one them Indian men be ownin'. Them forever watchin' us the minute we step in the store. Yup, and I swear I could see you stuffin' your pockets with quarter Now and Laters while the Indian men try to push drunk Jimmy out the store. Then we'd walk back down 123rd, back on home, past the Chinese restaurant, the train tracks, and the big empty house on the corner. You passin' out all yo candy, 'cause you always did share. You wadn't never greedy. Ricky and Man Man fightin' over the different colors they end up with, they always be wantin' what the other got. Yeah and me knowin' you had hid a purple piece in yo pocket fo Neicy, 'cause you know that was her favorite. Yup, I swear I was there. And the sounds. Man, Jovan, I could hear old Mrs. Washington on her porch talkin' 'bout, "You disrespectful children need ta stay offa my grass. Lord Jesus, have mercy on me. I'm getting tired, Lord. I am getting tired. Man Man, you better keep on walking past my lawn 'fore I call you mama." I could hear Chris tryin' to holla at all the girls that walk by. All them just gigglin', rollin' they eyes, and walking past. "Oh, so it's like that, huh? It's like that?" Yeah, then we'd all get home. Mama in the bathroom getting ready for work, and Neicy all bent over holdin' on to her knees talkin' 'bout, "C'mon, Javette. I gotta use it. I gotta use it." Yup, just like it used ta be. I swear I was there.

"Turn in here, Wilson. I better not hear about no trouble from you. You lucky I chose you for this program. Remember, lots a girls up on section just wishin' they could be down here 'stead a you." And that's all Ms. Hollister said. Then she pushed me through those big brown doors into the chapel, 'cept here, the chapel's just a big ugly room with, yup, big brown, brick walls. Usually for service, they have a table up in the front and all these chairs lined up. But don't nobody really notice, 'cept fo me, I guess. No one even notice what

Father Don be sayin', everyone too busy noticin' the boys or which girl talkin' to who. Yup, Jovan, up in here, girls be goin' with other girls!!! On my mama they do! Yeah, and they get real jealous about each other, too! Guess there ain' much to choose from when you always separated from the boys. What else you gon' do when you around the same girls all day, all night? You talk about each other, fight, and kiss, I guess. But not me. No way. I don't go like that.

Anyway, tonight all the chairs was pushed back 'cept for a circle right in the middle of the room. Not a big circle, but not too small neither. And you not gon' believe what I'm 'bout to tell you next. But sitting in the circle were some nappy heads from up on section and . . . some white women too! Now I'm talkin' 'bout them white women like you see on TV. Not like Miss Alvert from Songhai. But like them women we see on *Days of Our Lives*, when we sick or skippin' or whatever. Anyway they look like that! They not women, they ladies! Their hair was all pretty and soft and straight. They had on clean, pressed pants, some had dresses. They nails was all painted and cut the same. But they ALL had huge rings. I looked at ALL of them. And they all had HUGE rocks! Well, 'cept for maybe two. They looked real young, though. I remember thinkin' what the heck am I doin' up in here? I started tryin' to smooth down my hair and pull on my green shirt. I started shifting from side ta side, tryin' ta cover my feet 'cause I had on what the white girls give away free here. I didn't have no mama on the outside to send me real nice shoes. I just have what they give me. I just knew I looked a hot mess. I could feel my cheeks startin' to get hot. Then I kept looking around the circle and I saw Melinda, and Shirl, and this crazy girl LaToya. At least those were the girls I knew from section. There were a few others but they section B girls. So I was just standing there when one a the younger-looking white girls, the one that had a small rock on her finger, she told me I could sit. And the only empty seat left was next to Toya. Oh, Jesus, I had to sit next to that heifer. Toya always be gettin' into it with people. Just this morning she cussed out the teacher in the middle of class. Toya wouldn't sit still. She kept walkin' round and round the room . . . just walking and saying something real quiet. Just walking round and round. And the teacher, well, she real little and always scared like, she kind of quietly said, "Latoya, could you please sit down . . . please?" Just like that! Can you believe it, Jovan? Now if we was back in Songhai, wouldn't no one be askin' you ta sit. Remember when Mr. Hoskins shoved that boy Carl in his seat? Grabbed him by the back a the neck real tight. I swear I saw Carl tearin' up. Yup, dragged Carl to his seat and shoved him down. But not up in here. No way. The teachers here always be scared or somethin'. So Toya now, she just acted like she didn't even hear the teacher, can't remember her name, she probably quit next week anyway. And Toya she wadn't havin' it. She just kept walking. Well, the teacher asked again, but this time she coughed a little first. "Ahem . . . LaToya, will you please" and before she could say anything else Toya turned around and started walkin' real fast—I mean, real fast, almost runnin'—to the teacher, her hand balled up over her head like she fittin' ta steal offa her or something. And the whole time, the whole time she was just cussin' the teacher out. Callin' her all type a names. Then outta nowhere Q come bustin' in, I guess he musta heard all the yellin' from where he always sit down the hall, and he caught Toya and threw her to the ground. By that time we was all on top a our desks and jumpin up and down. It was wild. Yeah, then Q got up offa Toya and dragged her out. He was breathin' real heavy in and out on account a him bein' so big and all. Man, I ain't never seen Q move so fast. Anyway he drug Toya out the room and our lame teacher was just balled up under her desk. So yup, the only seat left was next to that crazy girl Toya, and she was already rockin' back and forth in her seat.

So I sat down, not 'cause I wanted to be there, but because I wanted all a them to stop lookin' at me mainly. And the lady that tol' me to sit down, anyway she started tellin' me that we was writin' a show together. A play. And tonight we had to write letters. Then she started passing out this paper. Well, I had no idea what she was talking about so I just sat there. All the other girls, well, they just moved around to different parts of the room and one a the white ladies followed them and sat with them. I just couldn't move. A play? Writin'? I kep' thinkin' this woman was crazy. Anyway she sat next to me real close, and she started whisperin', "So the other girls could concentrate," she said. I wanted to tell her that I have to live with these girls and they ain't nothin' but triflin' heifers. But I din't say nothing. I just stared at her. Then she told me that they all been meeting for months now and I was brought in 'cause Katie was DOCed last week. She said she understood that I might be nervous, but I should just relax and write. Relax?! This woman crazier than Toya. Well, she tol' me I should write a letter to someone I would like to apologize to. She said it could be anyone, about anything. Then she got up to "give me space."

Anyway I was just stuck 'cause no one ever talked to me that nice in a long time. And she smelled so pretty. Not all loud and flowery that make you choke. Naw, she just smelled real . . . clean. I ain't smell't that in a long time. And I kept staring at her lips. They was all red and shiny. Not all peelin' like the other girls in here. I wanted some of her lip gloss so bad. I started to remember how the one I usedta buy from the beauty supply store for a dollar usedta make my lips all sparkly and pink. It had REAL glitter. Yup, but Mama didn't know nothin' about it 'cause I always wiped it off before I came home. But now I an't got nothin' for my lips 'cept for some Vaseline I gotta keep on the back a my hand. And that's only when Hollister feels like being nice. Anyway, I was staring at the nice lady walk away when I started hearin' that click. Click. Click. Sound again. But it was strong this time. So strong, I thought I was just dreamin' it. But I looked over and saw Toya hittin' the leg a her chair with a pen like click. Click. Click.

And I don't know why, but outta nowhere I just started to cry. All slow and quiet at first, I just started to cry. I couldn't help it. It just kept comin' out. I tried to stop it. I tried to swallow real hard, pinch my leg, I even started prayin' 'cause I didn't want none a these girls to see me cry. But nothing helped. I just kept on cryin'. It was like my whole body started shakin', like this chill was runnin' up and down from my toes all the way to my head, up and down, up and down. And I realized I was rocking back and forth, just like crazy Toya. And I looked over to her. She was talkin' real fast and the white lady that was with her was writing real fast. And Toya the whole time was just bangin' her pen against that chair. I wanted to tell her to stop. Naw, I wanted to yell and scream at her to stop. I wanted to run to her like she did our teacher. I wanted to shove her down and bang that nappy head onto the floor. Just bang. Bang. Bang. Real hard with everything I got. I just wanted her ta stop. But she just kept on clickin'. Click. Click. Click. And then all the clickin' started to come all around me and wrap me up tight, but this time I was trying to fight it, tryin' ta get all that clickin' away from me.

But it just kept comin', more and more of 'em, click. Click. Click. Yeah, and they wrapped all around me, not like Mama useta do. They started coverin' my eyes and my mouth. And I felt like I was screamin', just hollerin' for someone ta help me, but no one could hear me on account a the click. Click. Click. That just kept growin' louder and louder. And now they was getting stronger and tighter 'til I swear on Mama it felt like I was being pushed and pulled, pushed and pulled. And I closed my eyes; the clicks were makin' every-thing dark anyhow, and when I opened them I was right on Ashland, right in front of McDonald's, across the street from Dominick's. You know, the one I used ta sneak you to after school when it'd just be the two of us? The one Mama said we could never go to. But we didn't pay her no mind, 'cause we knew we was smart. And besides it was your favorite place. And you are my favorite brother. You even liked that McDonald's better than Harold's.

Anyway I was back in front a that same McDonald's and it was your birthday last year. You remember that? You got up and begged and begged me ta take you to McDonald's. And I said, "Naw, 'cause Mama's home from work to cook for your party. And if Mama found out where we went, she gon' whup us real good." Remember that? But you was actin' real spoil't that day, and you started cryin' and sayin' how all you wanted was fo me to take you to McDonald's. So I told Mama we was goin' to the store and she tol' me.I had ta bring Neicy on account a Neicy gettin' into everything in the kitchen and gettin' in the way a her cookin'. So I rolled my eyes. Then Mama popped me in the back a the head wid her wooden spoon and dared me to do it again. So I said, "Sorry, ma'am" and started to put Neicy's coat on her. It was startin' to get real cold outside, so I put her scarf on her too. Remember that? I wouldn't even let you leave the house without yo hat. Yeah . . . so I was right in front a that McDonald's on my knees, one hand on Neicy's coat 'cause she forever wanderin' away, and the other hand looking for one a Neicy's barrettes . . . and I think you was already walkin' ahead some. I think I even yelled after you and tol' you to wait. But you didn't say nothin' back. Not even one a yo' smart comments that always get you popped in the mouth by Mama. Naw, you was just quiet. So I looked up and I saw you just walkin' up the street towards 123rd, towards home. You was almost dancin' some, so happy you got ta go to McDonald's. I remember thinkin' how happy you looked.

You was just sorta dancing along, eatin' yo chicken nuggets, like you ALWAYS get. Eatin' 'em with the hot sauce you brought from home. Yup, like always. And just past yo head, I saw a car creep up all slow. And I just know I seen it before. I just knowed it. And I sat there trying to remember where, trying ta hold on ta Neicy who was pullin' real hard from me now. And I remembered that car screechin' off in front a that court building when Daddy got locked up. I remember 'cause I had to wait in that car. That same car screeched off and Jahmel was yelling something after them. Yup, and I remember seein' that same brown car with dark windows screechin' off when Jahmel got shot, when Neicy was still up in Mama's stomach. Yeah, and I remember Mama just cryin' and cryin' at the funeral. And her holdin' onto her big stomach sayin' she ain't gon' name the next baby with a J just like our daddy, just like the rest a us, 'cause ta her J is a curse. First Daddy locked up and now Jahmel dead. And all 'cause a the gangs. And some Lord Jesuses or something more. Yup, and I saw it now. Only it wasn't screechin' it was just rollin' up slow. So I was thinkin' all this when I heard a voice yell out, "Ay, who you be about?" And I looked past yo head and saw one a the dark windows in the back start to roll down. So I jumped up and snatched Neicy by the back a her coat and just started runnin'. And I heard some real loud pop, I mean, real loud, and outta the side a my eye I saw some nuggets just fly up, real slow like. Like in the movies when it starts getting real good, and you all excited and the music is all fast, then everything starts to move slow motion. That what it was like. A few nuggets just flying up then slowly floating down. Only this wasn't a movie. So I grabbed Neicy even tighter, both my arms around her now. Her feet clear off the ground and dangling. Yup, I had that baby so high up, the back a her head was up against my face. I even remember smellin' the grease Mama just put in Neicy's hair before she braided it. Her barrettes just clickin' like crazy against each other now. Yup, I just ran and ran, just closed my eyes and ran, them clicks just leadin' me home. And I don't know how I even made it back without fallin' over nothin', them clicks just leadin' me home: Click. Click. Click.

You know, that was the last time I saw you. Mama sent me out the house before yo funeral. I was there, though. I sat across the street by the watermelon stand, hiding behind a car. Yeah, I watched all the people come in. And I waited two hours 'til everyone came out. I watched 'til that big car they put you in drove away. I wouldda been there when they put you in the ground too, but I didn't know where that was at. I just went to _____ funeral home 'cause it seemt like everyone that die on the South Side have they services there. Click. Click. Click.

So I was still in my seat. Just cryin' and sobbin'. Eyes closed. Rockin' back and forth, real slow-like. Back and forth. Then I felt this hand on my back and I jumped 'cause I was afraid it was Mama again come to beat me for takin' you outta the neighborhood even though I know better. But it wasn't Mama. It was Toya. And she just hugged me real tight. Didn't say a word. Just looked at me like she knew what I was crying about. Then she walked back to her seat, to that white lady still waitin' on her, her pen put down.

So this my letter, Jovan. When she said I had to write a letter to apologize to someone I could thinka no one but you. Not a day go by that I don't think about you and just wish I wouldda done things different.

Love,

Javette

A Letter From the Sea

Thomas Kemeny

Dear Mrs. K,

As my closest mate delivers you this message, I will be feeling the warm sun beating down on my face and the cool salty breeze off the ocean blowing through my hair. After much searching, I have found that there is nothing left for me on land. I have chosen a life of adventure and daring with my shipmates, and there is nothing that you or Mr. Stillbach can say to bring me back. This letter is simply to inform you of my whereabouts and to let you know that, despite my determination, I do this with a heavy heart and do apologize to those I have left behind.

I made this decision shortly before the end of lunchtime, when the true nature of the world revealed itself to me. Jennifer approached me as I was finishing my diagonally cut bologna sandwich. Her hair glistened like glitter on the floor after art class. She gave me a few kind words, and I gave her half my Fruit Roll-Up. Passions flared, and we shared an intimate shoulder punch. Life seemed beautiful, until Ms. Lee told us not to hit each other and tore my sweetheart far away from my adoring eyes. My friends tried to console me with chocolate milk, but it was no use. They tried telling me that I was better off without her, that she was nothing but trouble, but they did little to relieve my grief. I knew I would never be able to speak with her freely again, and with this knowledge I wept.

So you see, my dear Mrs. K, my decision was not much of a decision at all. I was heartbroken, and the only comfort I have ever found in times like those was the call of the waves, the crack of the wind as it catches in mighty sails, and the briny water crashing against the bow like a firework of tears. The sea has always been sanctuary for those with broken hearts, a wide expanse that soothes sorrowing eyes. Fear not, my good-natured mentor; my sadness will not drown the world, even if thoughts of days long ago flood my mind. If this incident had occurred in isolation, I might have been able to take the allotted fifteen-minute adventure as I had done in the past and return to the shore. Unfortunately, several other circumstances influenced this decision. Room 8B was not as it once was. There used to be a time when one could stand proud at our victories in the penny wars, but those days are long gone and have since been replaced by lice outbreaks and stale cookies. My men and I attempted to return us all to the glory days, but our attempts were thwarted by pirates who robbed us of the cupcakes we brought to share. Nothing is as it once was, nor am I.

I have also, of late, become disillusioned with nap-time. While it is true that my soul is weary, there is no amount of sleep that can mend my exhaustion. It seems pointless, and I resent having to lie there idly. Moreover, when I feel the wind blow in through the window, I can't help but wonder what awaits me on the other side of that breeze. I begin to drift off, and my uncontrolled dreams lead me to discover how small I am in this world. I start wondering what else is out there and whether somewhere, perhaps, I might find something to fill the hole in my life.

It is not only that I see nothing for me on land, but also that I adore the open sea. As captain of the largest vessel in the schoolyard, I feel an immeasurable sense of freedom and pride. My love of the deep blue yonder began accidentally one fateful day. I had made a habit of eating quickly so I could get out to the swing set, but I stayed a few minutes too long one day to savor fully an exquisite square pizza, and by the time I finished, the swings were all in use. I moped off and, without thinking, wandered onto a ship. I walked over to the steering wheel and almost intuitively spun it. It did something to me. I had to spin it again and again, and ever since then I could not be torn away from the helm. I assembled a small crew to help me on my journey, and we took sail.

My men are incredibly loyal and courageous. They never fear needlessly, and they do not scurry from wood-chip or kick-ball assaults from enemy crafts. I will never forget the sacrifices made by them, particularly Michael, who was injured on a scouting assignment I sent him on. He was walking along a narrow plank between the ship and the shore when he fell into the lava. Now, this image is with me forever, and I must come to terms with it every day. Thankfully, he only stepped down with his right foot, but now he walks with a peg leg, and I have to come to terms with being responsible for it. (With a long enough time sailing away, perhaps I can.)

I have all I need, the wind, the ship, the water, and two packages of Handi-Snacks. I am fully prepared to meet the world. My senses are finely tuned to the whims of the ocean, should it ever feel the need to test me.

The contents of my desk may be shared among my dearest friends, those who have accompanied me on my previous journeys. You can identify them by their iron will and tattoos done in berry-red scented Magic Marker.

I hope you think fondly of me in my absence, as I will certainly think fondly of you. Do not feel that our time together was wasted. I have learned much from your compassion and encouragement, and I cherish every gold star you have placed on my life. I do long to sit with legs crossed and have you regale me with great tales of inquisitive monkeys and felines in top hats, but not even that can tie my soul to the docks. I must go. If you look out your window, you might catch a wavering glimpse of me as I pull below the horizon. I will miss you all.

Yours with deepest sincerity,

Joey

Eureka

Philip Downie

DRIVING DOWN HIGHWAY 20 I'M GOING THIRTY OVER. IT'S NOT THAT I'M IN a hurry; believe me, I'm in no hurry to get where I'm going. I'm driving in a rusty blue '88 Sundance I borrowed from a friend. There's no AC, which is why I drive fast and, from time to time, with my head out the window. Inside the car it smells, another reason I go fast. The air thickens the second the wheels roll to a stop, clouding around me and clinging to my skin. It seems to be coming from the trunk, but I'm afraid to look. I smoke with my right hand and steer with my left. Occasionally I pull my shirt up to wipe the sweat from my forehead. My hair blows freely, crazily whipped around by the eighty-mile-an-hour wind coming in my windows. The gray T-shirt I'm wearing is still wet from the hour I sat in stop-and-go traffic just outside the city; dark circles hang from my neck and armpits. The radio is tuned to WBBM and the dial is broken, so it stays on WBBM. Every fifteen minutes for two hours the weatherman tells me it's a hot one.

"She's got cancer, Phil! Cancer! She's fucking dying!" Lately, for the past couple years, my sister only calls when there's some kind of emergency, so really whenever I talk to her she's either screaming or crying. This is how she got me to drive down here: a lot of screaming and crying. The sobbing started up hard, her words spaced by forced, painful breaths. "She's . . . fucking . . . dying . . . and . . . you . . . can't . . ."

I said, "There's no way in hell you're getting me out there." And two days later here I am, on a Tuesday, on vacation time. The air coming in the car smells like yeast, and I know I'm getting close to town. A couple minutes later I pass a large green sign: Welcome to Eureka, population 4701, home to beer, corn, Ronald Reagan, and my soon-to-be equally dead mother. Last time I was here must've been seven or eight years ago.

It was that Christmas when Uncle Chuck drank too much and wouldn't shut up about dung beetles. "They live in shit," he shouted and slammed his glass on the table. At the far end of the dining room next to a large, sliding-glass door, Chuck's wife, Phyllis, rested on her back on a raised hospital bed, covered up to her belly with a white sheet. (Their two daughters, both in their late thirties, still lived at home for their parents' sakes and their own; both were divorced and had no money.) There were four bedrooms in the house, one for Chuck, two for the daughters, and one entirely devoted to their cats. The family kept the house like an animal shelter; something like twenty cats lived in that room. On my way back from the bathroom I peeked in. There was no bed, just a random assortment of those carpet-covered towers with tunnels and platforms ceiling high. A rainbow of pine tree-shaped air fresheners circled the room, stuck to the walls with push-pins. A large plastic water dish and automatic feeders sat in a circle on the floor. The cats lay around the room, high and low, all motionless. I shut the door and walked down the hallway to the living room. Before I even turned the corner I heard the beeping and clicking of Phyllis's life-support machines. The house smelled like cigarettes, and even though I'd been there an hour I could still smell it like I'd just walked in. The dining room had wood paneling waist high, the rest was yellowing wallpaper with different images of ducks in ponds, taking off and landing. Around the table in the dining room were the four occupants of the house and the four members of my family, including me. A long, thin cigarette bounced between my mother's painted red lips; removing it occasionally, she'd flick the lipstick-stained end, ashing on the table next to her plate. My sister was sitting on my left asking me if I had seen some movie, but I didn't catch which one. "Um, no . . . I'll go rent it . . ." I was staring across the table at my middle-aged second cousin, Lynn, and the ridiculously thick layer of makeup she covers her face with. The longer I stared the more fake she looked, like a statue in Madame Tussauds Wax Museum. Her eyes were sensitive to all forms of light, so ninety percent of the time she wore a large, opaque pair of sunglasses. I couldn't tell where she was looking, she surprised me when she removed her cigarette and slowly said in a deep, raspy, smoker's voice, "What, never seen a pretty lady before?" Smoke exited her mouth in puffs as she talked.

"No, sorry, just really like your glasses."

She let the cigarette hang from her mouth, puffing rapidly, and said, "Uh huh."

Lyn M's sister Rachel started to talk. "So, Philip . . ." I raised my head from eating and looked at her. "How's your school going? Is it the eighth grade?"

I nodded my head, "I'm in high school, actually. It's fine."

My mother, sitting next to me, removed her cigarette with one hand and put the other to her chest. "Fine?" She forced a little laugh and continued, "A 'D' average is not fine." She looked Lynn and Rachel directly in the eyes and said, a little quieter and a little more seriously, "It's below average." The two sisters looked at each other and raised their eyebrows in concerned amusement. I felt like everyone sat three feet higher at the table, and I didn't or couldn't look up from my plate of mashed potatoes. The table quieted for a few seconds before Rachel started talking again.

"So, any girls at school you like?"

My mother calmly removed her cigarette again; her mouth opened slowly and deliberately, "Oh, well, Philip, why don't you tell them . . . ?" A metallic applause erupted as everyone's forks hit their plates, their heads swiveling to look at me. I leered at my mother, who didn't look back; started to speak when her hand flew forcefully over my mouth. In a hushed voice, like talking about death in front of the dying, she said, "He's gay."

A few miles into Eureka a large white building, six stories high with rings of black windows running down the outside, emerges on the horizon above a row of trees. Positioned in the center of Eureka, it's an odd match for a simple town. The modern structure doesn't fit with the other buildings, all two or three stories high and run-down. The hospital is clean and new, its windows dark and shiny. Driving through town I see that there's nobody on the streets, and that the shops are closed. I slow down for a lonely dog crossing the road ahead.

I pass the Diner Inn, Melville's, the post office, and then I'm there, at Eureka Memorial Hospital. When I park I see there are only a few other cars in the lot. By the entrance there's a large white conversion van with the word *Ambulance* on it. As I get closer I can read *Pittsburgh Paints* under the bad paint job. The hospital's automatic doors open, and cold air and the smell of antiseptic hit me as I enter. The first thing I see is that the lobby's empty. On the right directly next to the entrance is the front desk, but no one's behind it. There's a TV high up on the wall, inside a cage of bars that obstruct the view. In the moving vertical strips I can see Andy and Opie arguing. Across the room, to my left, three empty rows of lime green chairs watch me as I walk in. On the desk is a bell, so I ring it. A couple seconds later I turn to hear a rustling behind a door marked "Staff," and a chubby, bald guy pops his head out. "Help ya?"

"Yeah. My mom's in here, she's got cancer." The chunky man chuckles, pulling a miniature yellow legal pad out of his back pocket. "Cancer . . . Cancer . . . Cancer . . . Hmmm . . ." Flipping through the sheets of sloppy writing, the man looks up at me, then down at his pad, then up at me, then down at his pad. "Phil Downie?" he asks, pointing the chewed end of his pen at me. I nod my head, and he says that she's in Room 413. He says it's on the third floor, not the fourth, and that the room is actually marked 41, the three is missing. I thank him and walk over to the elevators. I stand there waiting for a few minutes, listening to Andy and Opie have one of their heart-to-hearts, until finally the front desk guy tells me that the elevators are broken and points to the stairs.

As I exit the stairwell, I am confronted with large letters made from red construction paper. Together they say "Terminal Ward." The third floor of the hospital is very plain; this is the death floor. Everything is either white or red, and the air has no smell. My shoes squeak like a kid's on a gym floor as I walk down the long hall, reading, "421, 420, 418, 417, 415, 414, 41, 41." There are two rooms marked 41; both are missing the last number. The doors to both rooms are shut, and I don't see any of my relatives around so I just guess and knock on the first, the one on my right. A weak voice says, "Come in." I hesitate a second, then go in.

My mother was pregnant in the winter of '81. She stood with the phone to her ear, her tilted head holding it against her shoulder, puffing madly at a cigarette. Her uniform no longer fit, and they didn't make bigger sizes, so Management decided she could wear a Santa suit, since it was the holiday season and all. The suit's material was terribly thick. Walking around the hotel checking the halls, sweat would stream from my mother's forehead. Walking back to the front desk she'd remove her hat and use it to wipe her face dry. I was at eye level with the front desk, so I stood on a box a foot off the ground and colored in black-and-white outlines of dinosaurs. My mother came over and stood next to me. She picked up the phone and dialed, resting her hand and tapping her long red nails as she waited. When there was no answer she hung up and took her cigarettes out of one of the suit's pockets. "Where the hell is your father?" Every couple minutes she anxiously glanced at the clock, then at me, then at the clock again. A loud crashing sound suddenly came from down the hall. It scared the crap out of me, and I shook with fear. My mother remained stoic, smoking a cigarette, resting her other hand across her belly. We heard a car engine turn off and then a set of doors flew open, slamming back against the walls. My dad stumbled into the entrance, backlit by the headlights of his car.

Gripping the walls, barely able to keep his balance, my father fell a few times before he was even halfway to the counter. My mother remained stolid, just standing and

smoking the same cigarette. Her belly stuck out, protruding out almost onto the counter.
I reached for her stomach, outstretching my small hand and arm. Looking down at me,
my mother saw me reaching for her belly. She noticed my deep brown eyes and was
instantly reminded of my father; instinctively she brushed my hand away before I could
reach her. Steady as ever, my mother did not budge from behind the counter, even with
her husband collapsing on the floor calling her name. I stepped down from my box at the
counter and walked out of the office into the hallway. There, passed out on the floor and
sprawled on his back, arms wide open to the ceiling, was my father. I slowly and cau-
tiously walked up to him, stopping when I arrived directly over his head.

Quietly I started to mumble, "Dad? Dad?" Not sure what I would get when he
woke up, I slowly bent over and poked his large, greasy forehead with one of my fingers.

"Leave him alone, Phil, he's fucked up." I stood up and stared at my mom.
"Hopefully you won't take after your old man, huh? Get back over here, Phil."

I went back to my coloring book at the counter as my mother made her way to the
hallway to pick up her husband. Now she was getting mad. "I ask you to do one fucking
favor and you can't, you selfish prick. Just to pick up your kid, all you had to do was
pick up your son and take him the fuck home. You know how hard I'm having it with
my new little girl." My mom grabs her belly and begins caressing it in long, soothing
strokes while she starts to kick her husband in the side.

The shades are drawn in the room, and it's dark except for the light from
the TV, which is turned so low I can only hear mumbles. Neither of us talk. I
listen to the rhythm of the beeps and clicks coming from the machines
attached to the bed. Every breath she takes sounds like the suction of opening
an airtight package. A curtain hung from rollers on the ceiling is pulled around
the right side of the bed toward the entrance, blocking my view of her. Scared
to look, I don't walk around to the other side of the bed, and I don't pull the
curtain back. The room changes colors with the light from the TV, and occasionally I can make out her outline through the curtain. Seconds pass like minutes as I stand in the doorway, wondering what to say. What do you say to a
dying person? How are you feeling? What's up? Anything good on TV? You
can't say anything to a dying person without it sounding petty, without you
sounding petty. I turn around and peek back into the hallway. Leaning on the
bathroom door, I say, "Not many people in the halls."

"Sunday."

"Does hospital staff get Sundays off?"

We're silent again, for a good five minutes this time. Eventually I get tired
and move around to the other side of the bed to sit down. When I turn around

and sit, I can't make out her face very well. She's looking up at the TV and the light is too dim to see her clearly. I can tell she looks different than I remember. Her skin is wrinklier and she's a lot thinner. I see her lips part but don't hear a sound. "What?"

"Do you know someone in here?"

"In where? The hospital?" She nods her head yes.

Just as I ask this, the TV's light gets bright enough that I can make out her face a little better and realize this is not my mother. She must be in the other room 41. "I'm sorry," I say and start to leave.

When I'm almost at the door I hear her voice sheepish and quiet calling after me. "Come back. Sit down." She pleads. The desperation in her voice is unbearable. How do you say no to a dying person? I take my jacket off and hang it over the back of the chair, sitting down again and staring at her as she watches TV.

"My mom's in here." I say. "She's got cancer." Not breaking her stare at the screen she gives a sympathetic sigh and I ask, "What's your name?"

She looks down at me, "What?"

"Your name."

"Penny."

"I'm Phil."

I'm in no hurry to get to my mom's room. It's evening, around five or six, and the sun is starting to go down. After a few more sitcom reruns, the woman falls asleep. Sitting in the chair I think about getting up and going next door, saying my good-byes, making my peace. Eventually I fall asleep.

I wake up and it's the middle of the night. The TV is still on and the woman is still asleep. I get out of the chair and leave the room, walking around the floor looking for the bathroom. There's still no one in sight, and it's very quiet. The sound of my walking echoes down the long halls. Eventually I see the men's room, and the second I open the door I hear someone whistling. I don't recognize the song, but I recognize the back of the man whistling it as that of my father. I walk up to the urinal next to his, unzip, and say, "Hey, Dad."

He turns his head to look at me. "Hey . . . she nagged the hell out of me. I wouldn't have been here otherwise."

"I know. Why do you think I came?"

"You missed the big show." I turn and look at him curiously. "You missed it," he said again.

"She's dead?"

"Yep."

I look back at the wall in front of me. "What are they doin' with the body?"

"Cremating her. You can fight your sister for the ashes."

"Yeah." I zip up, flush, and turn around to wash my hands. At the sink, scrubbing my hands under the faucet, I stare at the back of my dad's head in the mirror. "There a will?"

My dad and I leave the bathroom. He goes back to my mother's room where my sister is lying in the empty hospital bed crying into a pillow. I go down to the lobby for a cup of coffee. I decide not to go up and see my sister; she'll just be hysterical. When I finish my coffee I go back up to the wrong Room 41 to say good-bye to Penny. Before I even leave the stairwell I can tell something is wrong. I hear a few people running past the door, their footsteps reverberating down the hall. When I open the door they're already out of sight. I turn right, and then left, and can see down the hall where people are running in and out of Penny's room.

I run to the doorway and am pushed back by a nurse, her chubby hands pressing hard against my ribs, her eyes staring me down. "Your mother's had a heart attack," she says in a very abrupt way.

I raise my hand to my chest and push her hands away, saying, "Oh, she's not—"

"I don't think she's going to make it." With one of her hands the nurse grabs me by the arm, like she's going to catch me. She puts her other hand on my shoulder and looks me deep in the eyes. I don't know what to do. Instantly I realize playing along would be a lot easier than explaining why I sat in on a woman's final hours, a woman that I didn't know, so I say, "But she was so young." I think of her shriveled skin illuminated by the glow of the television. Standing in the hallway, just me and the nurse, I say, "She was so full of life." I raise a hand to my forehead like I'm about to collapse and then I feel it, a stinging behind my nose between my eyes. The nurse motions me forward with open arms. I stumble toward her and fall. Hugging each other in the empty hallway, my arms just able to reach around her, I burst into tears, my longing, wailing sobs echoing through the entire floor.

I'm the Jam

Cory J. Stewart

BELKO IS FROZEN. WELL, HE IS NOW. A FEW DAYS AGO HE WAS JUST LIKE YOU AND me: breathing, well-dressed, and of average height. Now he lies strewn on the cold sidewalk in bits like so many car parts. Who am I? The Jam. All hail.

A few days ago:

I'm the Jam. A week ago I saw Belko hit a homeless woman. She had called him a pig fucker, and if there's one thing we know about Belko, he'll not suffer being called a pig fucker. He pulled a brick out of his vest pocket and used it to beat the everlasting bejesus out of her. Just before she exploded into vast black rainbows, she uttered something I'll never forget: huagnifoooring kumplow excrackit! That's vagrant for: In a week, you shall lie frozen in bits on the sidewalk. Belko looked slightly aghast as he heard this curse, but he regained his composure and killed her anyway. How do I know? I'm the Jam. Bow down.

Belko lives in this town of ours. I like to call it *Ye Olde Stockyards*. Has a river through it, like most cities, and has that puffy pink toad who is his father's son and runs us accordingly. Belko thinks of these things as much as a rock worries about being struck by a car, for Belko is not the thinker by whom others are measured. He does live under a large rock, however. His apartment is a water-soaked mess, and the builder was a clown. Dennis Klonowski put up his building during the Depression, mostly with whatever he found on the street or pulled from the rail yards when the bulls could be bought. About two thirds of Belko's ceiling is a big slab of Depression-era granite. His walls are railroad ties and road rebar and stolen fence boards all tied together with discarded pig intestines the 'yards found too fucked up and awful to make hotdogs with. Over the years moisture has caused the intestines to stretch, lowering the slab ever closer to the floor. Belko lives there because he wants to die, not the other way. He knows the slab will crush him as he sleeps once those last things give way. Belko is also comforted by taking a building full of people with him.

Belko, having considered these thoughts of self-homicide, went out in search of a hooker. He long ago tired of alcohol and had an appetite for hard drugs which, due to a quirk, he had to do off the tits of the most repulsive, diseased, scum-of-the-earth hooker he could find in his first ten minutes on the street. When you live in a building of discarded pig guts and stolen lumber, you don't have to look far. The Jam knows this, and knows that Belko had a pocket full of Tatersmach, and a syringe of Pollycrumb, and an appetite for Christine.

Christine is the multiple-decades-old call-hag who lives in the doghouse behind his building. She growls when she sucks cock and barks like a rabid pit bull when you fuck her in the ass. She had a gangrenous pair of negatives on her; negative because the shriveled hag-bag's just-waiting-to-drop hung to her elbows.

Belko approached his score carefully. She came running at him, and he smacked her on the side of the head. Hard. The emaciated Christine went down like a Jenga tower colliding with a bat. She was knocked out, so he moved fast with the Tatersmach. He dropped a fistful on her and watched the pile of powder absorb her filth upward, and licked it from her rotten flesh. He felt his capillaries rupture under his skin; Tatersmach makes you feel warm because it makes your capillaries burst under your skin, which makes your warm blood pool around your joints. It also gave you more violent energy than you knew what to do with. Belko exploded on Christine, kicked her and bit her, and she tore apart like a paper doll. He ripped her degenerated, parasitic scalp from her skull and wrapped it around his neck like a scarf.

The Jam feels the need to explain Tatersmach. Potatoes are the roots of a plant that belongs to the nightshade family, many of which are toxic. The top plant is usually discarded or re-used in some manner once the root is harvested, and one of the uses is Tatersmach production. The tops are cleaned, chopped, crushed, and mixed with coca leaves. The same method used for cocaine production is applied to the mix of coca and potato plant, and the result is Tatersmach. The potato plant provides a substance which, when mixed with coke, has dramatic effects. The product is also much cheaper since it doesn't require much coca, and potatoes are dirt cheap to grow and legal everywhere. So there you go. The Jam says you're welcome.

So Belko, his head full of violence, ripped apart his favorite whore. He giggled as he thought of Jack the Ripper. The difference? A dead prostitute goes nearly unnoticed in this city. The London police actually cared about dead whores.

Belko disappeared from me into the distance, running into the creamer-stained black velvet of city lights and night.

The next day

When I caught up with Belko, I found him passed out from Polly's embrace on a burning horse carriage. Pollycrumb is the only way to counteract Tatersmach; enough will neutralize Tatersmach, a little more will put you to sleep, but too much, and you won't wake up. The Jam knows this, and Belko knows this, and Belko always wakes up.

The Jam needs to explain Pollycrumb as was done with Tatersmach. Pollycrumb is also known as a poor man's heroin. Heroin, in our city, is fashionable and expensive. When the Fabulous Fantastics made it chic, dealers realized they could charge more and carry less, which meant the same profit without sticking their necks out quite so far. The street men came up with a little number that could still bring them down: Pollycrumb. Pollycrumb, in essence, is just a little herbal cocktail of common plant-world poisons: foxglove, passionflower, chamomile, nightshade. Boil it all with a gallon of water in a big pot and pour into another big pot, but strain it. Discard the boiled herbs. Boil the liquid in the big pot until it's reduced by two thirds. When the last third remains, gather the same amount of fresh herbs in cheesecloth and add to the mix. Boil for six hours. Remove herbs, and leave the sludge on low heat until it crusts to the pan. Let it cool, cut it, freebase it, and inject it. The Jam is pleased by your gratitude.

Fabulous Fantastics are the people who have different names in different eras but always have the same characteristics: vanity, money, prestige, attitude. They are the people your mother wishes you'd date and marry and have kids with. The Jam hates them and Belko hates them more—the males, at least; he loves the females. He's only human, after all.

Belko woke from his slumber when the fire tore at his shoes and nipped his toes. He stumbled from the carriage in a haze and walked, his shoes still painted with leaping orange, to the Snakehead.

The Snakehead was the name of a cafeteria-like establishment that squatted inside an abandoned Burger King. It served all manner of food to all manner of junkies. They used the nastiest of the rancid, the spoiled, the *freshly hunted* foods and cooked them until they went down warm. This was actually a menu with a purpose—why feed a junky something he probably won't keep down long anyway? As long as it tasted slightly better than the insides of their mouths (and considering what they would do for a fix, it usually did), you'd be doing them a service.

At the Snakehead, you pay your fifty cents at the door and you get a Styrofoam bowl and a plastic spoon. You do your little junky-shuffle to the enormous pot filled with whatever the slurry of the day was, fill your bowl, and shuffle to a stool. The Snakehead also sells drugs, naturally, in case you have cash left from your bender and you need to chase the shakes.

As Belko entered, he paid his fifty cents and acquired his slurry. He shuffled over to Bean. Bean sold the drugs at the Snakehead, and despite his name, was one big, tough motherfucker with a bigger shotgun just under the counter. Belko ordered up four NoDoz. A thousand mgs of caffeine was just the thing to kick him from his Polly haze. He swallowed them in one gulp and washed them down with a spoonful of rat slurry or discarded-meat-from-the-dumpster-stew or whatever it was he was eating. One thing he had learned is that when you eat at the Snakehead, you never visually inspect your slurry. Never.

I sat, or rather hovered, next to Belko as he waited for his caffeine jolt to kick him in the ass. Even if he chooses not to look at his fetid stew, the Jam needs to know these things. The Jam watched as he hoisted a section of rat tail to his lips. The Jam heard the crunch, and watched Belko wipe away a tear after convincing his gag reflex not to push the issue of swallowing whatever it had been that crunched.

This is Belko on a thousand mgs of caffeine:

Now running, now pausing and talking, gibbering to no one like mad and wanting to fuck something. He had three more caff pills from Bean and a thumbnail of Tatersmach ready to go. He took a bus to this famous street we have in Ye Olde Stockyards where the Fabulous Fantastics go to buy their new plastic outfits and show off their new plastic tits. And Belko was hot for a Barbie to call his own.

Belko poured himself from the bus and crept along, ever the human puddle. He seeped along and found seemingly innocent ways to cop feels of all the Fabulous Fantastic ladies who were out.

The heroin-hooked Skinnies were considered the height of style and envy. They were so skinny and weak, many of them, that they struggled under the weight of their saline chests and could barely carry their petite credit-card wallets. Their blue-black-green needle tracks gave away the severity of their commitment to fashion; inner elbows with a few pokes were hardly vogue anymore, having become fairly common on Fabulous Fantastic campuses: Yale, Dartmouth, Vanderbilt, Northwestern, etc . . . No, these days it was inside the knee, back of the hand, top of the foot, side of the neck. The eyeball was too severe, the tits full of fluid and too risky for the needle.

Belko would move along and innocently knock into a Skinny; she would end up sprawled on her back spread-eagle, and he'd take a good long look before picking her up, telling her he hadn't seen her, and going on his way. Most of the girls hardly even noticed.

The Jam watched Belko knock one down, and apparently seeing what he liked and deciding she was too high to notice, he led her down a side alley and bent her in half over a sawhorse. He removed a bit of boot string from his pocket and tied her hands so she wouldn't stand up. He pulled two one-foot sections of coax from the Dumpster and tied her legs to the sides of the horse. He pulled out his Tatersmach and licked it off her ass. Once he felt the rush he pulled out his rocket, lined it up, and exploded like a maniac.

The Jam knows something he must share: Belko is missing the toes on his left foot. During his run into the city high on Tatersmach, he had lost them. Thinking they were pebbles rolling around, he pulled his shoe off, dumped out his toes, and kept running.

Having exploded in the Fabulous Fantastic Skinny, Belko felt brought down a little. He popped the other three caff pills and the Jam saw him pick a fight with a Fabulous Fantastic Alpha Male, and strengthened by Tatersmach and pepped by caff, he punched the guy in the back, broke his spine, and ran like hell. The fat little boys with the uniforms and big brass badges tried like hell to keep up but were left behind huffing and puffing in short order. All you need in Ye Olde Stockyards is a half-decent brain and a good pair of legs, and you can get away with just about anything. The Jam knows this and Belko knows this.

The next day:

Belko woke in bad, shitty shape. He had a headache from the caff-related dehydration and withdrawal from Polly, and the runs from the rat slurry. He crawled to the toilet and sat down. The Jam thought he looked a little pale as he expelled the stew that hadn't been fit for a dog. Belko reached for the roll in order to wipe himself, and noticed his left hand was gone. Gone. All he had left was a stub of his left arm. Belko, not one to emote, just kinda stared. He shrugged and reached out with his other hand, and in doing so, saw he had no toes on his left foot. At that he jumped a little, held up his foot, and saw he had lost all five toes. Once again, he had healed and all he had left were little blank spots—no scars, even. He remembered the pebbles, and realized he had dumped out his toes. He chalked it up to himself being a moron, and went back to bed to sleep his drugs off. He slept the rest of the day, waking only once around 7:00 P.M. to have a few crackers and chug a liter of water. Polly was a bitch the day after. The Jam knows and Belko knows.

Morning

Belko woke up, swung his legs out, and tried to stand. Upon discovering the floor, hard, he realized there was something wrong with his balance. He gathered himself back together, put his feet under him one by one, and teetered. He inspected his left foot: sans toes, like yesterday. His right foot: sans toes. Ah, so this is the problem. Lose five toes, the other foot picks up the slack, but lose all ten, good luck balancing. He found his knees and maneuvered back to his bed. He felt through his sheets with his hand and stump, half expecting to discover a rat the size of a collie that was snacking on him. Instead, he found his toes; they were black and as hard as coal, and had a curious coldness to them. They looked frostbitten, as if they had just frozen and fallen off as he slept.

The Jam watched as he picked up his former extremities and flushed them down the toilet. He crawled to his closet, dug out his old walking stick from Bear Scouts, and used the ancient staff as a cane. With a little doing, he got himself out to the cold and frozen winter sidewalk. COLD it was, the Jam knows. Fucking COLD that day. Belko began stumbling and tripping down the sidewalk, and froze a little more with each step, froze to the sidewalk. The Jam lit a cigarette, blew the smoke at Belko, and Belko fell, shattered and scattered like so many used-car parts.

Belko woke from the vision of his breaking into frozen pieces just in time to scream as he was crushed to death by a slab of Depression-era granite.

Meeting the Duke

Mark W. Anderson

THAT NIGHT, THE WHOLE SECOND HALF OF THE SHOW SEEMED TO BE ABOUT Rab. After a couple of pure dance numbers, the maestro started calling out one slow ballad after another, and everyone in the whole place settled into one of those dreamlike states where everything in the universe just seemed exactly right.

A couple of tinkling notes on the piano to lead in the tune, a knowing nod, and Rab stood dutifully each time, behind one of those little wooden music stands that had the letters "DE" painted on it, and poured out. Dressed in a finely tailored wool suit, a silk tie hanging over the buttons of his jacket, he uncurled one long, slow, creamy solo after another, spotlight on, eyes closed, pointing his horn towards some of the women at the little tables up front, the lightest beads of sweat forming around his collar.

No Gonsalves. No Cat Anderson. In fact, no one else, really, after the fourth or fifth tune after the break. Just Johnny "Rabbit" Hodges, plumbing down into the lowest depths of his sax he could find, the notes wide and vibrating and just flowing out of that bell.

Later, I heard he left the Duke a couple of months after to head out on his own. But that night, no one imagined anything could have been wrong. All everyone up and down Forty-seventh Street knew was that Ellington was back,

Johnny was blowing, and that there would be two shows nightly—but make sure you caught the second one, because the first one was always for the kids.

Myself, I knew he had been coming for a couple of weeks. I'd heard on the street that the ballroom at the Sutherland Hotel had been booked for a ten-day stretch in November, and by the time the air started to get really cold we all knew who it was. I had been kicking around the South Side of Chicago for about six months by that point, living in a place called Rat Alley, a little warren of apartments that mostly catered to artists a few blocks north around Thirty-fifth and Cottage Grove. It was a little more white up there, not like down here, where I'd sometimes get a look out of the corner of an eye or a moment's hesitation when I'd ask for a Coke or something. Not like Forty-seventh Street was off-limits to white folks or anything. Just that a scuffling guy in work clothes wasn't always the preferred clientele of a swank place like the Sutherland, even if it was black.

The army hadn't done me any good, not in regards to figuring out what it was I was supposed to be doing, but I had recently come across one of the best strings of luck I had had up to that point. On a tip from a guy I ran across one night in a bar who was from my home town of Muncie, Indiana, I went one day, a couple of months ago, and applied for a dishwashing job at one of those big downtown hotels. The manager, this little mousy guy with a pencil-thin mustache, said he felt the best thing he could do since he couldn't serve in the fight was to hire guys who had gone "over there," as he called it. I could tell right away he meant Europe, but I didn't have the heart to tell him I had served out the war peeling potatoes in the mess of a destroyer in the Pacific. He asked me a bunch of questions, writing stuff down about my answers in a little notebook he carried around, as we stood in the greasy hallway between the steaming kitchen and the big ballroom where they held weddings and stuff. He said he liked how I looked, too, commenting on my broad shoulders and "nice, thick neck," saying I'd need it for the job. But all I needed was the dough, so I didn't ask him whatever it was he meant by that.

So I had scratch, enough to eat more than once a day, a place to stay, some clothes that fit, and a dime beer wasn't too much every now and then. I tried not to think too hard about the fact that even though I'd gotten out of the Navy in '46, here it was 1950 already, and I was wearing the first pair of shoes I hadn't found or stolen in a long, long time. Thinking about stuff like that didn't do anyone any good, I figured, and whenever it got too much all I had to do was make sure I had enough dimes in my pocket to make it go away.

So things were going well for me when I showed up that night. I'd even met a little looker, some girl who'd lived in Chicago all her life and was just mad about jazz. Doris would go to see anybody, anywhere, even if she did end up looking a little more the strange bird in some of those places than I did. She was big on all the names that came through—Basie, Cab Calloway, Louis Armstrong—anybody. She knew who all the smaller bands were, too, groups like Boyd Raeburn and Horace Heidt, guys who you really had to follow music even to know when they were in town, let alone who they were. One time, she dragged me to see some guy named Andy Kirk and His Twelve Clouds of Joy at the Sherman downtown. It didn't do nothing for me, though, but waste a buck twenty-five. She beamed like a schoolgirl the entire time. Sometimes I wish she'd look at me like that more often, but at least I didn't have to support her.

Me, I liked things that swung a little hotter, even if it was sweet every now and then. Like Johnny. He could blow fire and ice with the best of 'em. Hell, Ellington was all right in my book. Nobody else out there could match up. He was a great piano player; he spoke like royalty, dressed like it, too, and even white musicians said in all the papers that he was the best there ever was. When he and the boys traveled, they went by special rail car, real classy, and I'd heard that when the war started he refused to play any places that wouldn't let Negroes in. Which I guess I respected, kind of.

I figured by that night I'd seen at least one show every time he'd been in Chicago since the end of the war, and I'd always try to squeeze in a couple more if they were sticking around for a while. That meant I'd seen band members come and go, and even had a drink with one or two of them. I'd head back after the show if I had some dough, looking like I was waiting for someone else, and then maybe catch Russell Procope or Jimmy Hamilton or somebody. One time, "Floorshow" Nance even invited me to a card game, but I pretended I had something else to do since I didn't have any money to lose that night.

And the Sutherland was great back then, too, even if a lot of the folks there tried a little too hard to be swank when they really weren't. I didn't have Doris along with me the night Ellington asked to see me. She had some meeting up north where she lived, with some church group. I ended up going to the late show alone, walking the entire way from Rat Alley to Forty-seventh and Drexel Boulevard with my coat up around my neck, not paying attention to the street, or the wind, or the guys who were hanging out on the corners and staring at me as I walked past.

But as soon as I walked into the lobby, before I got my coat off or turned right into the ballroom, a black boy of about sixteen or seventeen ran up and surprised the hell out me. He must have been waiting for me, because he came right up to me and stuck a piece of paper with my name on it into my hand. Before I could even say thanks, he was gone. When I looked at the words "Butch Otter," in just about the neatest handwriting I'd ever seen, the first thing I saw was how foolish my name looked in such fancy letters. I looked around to see if anyone was watching, and I noticed that the lobby, which moments before had been filled with guests and bellboys and show-goers and cigarette girls, had suddenly gotten a lot quieter. It seemed to me that some kind of momentous message was about be revealed to me, and right then and there I almost didn't open it. I almost put it in my pocket still folded up, or found a trash can, or chased the boy down and gave it back to him. I almost did a lot of things. Sometimes, it don't do no good to take in a surprise.

But I didn't. I drifted off to the wall by the door, natural as I could, and got out a smoke. When I opened it, all it said was:

Meet me after the set. Charlie the bartender will keep you occupied until I'm ready.
-DE

I didn't read it twice. Just folded it back up and put it in my pocket and finished my smoke.

I stopped by the bar on the way in, which looked real smooth since it was right inside the door. Charlie, the regular guy I'd seen a dozen times before, jerked his head in my direction for the benefit of the floor manager, who in three easy strides was by my side, leading me to a table off to the right of the raised bandstand. Before he left, I slipped in an order for a Scotch and soda on the rocks, which appeared almost before I was done saying the words.

The ballroom inside the Sutherland wasn't the biggest I'd ever been in, but it was pretty big nevertheless. A couple of hundred tables maybe, all of them, except for the big ones in the back, the little round kind just big enough to fit a candle on and maybe a couple of cocktails. The ones in front, like mine, were right below the edge of the stage, so when you looked up it seemed like anyone up on stage was larger than life. And when the lights went down, the whole place, too, seemed to open up and get bigger, like the ceiling was really outside and the night sky was all you could see. Across the room, behind a pair of swinging doors, shone the tiny light of the kitchen, the staff told every night before the doors opened that they had to pay attention to what was happening on stage so they didn't break a glass during a quiet part and get cashiered on the spot.

He didn't look at me once during the entire show. Just looked at Rab and whoever else was soloing. And that big, charismatic smile at the end of each tune, just like he had never heard applause so genuine before in his life. And when he spoke to the audience, he made us feel like we were the only friends he had in the world, that he and the boys were playing just for us, and hell, here's a tune they don't play much anymore but they thought they'd pull it out just because this was the most special of all possible nights and we were really just the most special of customers he'd ever run across. So, here we go—"Mood Indigo," featuring Johnny Hodges!

Everybody, me included, just ate it up. But by the time the set was halfway done I'd worked myself into a state. On the one hand, I couldn't fathom for the life of me why he wanted to see me. I hadn't dressed, not that I had much better than I had on. Would he notice the scar across my cheek I got that night in Manila, when that goon of an MP tried to take the girl I was with away from me right under my nose? What was he going to say? What was I going to say? Hell, what was it that he even wanted in the first place?

Four or five Scotches later, though, by the time the band was breaking down and the house lights were up, I was feeling pretty full of myself, noticing how other people shot me what I thought were envious glances on their way out. Ellington had asked to see me, had a boy wait for me, knowing I was coming that night, after all. Look at my table, I thought—I would have been standing along the back if it wasn't for him, since a fiver for a table up front was never an option. He asked me to stay. He wants me to stick around to talk. Plus, the drinks were flowing from Charlie, and when I pulled out the only folding money I had on me, it was waved off every time. That had to mean something.

Between the time the set ended and he arrived, I watched the room around me as if in a vision. Every detail seemed clearer, somehow, the Scotch and my mounting nervousness throwing everything into sharp relief. The band broke down as if every man was solving a math problem in his head as he moved: slow, methodical, quietly; too slow, maybe, like they were killing time, or waiting for some kind of shoe to drop. Off in the background, the sound of dishes clattered, mixing with the hushed conversations of show-goers offering their companions their take on what they just saw and heard while they slowly got up from their tables and shuffled out. The fresh ice crackled in every new Scotch and soda that made an appearance, and even the cigarettes I began to smoke every five minutes hissed slightly as they burned down in one of those little glass ashtrays that was stamped "Sutherland" across the bottom. For a moment, as one of the spotlights was turned on and jerked quickly around the room as if to test it out, I thought it was going to land on me and reveal to everyone that I was waiting for the great man himself, not just some schmuck who was trying to stretch out the last few moments or his last few dollars.

When he came, he appeared from somewhere off to the right of the band-stand like a prizefighter coming out of his dressing room after a fight to inspect the scene of his triumph. His checked suit jacket was nowhere to be found, just his still-crisp, white shirt with his tie hanging limply, undone around his neck, and a towel draped over his shoulder. He moved through the room a big man full of grace, nodding to acquaintances and calling out to some of the waiters like long-lost cousins at a wedding. He navigated the tight spaces between empty tables and walked right up to me, taking me by surprise even though I had done nothing but watch him since the moment he had come into the room.

"You Butch?" he asked, sticking out his hand through the smoke of a burning cigarette.

"Duke," I said, feeling slightly foolish but offering my hand in return and rising slightly, only to find that my legs felt weak under me from too much sit-ting. His own hand was big and strong, with long tapered fingers soft from years of manicures and lotions and the recognition that those fingers were what put bread on the table for not only him but the eleven or so men who played their hearts out every night.

"Call me Edward," he said, looking me straight in the eye. His voice had that sort of detached quality that seemed like he was thinking a million things at once. "Only the fans, the ones I don't know—only they call me Duke."

I nodded, not knowing what to say. "Let's go over here, Butch," he sug-gested in a voice that was used to telling people what to do. "I need to eat."

A fresh table towards the back of the room had been prepared, with clean white linen, two chairs, and a pinkish-white rose in a slender vase no thicker than one of those soft, talented fingers. I had to stop and go back halfway across the room for my drink, and reminded myself not to spill it as I followed him.

He sat down, pulling the towel off his shoulder. Immediately, several waiters appeared, and began a ritualized dance of service: as if by magic, a freshly-grilled steak appeared, as did half a grapefruit, some toast, a huge plate of French fries, and a bowl of steaming water with lemon. I looked down at my Scotch and soda and fought off the urge to light another cigarette.

After a few bites of steak, he got to the point. "What did you think of the show?" he asked, chewing thoughtfully. "Did you like it?"

Without skipping a beat, through the steak and half the French fries, I found myself talking about jazz with Duke Ellington for the next fifteen minutes or so. More of a monologue, really, as I talked about everybody I had ever seen and how they compared to the Great Ellington Orchestra while he chewed and listened and occasionally nodded back. His slicked-back hair glistened in the remaining light from the stage and the candles on the table next to us, the eyes in his open and somewhat cherubic face switching back and forth between his plate and my own eyes. And whether it was from the complete command of his body he needed for effective showmanship or something else, I noticed dimly through the sound of my own voice that the shoulders spread across the large expanse of his back hardly moved, no matter what his hands or any other part of his body was doing.

Right around the fourth time I had made the same point about how the Glenn Miller Orchestra was nowhere near his league and never would be despite Glenn's noble act of dying in the line of duty, I caught myself and decided to shut up. He decided he was done with dinner at the same time, and the dance of waiters began again. They whisked away the plates and brought fresh hot water and lemon, a pack of imported smokes, and another Sutherland-stamped ashtray.

"I'll tell you why I'm asking," he said after a moment, lighting up a long, finely wrapped cigarette. "Ah, I know you've been to a couple of our shows, and you're a neighborhood guy, from what some of the guys in the band tell me. Most of the white folks I meet are either in the business or work so hard to tell me how great I am for a Negro that I can't ever tell what they really think." A new glass arrived for me, along with what I felt was a wave of confidence that swept over me. So this is what I was here for, I thought—the only thing I could ever really claim as all my own. I was a regular guy. He needed the advice of a regular guy. Duke Ellington, the greatest bandleader in the country, one of the greatest musicians of all time, was cocooned in his show-business world and needed the expertise of a guy who was out there in the world. A regular guy who hit the streets with some regularity, not some fancy-pants downtown guy who only cared about money and cars and swell women. A guy who served, maybe. A guy who knew how to read a box score, shoot a game of pool, knew how to have a couple of beers or Scotch and sodas and not let it change him in any way.

I had almost forgotten he was speaking to me when I heard his voice again. "So we find ourselves in a bit of a spot, the boys and me," he went on. "Well, me really. Besides the band, I've got another ten or so people that I need to carry. There's Strays—Billy Strayhorn—our arranger. Tom Whalley's our copyist. There's a road manager, a guy at the publishing company, and even Mercer, my son, who's helping out." He paused for a moment, and looked at me thoughtfully for a moment. "There's a lot of people now, and, like the song says, things ain't like they used to be."

Somewhere in the back of my mind, through the thickening haze of distilled Scotch and cigarette smoke, I realized that the members of the band had finished storing away their equipment and had sat down in a line on the edge of the stage, watching us like some Greek chorus waiting to pass judgment, or a line of condemned men, awaiting their fate. The room had grown silent, with all of the waiters slipping behind the kitchen door or out to the lobby, not wishing to disturb us. Somehow, I longed for the spotlight to make another appearance and sweep the room, just to see if there were any other pairs of eyes looking in, waiting to see how suddenly the very real drama was going to play out.

"That's interesting," I managed to get out. "But I'm not exactly sure what you mean."

"What I mean," he said, "is that when you get right down to it, there isn't any money to be made in this racket anymore. There used to be, during the war, and before, but not now. The music's changing, and I can't even begin to guess where that's going to end up. Booking agents don't want to pay anymore, and I'm down to less than a thousand dollars a week in some places. That just isn't enough for me to meet payroll. These cats, they got to eat. And travel's getting more expensive, especially since the price controls on all kinds of stuff have been lifted. There's more bands out there, too, scrapping for places to play, especially since all the guys who came home from overseas who where thinking about getting back into the game have done it."

"I see," I said, hearing my words slur. I tried to peer into the darkness behind him, but couldn't make out anything past his face.

"But, really," he went on, smoothing back his hair with a pass of his long fingers over his brow and beyond, "I don't think the public wants to listen to this kind of music anymore. I don't feel it. Sure, they come. You come. But the days when we could get five thousand dollars for a couple nights' work are over, and I've been at this business for over thirty years already. I'm not sure it's even something I can do anymore." He paused, looking straight at me. I looked straight back at him, and felt my head rotate slightly. "Or even if I want to."

"You're a regular guy," he said again, with an air of finality, as if he had already made up his mind and was looking for me to finish up the conversation. "You tell me—do you think we should hang it up? Are we done?" He looked down at the ashtray where he stubbed out his cigarette.

For long moments, I didn't know what to do. I wanted to jump up and shake his shoulders, run around the room and tell him what a fool he was, even if he was the greatest bandleader the country had ever known. I wanted to shake his shoulders and tell him about the secret joys he had given me as I walked down the street humming out, "Don't Get Around Much Anymore," and "Take the 'A' Train" in my head. How I had thought of his music all those nights, crammed into a steel bunk on a destroyer somewhere in the Pacific, the sweet and sour smell of other men's sweat wafting through the pitch blackness, keeping me awake on the rolling sea. I wanted to tell him about the women I had seen outside the Metropole Theater one summer night in 1947, when I snuck in around the back by pretending to be one of the kitchen staff and watched as Rab had pulled another one of those miracles out of his pocket, and how the women couldn't contain themselves afterwards and dared each other to do their own sneaking into his dressing room after the show. I wanted to talk about joy and beauty and human emotion, the feeling of being alive that comes from knowing that you have a destiny to achieve and a duty to those who surround you as you work to achieve it.

I wanted to tell him what it meant to be an average Joe and how important it was to have somebody out there on the horizon who you respected and idolized and followed who you could pretend would one day pull you aside and ask for your advice, validating that roll you were on and maybe, just maybe, let you think that you weren't so worthless after all. And that all of the choices you had made in life up to this point weren't wasted. And that you had something of your own to say.

I wanted to tell him all those things, but as I opened my mouth to start, a wave of reluctance came over me and started to take root in the pit of my stomach. Duke had picked up the lemon from the saucer beneath the cup of now lukewarm water and squeezed it gently with those long, tapered fingers, releasing a steady stream of lemon juice into the cup. I was a regular guy, after all. I had seen the streets, had seen war, had been around the block a few times, and now it was important for me to remember why I was here and who, exactly, who Mr. Edward Duke Ellington thought I was.

And then I realized, with a start, what the horror was. My alcohol-soaked brain snapped into focus with startling speed, the dreamlike state being tossed aside for the full range of the trouble I had suddenly found myself in. The steady stream of lemon had steeled into a trickle, and the man across from me dropped it onto a napkin on the side of the saucer and wiped his hands on a cloth napkin he retrieved from his lap. Off to the side of the room, somebody pulled a horn back out of its case and started to silently finger the keys, as if the spotlight was back on and the heat of the moment was once again upon him.

There had, no doubt, been a long line of hangers-on who had been asked the very same question and who had told him exactly what they thought he wanted to hear. Who had said "Stay the course," and "Your fans need you no matter what." But he had sought me out, had come to me, here, in my new hometown, blocks from where I lived, bought me drinks and asked me to wait. I had to tell him what I thought.

No matter what the price may be. To me. To him. To all of my dreams and beliefs about how the world should work, about what we're here for, about what beauty was. Or about the cold, hard realities of what it took to make it in this world. And how you'd always lose in the end. And about those who you thought were out to help you were really just in it for themselves. About how, when you opened yourself up for advice, you were really just asking for it.

"Hang it up," I said, pushing myself away from the table with as much authority and confidence as I could muster. The table shook slightly, and the lemon water in the cup sloshed slightly over the rim. "Hang it up. You're right. It's over. You'll do nothing but bleed yourself dry." I stood there, not knowing whether the drama I had hoped to create was being broken by the tyranny of too many words or not. "You said yourself—no one but the few of us left who care wants to hear this music. Do yourself the favor."

And with that, I fished into my pocket and pulled out every dollar I had in the world, the crumpled five spot I had tried repeatedly to pay with for the ten bucks' worth of drinks I had already had. I threw it dismissively onto the crisp white linen where a moment ago I had sat. And turned on my heel and walked out, past Charlie, past the floor manager who was chatting up the cigarette girl in the lobby. Through the revolving door, and out into the cold night air.

A number of years later, maybe six or seven, I was pulling an overnight shift in some run-down diner on the West Side, around Madison and Halsted. A well-dressed man came in and took a seat at one of the stools that lined the counter in front of the grill. Seeing how it was after midnight and I didn't have a waitress, I just called out from the kitchen to see what he wanted. There were only a couple of other customers in the tiny place that evening, mostly due to the steady drizzle that fell through the June night. Instead of answering my call with a BLT on rye or something else, the man, who was wearing a suit that clearly cost a half a year of my salary, simply asked, "You Butch Otter?"

When I heard my name, I put down my spatula and peered through the little window that separated the kitchen from the dining room.

"Yeah, that's me," I said in a voice that had seen too many cigarettes and quarter beers. "Who's asking?"

"I have a message for you from a friend," he replied, reaching into his suit and pulling out the biggest wad of cash I'd ever seen in a year. "His name is Duke Ellington."

At the sound of the words, a million thoughts flooded my brain. How I'd followed his career with diminishing interest as the years went on, but was still able to catch the news that he had ridden out the tough times and had come back out on top. How he had beaten back bebop and West Coast cool by sticking with the Ellington Sound. How he had made the cover of *Time* magazine, how he had wowed them at the jazz festival in Newport one year with twenty-seven honking, screeching choruses on Paul Gonsalves' saxophone on "Diminuendo in Blue."

How he had come through Chicago any number of times, playing the Regal Theatre on the South Side or the new Blackhawk downtown. How he still had it, how Rab had come back, how much people couldn't believe that he was still going strong after all these years. How I never went to see him again. How I had never even uttered his name or listened to a record after that fateful night.

"He wanted me to find you. He has something for you," the man said in a voice that sounded like I was simply one in a long line of stops he had to make that evening. I watched him, craning my neck through the little window, as he straightened out his coat and prepared to leave.

"Here," he said, dropping it on the counter with a wave of his hand. "He says this is yours."

And, with that, he turned and went back out onto the street, pausing a moment to cup his hand around a match to light a cigarette. He looked each way before crossing the street to a waiting cab.

The eggs I was cooking had started to sizzle, and I could tell by the smell that the bottoms had already turned black. I turned the flame under the skillet down and reached around to untie my apron before pushing through the swinging door that led into the brightly lit, tiled dining room. And I sensed it was there before I even saw it. Knew what it was before my eyes even had a chance to do their job.

There, on the countertop in front of the stool was the message he had come to deliver: A crisp, new five-dollar bill.

I tied my apron around my back and, thinking about the eggs, left it there. For the morning waitress.

Don Simon

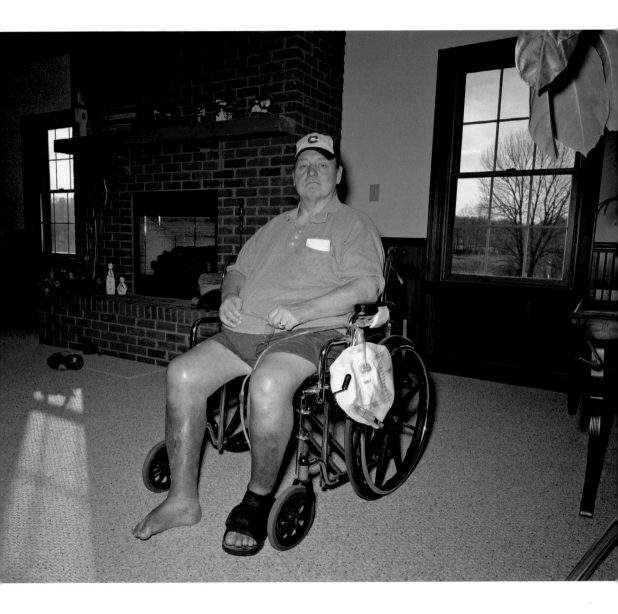

From the *Iliad* onward, war has been a major theme in art and literature. I hope that my photographs and interviews
will make a contribution to our understanding of how the trauma of war affects combatants, and civilians caught in
literal and philosophical crossfire. Many important issues of war and peace emerge in the stories of these veterans
and in the portraits themselves. Many veterans suffer from Post-Traumatic Stress Disorder. Some still wear their
Vietnam War medals. Some fight for veterans' medical issues or make art or write books about their experiences.
Others have found ways to put their experiences behind them, often with significant struggle, and to successfully
return to civilian life. All were deeply and permanently affected by the war, but the majority are proud of their service.
In a significant way, this is an exhibition about the inability of photography to record life completely, and especially to
record the human consequences of war. – **Jeffrey Wolin**

This project will be published as a book by Umbrage Editions in 2006. For the stories behind the photos,
visit www.jeffreywolin.com or www.mocp.org.

James Claude Arnold

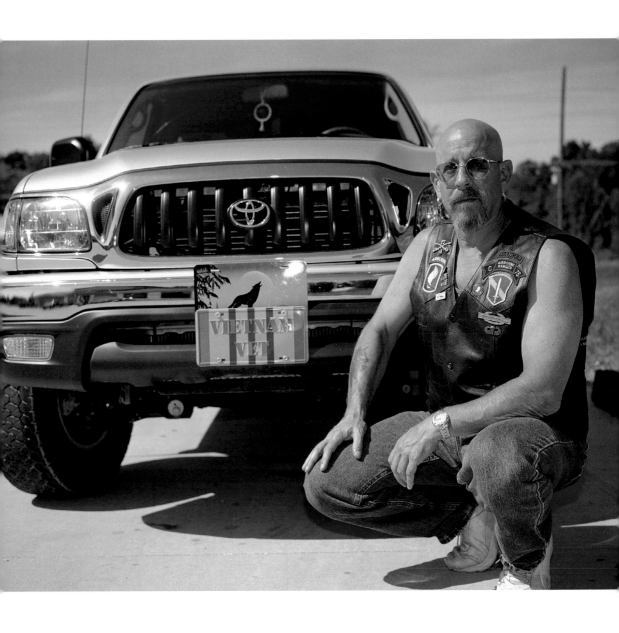

R. Michael Rosensweig

Simba Wylie Roberts

George "Tom" Boone

Jeanne Urbin Markle

Owen Mike

Jerry Kykisz

The Top Three Reasons
My Dad Thinks I'm Gay

Fritz Tucker

INTRODUCTION—UNTIL A COUPLE OF YEARS AGO I NEVER REALLY BROUGHT girlfriends home. It was no reflection on them, it's just that I didn't want my family going "Ooooooooooh, she's your giiiiiiiiirlfriend" every time I brought one of them over. Also, if a girl was introduced as just a "friend," it would enable us to spend lots of time behind closed doors without parents thinking there was mating going on. So my parents, particularly my dad, thought that I didn't have girlfriends, just lots of friends who were girls. As if that wasn't enough to make my dad think I was gay, the following situations didn't help either.

Chapter 1: Sucking Dick—So it's freshman year and I'm visiting my brother, Kevan, in college; he goes to Hampshire College in Massachusetts. My long-time friend Robert came along with me and my family on our trip. We had known each other since nursery school, and he was close with everybody in my family. So me and Robert are walking to my brother's dorm room from the dining hall, and I'm talking to Robert about a story that somebody else told me, or a joke, or something that has absolutely nothing to do with my life. So we get there and I am under the assumption that nobody is in Kevan's room; little do I know that my dad is sitting on Kevan's bed, reading. So we open the door and walk into the room, and I continue my story by saying, so I'm sucking this guy's dick, right? And I, "Ahhhhh!" I scream, seeing my dad looking at me now. Then instead of playing it cool and finishing my sentence I turn around and run right back out of the room and keep on running. I then avoid my dad for two straight days. The conversation was never mentioned again.

Chapter 2: Touching My Titties—By now my dad must have been suspicious, but it's not like he had caught me performing any homosexual acts. So a couple months later I'm chillin' with my friends. Most of my friends are in my basement, but I'm in the kitchen getting something to eat with my friends Arian and his girlfriend Sara Green—Sara also happens to be my mom's name, but that's another story. We're talking about how her ass is enormous but she has no titties. She's all like hey, I have nice tits, and Arian is like, eh, they're decent. I'm like, pshaw! My titties are nicer than that shit. She's all like, oh yeah? We'll see about that. Arian, who has nicer titties, me or Fritz? So Arian puts his hand on Sara's chest, testing the weight, the shape, the fluffiness, the perkiness, and the size of the nipple. After a couple minutes he turns to me. I'm wearing a wife-beater, so I make my best titty muscle, and just as Arian's hand is perfectly cupping my flexed teat, my dad walks into the kitchen. Again, I could think of nothing better to do than to scream like a schoolgirl, run out the back door, and stay in my backyard until my dad left.

So by now my dad must have had serious doubts on the subject of my heterosexuality, but it's not like he had ever caught me in my underwear, in the bathroom, with another guy, at three in the morning.

Chapter 3: Catching Me In My Underwear, In the Bathroom, With Another Guy, at Three In the Morning—So about a year later my friends are over again. This time it's Oliver, Theo, and Arian once again. They're all sleeping over and we're doing what we normally do, which is play Golden Eye and listen to Too Short, but tonight we also have something else to do. A couple months prior to the occasion my mom had gotten me these Pierre Cardin boxers that were the biggest piece of crap boxers in the entire world. They were maaaaad short, so they kinda looked like loosey whities, except that they were green. They also left me with maaaaad penis lint no matter how many times I washed them. As you can tell, I was not a big fan of these undergarments, so I decided I was going to burn them. But before the sacrifice there obviously had to be a ceremonial last wearing of the boxers in order not to piss off the gods. So it's like three in the morning and we're sitting in my basement, chillin', doin' our thing as usual, but all we're wearing are these loosey greenies. All of a sudden I hear my dad about to come down into the basement and for no good reason at all I yell, "Hide." We all stop what we're doing and run in opposite directions.

Theo runs into the furnace room, Arian runs behind a bookcase, and me and Oliver run into the same bathroom. My dad comes into the basement to find it completely abandoned of all human existence. He walks over to the bathroom and opens the door to find me and Oliver in our underwear, huddled together in the corner of the bathroom, at three in the morning. This time there was nowhere to run. "Ohhhh," said my dad, and walked back out the door.

The Sears Outfit

Mary Beth Hoerner

IT WASN'T AS IF I HAD BEEN ASPIRING TO WORK AT SEARS ALL THOSE YEARS. MY sister had worked there in the Notions Department—an entire department devoted to needles and thread—so I had no delusions about the glamour of the work. But it required zero skills, which is how many I had; it didn't involve French fries; and since some people knew my sister, maybe they would be nice to me.

I was not destined, however, for the Notions Department but for the Boys' Department, which turned out not to be the selling of actual boys, but their clothing. I was sixteen, my boss was in his sixties, the full-time ladies were in their sixties, and the part-time ladies were in their seventies on a good day. A rivalry had been brewing in recent years between the two full-time women, Tanya and Doris. Tanya had spent her entire career in the Boys' Department; there was nothing she didn't know about Toughskins. Doris was an implant from Hosiery, so although she could hold her own when talking socks, she would have to refer secretly to the manual regarding the finer points of suits and underwear. On my first day, each woman tried to recruit me to her camp.

"The full-timers work on commission," Tanya said. She was elephant-like, with blond beauty-shop hair that crushed pillows, and just a hint of an accent from the Ukraine. She slipped a note into my hand folded to the size of a pencil eraser. It said "58321."

"I work on commission," she repeated. "Vanya and me left the old country liking the idea of economics in U.S."

"How long have you been here?"

"That's not the point," she said. "The point is I work on commission and you don't. That's my employee number. When you ring a sale, you sometimes can punch in my number instead of yours. That way, I get commission, and it's no skin off you."

"Won't it look like I'm not doing my job if I don't have many sales racked up to my number?"

"No . . . Who cares? You part-timers got nothing to worry about. Nothing!"

I was tempted to confess my worries to Tanya. My parents' pockets had been turned inside out from two decades of nonstop private grade school, high school, and college tuition, a couple of weddings, and rotten luck in all its economic forms. So I had two years to haul ass to save money for college. As a math problem: 0 skills + 2 years = \$40,000. But I figured my middle-class struggle didn't compare to her Bolshevik one.

Plus, I was arrogantly certain that stacking packages of boys' briefs was not my life's work, so I had no problem obliging her, even if it made me look like a slacker. I just couldn't get fired. My father had just gotten fired; I overheard this—no one was supposed to know. He continued to get dressed for work and pretended to go there everyday so we wouldn't know. But I knew, and I couldn't get fired.

Moments after Tanya's shift ended, Doris cornered me. She looked like a tall, white-haired man and dressed in monochromatic, unisex slacks and mock turtlenecks. "Tanya gave you her number, didn't she?" I feverishly dusted the counter and looked up only long enough to examine her chest and crotch, looking for signs of gender. "She's got more than I do," she said, stroking a stack of twenties with her thumb. "She has a husband. They travel. Every summer, Geneva."

"Switzerland?"

"Wisconsin, Lake Geneva, and I'm sick of hearing about it." She slammed the cash drawer shut and placed a laminated version of her employee number in my Annie Hall vest pocket. "Don't use my number when I'm not here, it won't look right."

If I was going to be two old ladies' bitch, I was going to need some candy.

I followed the smell of roasting Spanish peanuts into the Candy Department, which was separated from the Boys' Department by an aisle that led to a little-known exit. Even though I ordered fifty cents worth of Red Hot Dollars, the surprisingly young, curly-haired girl behind the counter hurled a huge, loaded, pink-and-white-striped bag over the counter and said, "It's on me," and winked. "Tell John that Cece says hello."

So much petty thievery. So much candy. Petty thievery. Candy. As active as my guilty conscience was, a different part of me was more active—my heart—which became supercharged with the mention of someone named John. There was a John on this island of misfit bluehairs? A John who must have something to offer if this cute, perky Cece bothered to send him good tidings.

"You sure about the candy?" I said, my mind elsewhere, conjuring up John's different possibilities. Black hair? Brown? Blond? Short, medium, tall? Gray, green, blue, brown, hazel? Jock, brain, nose-picker? Cubs or Sox?

It mattered not. It was a boy—who would be forced to talk to me. A boy, which was a novelty absent in my house full of sisters and high school full of nuns and sixteen-hundred other girls.

As Doris riffled through the bag, I feigned boredom and asked, "What kind of candy does everyone like? I'll make a note of it. John, for instance—"

"John? Was he in? Hardly ever works here anymore now that he's with the FBI." This needed clarification. Doris stored one malted-milk ball in either cheek and, instead of chewing, she let the balls disintegrate, impairing her speech.

"FBI?"

"Mmm-hmm."

OK, so he's not in high school. How not in high school is he? Cool job, though.

"John at the FBI. Can you believe it?"

"No," I said, hoping he was some kind of criminologist prodigy, still within my acceptable age range, which I had calculated to be four years older because my sister was four-and-a-half years older, and the thought of dating someone her boyfriend's age was creepy. Not to mention that anyone old enough would fall in love with her, not me, and then I'd be forced to commit a crime of passion. I have a gift for seeing how things will play out.

"John's a nice young man," Doris said, and she was turning into a fine work companion. "His girlfriend's nice, too. Tammy. Works in Hosiery."

Right to the jugular. Him having a girlfriend. That's a bad thing. Her working in the Hosiery Department—if she's not going to college—is a potential good thing because it means they're not on the same intellectual level and he'll eventually outgrow her. Her name, Tammy, works in my favor. It's a low-budget name.

"You got a boyfriend?"

I had been asked this question so many times already that my head responded "No" of its own accord.

"Good girl," she said, packing two more malted milk balls into her jowls. "There's John now. Here he comes."

I returned to intense counter-dusting, out of nervousness and the desire to appear hardworking. Then he spoke. "I heard there was a new kid," he said, in a voice that would make Barry White tremble.

Meeting John only confirmed what I had suspected all along: I was in love with him. I was a little mad at him for being out of college already, and I had always pictured myself with someone who had a little more funk, but we don't get to choose who we fall in love with, now, do we?

He held out his hand. "The whole store's a-buzz."

A-buzz? I'll show you a-buzz. When we shook hands, skin-to-skin, the Earth didn't stop spinning, everyone around us didn't freeze, but I did feel a very simple happiness take hold of me. Despite their disparity in size, our hands fit together well, and there they floated over the clip-on ties.

"Do you go by Mary or Mary Grace?" he asked.

I had been called Mary Grace since conception, but when he said it, it sounded like the name of a fat farm gal from the 1830s. It had even less panache than *Tammy*, so I rechristened myself. "Grace," I said, "just Grace."

John reminded me of a tall, black-haired, mustached version of Steve Martin, with eyes that creased up when he smiled, which was often. And nice teeth. Nicer teeth than I had ever prayed for. Almost intimidating, teeth like that, like they had never seen candy.

"You working Sunday? Try to work Sunday. I'm down to working Sundays, if even that."

"I'll be in Sunday," I said. Whether I was on the schedule or not, getting paid or not, I'd be working Sunday.

Sunday was the happiest day of my life. We exchanged life stories, his being far superior to mine, but he acted as if my life story was as engaging as Jesus'— but better because mine had some comedic episodes. His father had been a vice president of Sears but had left for some reason. John stayed on because it was easy, close, and he knew everyone. But he couldn't stay there forever.

It was spring and the polyester was in full bloom. Shiny, fly-away-collared shirts in uncomplimentary greens and browns and rusts had come in, the arms of the hangered shirts fastened behind the backs. They were criminal.

Putting together a miniature ensemble in silvers and blacks, John asked, "Do you know any seven-year-old boys going to discos?"

"Nice. Does this come in your size?" I said, hangering a shiny white shirt to a pair of white pants with contrast-stitched pockets. And the Outfit Game was born. We would compete against each other to see who could put together the most egregious outfit. The winning outfit we would display each week in a place of prominence, a mascot. When we didn't work together, we would leave an outfit for each other, a love note of sorts. I was trying to get up the nerve to use actual words instead of funny clothes to express my feelings. He seemed content expressing himself with the outfits. Until one Sunday.

He walked in excited, only the counter between us. "I've got something for you!" He had been working on a hush-hush assignment that was "Big. Huge. Can't wait to tell you about it."

I stood there grinning, leaning a little toward him over the counter to make sure I was breathing in some of his exhaled air, and let me tell you, it was erotic. What could be more erotic than filling up your lungs and therefore your whole body with air that had just been through someone else's—John's? He had refined it for me. Breathing was meaningful. Inhaling was arousing.

"Take a break. I have something," he said. We took the long way downstairs, avoiding the Tammy department, to the Sears Country Inn Cafe. "Hope you're hungry," he said, filling up our tray with two turkey sandwiches and two chocolate donuts. "Can we finish all this before we get to the cashier? I've always fantasized about doing this," he said, cramming half of the turkey sandwich into his mouth. Then he held half of a sandwich up to my mouth, which I obediently opened. The line started moving quickly, and he added a large blue plastic bowl of peaches and cottage cheese into the fray.

"I can't eat that," I said. "I'll gag." The sandwich and donut were backing up in my throat. I slammed a sixteen-ounce glass of tepid tomato juice on the tray. "Are you a boy or a man?" We were only a couple of moms and toddlers away from the cashier, Mabel, who looked like she just stepped out of the original Sears catalog.

"A man?" he said, forcing down the juice.

Mabel was skeptical. "One peach medley between the two of you?" she said, stroking her mole. "John . . . how's Tammy?"

We walked quietly to the table now that Mabel had hit us with the harsh reality that was Tammy. The age difference was something we could perhaps outgrow, but Tammy seemed insurmountable. "So," he said, "you heard about that John Wayne Gacy?"

"Yeah, of course. Is he related to Tammy?"

He smiled. "No. That was the big case I was dying to tell you about. I've been on it for weeks."

"Oh, my God. Can you talk about it? You don't have to. How bizarre!"

"The story's pretty much what they've told on TV. Unbelievably gruesome. But I don't want to make it any worse. I brought something back for you." He handed me a rock with a red ribbon tied around it.

I untied the ribbon and held the rock in my hand. Cold. What was the proper etiquette for responding to a rock? "Cool," I said in an exaggerated voice.

"It's from his house!" he said. "It's a Gacy rock. They're tearing his house down. It's like a relic, a part of history, and you're always talking about your history class. I thought of you, and I pocketed it. We weren't supposed to, obviously. So what do you think?"

A rock from a serial killer's house. It's a start.

There is no misery like the misery of a boy shopping with his mother for a suit. What turns this misery into gut-wrenching tragedy is when the suit goes by the name of "Husky."

On this particular Tuesday night I worked alone. John said he might stop in, so I wore the Gacy rock just in case. I had asked a man in the hardware department to weld it onto some mesh wire and wore it as a bracelet. I didn't really like it that much; it terrified me, actually. But I was afraid it would accidentally get thrown out otherwise, and that might have hurt John's feelings and would have devastated me. I couldn't exactly count on getting much else from him.

The suits were hung on an enormous round rack in the back of the department. A mom was inspecting every suit even though only two suits had even a chance of fitting her son—the Husky 16 ice blue and the Husky 16 fleshy peach. That the Husky line cost more and offered so few choices seemed mean, created by someone with a "Kick 'em when they're down" mentality.

"Do you need some help?"

"Yeah—I need Porky to go on a diet. Can you help me with that?" The mom shook her head in disgust. "Try this on," she said, handing her son the fleshy peach.

"It'll fit," the boy said, holding it up to his shoulders.

"Get your fat—" she caught herself. Twenty minutes later the boy shuffled out of the dressing room staring at the carpeting. He had taken his shirt off, the jacket refused to button, and the pants were hiked up to right under his chest, but still they dragged on the ground a good four inches. "Get a load of this," the mother said. "Take it off. I'm not paying that kind of money and then paying a tailor."

It was just about closing time and still no John. Tammy was on her way out and forced a toothless, my-underwear's-too-tight smile. I wondered what he saw in her and why an aspiring FBI agent would steal.

I walked through the department one last time before closing, looking for garbage or disheveled shelves, and one thing did catch my eye back by the suits. It was the boy's mother and the largest suitcase ever; a camel could have fit in there, and she was lifting suits five at a time off the rack and into the suitcase. The only thing separating her from the side door was a metal railing. She was fast. No novice. Five. Five more. Confront her? What would John do? Call Security? Could they make it that fast? I ran to the phone and called Security. She couldn't close the suitcase. Too greedy. A young-looking bum in a floppy Miller Lite cap approached me and, I thought, I don't have time for you.

"Security," he whispered. I looked doubtful but pointed to the woman when he flashed his ID. She was kicking the monster suitcase under the railing, and he was letting her.

"What?—" I attempted to move toward her, but he held his arm out in front of me, rigid, like a toll gate.

"Let her go. We sent guys outside." Buzzers wailed, a getaway car sped up to the door, and they got him and her, and all the suits were saved. The Security guy's name was Bill, and who would have guessed Sears was such a magnet for young spies?

On Sunday, the BIGGEST SUIT SALE OF THE YEAR began, and Tanya, Doris, John, and I were huddled around a smorgasbord of candy. The foiled heist was all they wanted to hear about. Tanya and Doris agreed on one thing. "Next time," Tanya said, "look away, go to the toilet—"

"That's right," Doris said. "You got a life ahead of you. You take chances—for what?"

So much for company loyalty.

"What they give you for it?" Tanya asked.

"A gift certificate for a cup of coffee at the Country Inn—"

"That's what I'm telling you!" Tanya said. "You risk your life, you save them, what—$2,000? and they give you fifty cents for that? Not even in

Ukraine do you get such treatment."

"Who did you work with from Security?" John asked.

"Bill."

A woman's head popped out from behind a stack of suits. She threw them down on the front counter, and Tanya and Doris, combatants once more, hustled over to pounce.

"Bill?" John said. "He didn't try to make any moves on you, did he?"

"People don't make the moves on me." Was this jealousy or fatherly curiosity?

I started catching thieves regularly after that—regularly enough for the Security force to take notice of me. Maybe it was too much notice because one day, out of the blue, Cece got fired, and Bill asked me if I could help them with an internal Security problem. "We have our suspicions—an inside outfit—so keep your eyes and ears open. We might even have a few tasks for you."

I was kind of honored—like maybe they know I have a brain—and kind of insulted—like maybe they think I'm a Nazi-informant type. In any case, my new responsibilities would raise my esteem in John's eyes. And what if . . . ? A horrible, intriguing thought occurred to me. What if Tammy was involved? I pictured her bouncing out of the store, her purse crammed full of unpurchased L'eggs pantyhose. I rehearsed ways of putting it delicately: "Darling, Tammy's a rotten, stinkin', pantyhose thief. Pantyhose!" Then I would pat my shoulder, and he would know his head belonged there.

I decided to do a little pre-op on Tammy myself and hid behind a display of nylon samples. She strutted around the hosiery department sober-faced with a clipboard. Every few seconds she'd make an extreme checkmark on her clipboarded page. She checkmarked with the conviction of Goebbels, and I pictured her at home in a pink canopy bed with her clipboard and checklist of acceptable attributes her boyfriend must have, and only after tabulating does she realize that John has a few more of the mandatory attributes than her previous boyfriend, thereby moving him up into the husband range. Since one of his characteristics is that he's polite, I think that's why he likes her—because it would be rude not to. Maybe I should tell him I like him—his teeth, yes—but mostly the inside of him—his guts, his liver, not the checklist parts.

All smiles, Tammy came over and said, "Are you old enough to wear hose?" What would she look like with one of the samples stretched over her head? I doubt she went for the nylon-over-the-head criminal look because her hair would lose its bounce. I would steal nylon-faced, just for the drama of it, for the distortion, but it wouldn't be at Sears. The object would have to be worth my while—maybe the statue of David.

"Do you have a boyfriend?" she said, checkmarking violently, not looking up, not waiting for me to respond. "John thinks you need one." She couldn't realize the devastating effect her words had on me. She couldn't. "It won't be the same around here without him," she said with false sadness. "He's dying to get out of that ridiculous Boys' Department."

She could. I was no match for her. I drifted away to the Country Inn to cash in another coffee coupon and moved robotlike down the line. I'm sure John would not talk about me condescendingly. Not John, who in this very spot force-fed me the turkey sandwich. I felt someone standing too close behind me and turned around. It was Bill.

"Just go ahead and sit down," he whispered, as if I had other plans. He sat at my table but kitty corner from me and asked, "Got anything to report?"

"What do you think about hosiery?"

"I like it." He smiled. "You have a boyfriend?"

Again! "In seventh grade I did. He gave me a hat just like the one you're wearing. We took turns wearing it, tossed it around, hid it on each other—"

A cryptic numerical sequence came over the intercom, and Bill jumped up, paged. "Pay attention in your own department. I don't want you to end up like Cece."

End up like Cece? What—was she in Gacy's basement? Would they fire me for punching in the old ladies' numbers?

The next morning when I opened the department with John, a surprise was waiting for me on the counter: Bill's Miller Lite cap. "What's this?" John asked.

"Bill's cap," I said.

"Why is it here?"

"I'm not sure." I saw Bill walking down the main aisle, hatless. I hardly recognized him. The hat had been serving a dual purpose—helping him blend with the masses but also camouflaging a hairline that was in the earliest stages of receding. He was a young Bill Murray.

As he walked by, John said, pointing, "That your hat?"

"It's hers now," Bill said. "Gotta do my walk-through," and he went to tip his hat, which was no longer on his head, and left.

John said, "Is he moving in on my girl?" putting his arm around me. We stood there like that. I, of course, unable to speak, was trying my best to breathe, trying to determine, fatherly? brotherly? All of a sudden incest didn't look so bad.

"So this is what goes on when I'm not here," Tanya said, throwing a tote bag full of rattling pill bottles on the counter. "You be careful, John. She going to get ideas in her head about you. You got a young girl here."

"I asked her to hurry and grow up, but she's taking her time," he said, squeezing me tighter.

I was touched that Tanya was looking out for me. I was more touched by John's touch, by the fact that he had thought about accelerating my growth, as I had, and by his barbershop-clean, mint-powdery smell.

Tanya cried to us for help, "My bunions!" and kicked off her black nurse's shoes. With his arm firmly on my shoulder, John turned toward me for a response, but I had none. His magnetic field at close range was a mighty pull. If he didn't kiss me then and there, I would have to kiss him, even with all those religion classes in my belly. Buzzers started to go off, real buzzers, like a nuclear meltdown was underway, spoiling the soft-focus moment. We both rushed toward the door, but it was a false alarm triggered by the recently installed clunky white Security tags. John escorted the innocent shopper to the negligent department.

"Tanya, when're you going to learn how to work the Security tags?" Doris said, strolling in.

"It wasn't me! Why are you here on your day off?"

If not for the baritone voice, I might not have recognized the off-work Doris, but I can report with confidence that she is, in fact, a W-O-M-A-N. Although she wasn't without androgynous gym socks, gym shoes, and a White Sox T-shirt, the off-work Doris wore black-and-rhinestone, green–tinted sunglasses indoors, white culottes, and a Sox clutch bag. Under all those slacks she had been hiding legs that could stop a train. "Go to Hosiery and get some slipper socks, for Christ's sake. I thought you were having the bunions scraped."

"With Cece gone," Tanya said, "I'm low on cash. My foot guy, he works on cash. From Ukraine."

"That's why I'm here—so we can put our heads together and come up with a Plan B now that Cece's AWOL. Didn't squeal though, good girl. Where's John?"

I wasn't sure I wanted to hear this. "John was helping that woman with the Security tags," I said. "Then, I think he was going to the stockroom. Do you want me to get him or keep him away?" *Please say keep him away, please . . .*

"Get him," they said in unison.

As I opened the stockroom door, he was in the middle of putting together a red Shaft outfit, complete with mirrored belt. "I wanted to surprise you with this." His face was all lit up, and I couldn't picture him doing anything as un-fun-loving as stealing.

"It's a bad mother." How could I not like someone who tried so hard to make me laugh? Mortified, I realized that thinking he was a thief didn't change my feelings for him. I was a love junkie, incapable of determining right from wrong. We left the stockroom in an awkward silence.

"You going to Doris's 'Twenty Years at Sears' anniversary luncheon tomorrow?" he asked.

"Yeah. I didn't know it was optional." Are they stealing cash or wrench sets? Mug trees? Booties from the Pooh collection? "Tanya and Doris want to talk to you about a Plan B now that Cece's gone."

"Is that why you're so quiet?"

I kept walking toward the counter where Tanya and Doris were waiting. "Let's figure this out," Doris said, "so I can get the hell out of here."

"Here is probably not the best place," John said.

"Downstairs then. Coffee," Tanya said. "Doris owes me a dollar. I'll call Mel to cover the register. He's got nothing to do over there but dust shoes."

"I don't need to go," I said.

"No, come," John said. "It's no big deal, really."

"*You* owe *me* seventy-five cents," Doris said to Tanya, "but do I bring that up?"

"You're going to leave me to referee between these two?" John asked. I nodded. He knew I knew something was up, something not good, and we didn't talk again until Doris's luncheon.

So you give your heart and soul to your job, you give your life's blood eight hours a day, forty hours a week, fifty-two weeks a year, twenty years, and for that you get a luncheon in an austere room that in its off hours is used for interrogations. Being in that room for any length of time—no windows, one buzzing fluorescent tube flickering—would make me confess to crimes against humanity, much less pilfering. For twenty years, you also get last year's model of the Parker pen and pencil set, and I wondered if I should just quit now, dis-pose of the middleman, and start selling my own blood.

I had to talk myself into showing up to the luncheon, but I did not want to endure Doris's wrath. I was afraid of being around the Gang of Three and discovering things I couldn't undiscover. I was afraid of running into Bill and having him ask me to squeal and tell how I liked the hat. I was afraid John would do something that would only endear him further to me like burp or breathe.

After saying hello to Doris I got in the buffet line so I could leave quickly, but John came up from behind. "Save me that furry piece of chicken." His whisper, his breath on my neck—

"Smile!" Doris accosted us with a large Polaroid camera. John threw his arm around me and smashed his cheek next to mine. Cushy and ruggedly nubby. "Look at this turnout!" an ebullient Doris said. "Where's Tanya? I'm photographing this huge line and everyone in the room because if she comes in at the end and the crowd's thinned out, she'll tell me she had more people at hers." She waved the photo dry. "Here we go. Which one of you wants it?"

"I'll take it," I said with brazen selfishness. The photo would provide me with countless hours of viewing pleasure and the accompanying heart palpitations, while John would only put it in his back pocket, fart on it, and send it through the cleaners where it would end up ignobly in a dead-letter-type bin. The photo was proof that at this moment in history there were these two people cheek to cheek, their lips only a millimeter apart. If I could freeze this moment in history I would, except I'd erase the suspicions in my head. Would there ever be a moment to freeze that would not be tainted?

The next moment in history we were sitting at a table, John serious, scooting his chair close. "Tanya, Doris, I need you," he said, pepper-packeting his lettuce. "When Cece was here, she put cash at the bottom of our big candy bag—regularly. They have no concrete tracking system of what's going in and out of that department. There's no scanning. It's almost all cash transactions. When Cece started, all of a sudden we were finding fives, tens, and twenties hiding in our bags. We didn't ask for it. She saw how the department worked, had virtually no supervision—"

"Until she got caught," I reminded him. He leaned his tall body across the table, and the whole air-sharing thing started up again, and I looked at his goldish eyes, and his animated, mustached mouth, and his acne-free nose—a nose that had boogers in it just like everyone else's so why did I feel compelled to kiss the round tip of it, and who needs the statue of David, and what is he saying? . . .

"They still haven't changed a thing in that department—thought she was just a bad seed. If you replaced Cece . . . They'd never suspect you."

I put my fork down. I removed my Gacy bracelet, as it seemed to be interfering with my pulse, and put it in the pocket of my Annie Hall vest. I leaned back, trying to find some air of my own. "It's not much money, but they've come to depend on it. No one's getting rich or being greedy. Tanya wants to have her bunions done. Doris has perpetual car trouble, and she can't even afford to go to the Sox games."

"And you?" I said, looking him in the eyes, wondering whether I could even tell if he lied to me or not.

"This place has made a fortune off them—"

"And you?"

"I'm doing this . . . I guess you'd call it revenge—for my father who got walked on and screwed here."

So these were the workings of the grown-up mind. "John, what would the FBI say if you got caught stealing from Sears? How would that help your father? They've got a lot to lose, too. They can retire soon—"

"Don't do it if you don't feel comfortable about it. I just—you're the last person they would suspect, and I knew you needed the money for college."

Low blow. "What did Cece get out of this? It seems like she was doing all the work."

"That's the way to think—from a practical point of view. We pooled the money and divided it. Cece kept tabs on the totals; Tanya and Doris watched each other like hawks." Rumblings came from the doorway. Tanya had arrived, and Doris was flaunting the Polaroids.

"Did you ask Tammy to do this?"

He shook his head. "She'd be afraid to. Afraid of scandal. And she would never share it with Tanya and Doris. Besides, I want to loosen my ties to her, not tighten them."

Good answer. Tanya and Doris had apparently patched things up for the common good and headed to our table. "We have a foursome now?" Tanya asked.

"I'm just hearing about it," I said. "It's a lot to think about."

"That's not the point," Tanya said. "The point is, you been catching shoplifters left and right, and these higher ups, they take and take. You want to give and give until you're my age and you think about stealing so you can stand on your feet long enough to get your job done? This is not the economics we came for."

"Grace," Doris said, "you should have heard John talk you up."

Did he talk me up like, "She's a nice person," or talk me up like, "She'd be good at stealing"? Knowing John and all of them wanted something from me made me suspicious of any compliment or kindness. Bill came in and tipped his imaginary hat my way. Even he wanted something from me. Maybe his hat was advance payment for being a snitch. I must come across as the cheapest of informants. Their eight eyes were staring at me in a pleading, hungry gypsy-child kind of way. "You think for a minute," Tanya said. "We'll get you seconds. Doris, make Skinny here a plate."

"You make her a plate, it's my luncheon!"

Yes, they were buttering me up. I had a couple of good characteristics, but skinny wasn't one of them. Honesty, actually, was the only characteristic I had been vaguely certain of. "How did Cece get caught?" I asked.

Doris said, "She wasn't paying attention, got sloppy."

"She moved the money from place to place in drawers and cubby holes," John said, "never straight from the register to the bag. One day, your friend Bill hung out at the candy counter too long." Doris and Tanya turned their heads in unison to glare at Bill. "He figured she was stashing it away for herself. They never caught her red-handed—"

"A bunch of amateurs, that Security team," Doris said. "Now say yes so I can mingle."

Bill came over to the table to shake Doris's hand and sat down right next to John. "I'm going to make a plate for myself," Tanya said. "No one in line, look at that."

"Looked like quite a powwow the Boys' Department was having," Bill said.

"You didn't miss anything," I said. John gave me an approving smile. "Just Tanya and Doris butting heads."

"I have to take off," John said. "You'll let me know in the morning?" I nodded.

"What's going on?" Bill said, wasting no time.

"Nothing . . . I need to go myself," I lied, fearing I would crack easily and messily.

"Forget I ever mentioned it to you. I'll tell Security you can't help us. For me, the point was to get to know you better. I don't want you to have to rat on anyone for that to happen."

"There's no one to rat on, and I wouldn't anyway. My sisters beat me up enough times to learn that lesson."

He nodded. "Thanks for the hat." As I stood up to leave, Bill grabbed my hand. His was an intense hold, and for a second, I thought he might kiss it, as if I deserved it. No kiss. Just a little squeeze as he said, "Don't end up like Cece."

I tossed and turned in bed that night. Tossed and turned. The full moon poured through my window, silhouetting the muntin bars onto my ceiling, prison-like, and I pictured Tanya and Doris in the orange jail jumpsuits, shiny, with flyaway collars, their employee numbers plastered across their chests, Tanya barefoot and bunioned, Doris with sunglasses on, as both the male and female prison population called for a piece of her. And there I am in the big communal shower with John next to me but we're wearing bathing suits, orange prison bathing suits, and the boy's thieving mother's there nude, so it's not romantic at all, and we're in the prison food line but it's in Doris's luncheon room, and there's empty stainless steel food trays, and at the end of the line is Bill, and he hands me a folded-up note, and I think it's my ticket out, but it says only, "There is no candy in prison."

I sat up in bed. Heart pounding. Head pounding with the certainty we'd get busted. I heard my dad's alarm go off, heard him shuffle downstairs to make coffee, heard him get in and out of the shower, get dressed and leave, and as much as I didn't want to go to work, how could I not?

Slowly, disheveled, I slouched through the magic doors into Sears. That's the mysterious thing about work—you just keep showing up. You show up and smile and act polite, and no one knows what's going on inside of you. I trudged toward the Boys' Department, and there was John charming a customer. What if I didn't have a gift for seeing how things played out? What if orange prison-wear wasn't in our future, but a house full of Steve-Martin-look-alike kids was?

"Are you sick?" John asked.

"Allergies," I said, "and sinus trouble . . . and allergies." John waited on the customer, making jokes, looking robust—rosy cheeks, every hair in place, crisp, ironed shirt. You know how food looks better when you're on a diet and you can't eat it?

As he sent the customer away happy, I propped my butt on the counter for support. He took both my hands in his. They still had that hand-in-glove feel. I wanted to get it over with quickly, like a Band-Aid or a vaccination or a bullet, so I tried to focus on something other than his eyes. "You're probably going to think I'm a jerk," I said fixated on his hands. "I hope you won't, but . . . I'm not going to be able to help you out." He nodded slowly. "The only reason, really, is that I'm hoping if I don't do it you'll let it die, and then you won't get caught. Bill's eyes are open, and I don't want you to get caught." I paused so he could say, "OK, let's forget about it," but instead, he squeezed my hands. "I found a ten-dollar bill on the sidewalk," I rambled on, "and I ran up to the guy in front of me waving the ten dollars in his face, 'Did you drop this?' and to the guy in front of him, 'Is this yours?' They looked at me like I was insane, but that's my instinct. My instinct would get us in trouble. I thought maybe I should put the money back on the sidewalk where I found it but realized it would just blow away—"

"You kept it just the same," John said. "If you find money, you keep it.

That's what happened to us."

I didn't tell him the part about me giving half (half!) of the money to a homeless guy, which I did mostly to ease my conscience, like it could be bought for five bucks. "Just keep thinking about it," John said.

Maybe his conscience wasn't the loudmouth mine was. His eyes were loud, though. Loud and penetrating, and when I looked into them I lost all resolve. When I looked into them everything he had said made sense, and I knew that if I stayed at Sears I would eventually lie, cheat, steal—wear Toughskins if he asked me to. So before I even knew what I was doing, I let go of his hands, grabbed the hat, and turned to leave Sears for good.

"Wait," he said softly. "I was waiting until you turned eighteen to ask you out." That touched me. Even if it was a lie, I held onto it. Emboldened, I kissed his hand before leaving. It was a moment of courage and brilliance because I landed a commemorative hand hair from the kiss. Between my super-glossed lips, I felt a lone, stray strand of John's DNA. To eat, or not to eat. No, I wanted to look at it, perhaps pet it, examine it in case its origin was south of the hand. I coughed it into my palm and scurried away.

I'm 16-3/4, and after extensive pavement pounding and a tour de force of acting—my parents never found out I quit Sears—I filled out a job application at an offbeat store that sells posters of Einstein sticking out his tongue, framed movie stills of the Three Stooges, and Picasso's entire Blue Period in magnet form. There is no way anyone over fifty will ever work here. Probably no one over twenty.

I wore the Miller Lite cap thinking it might give me a funky edge over the other applicants, and it worked. When, for more personal reasons, I went to put on my Gacy bracelet, I discovered that my Annie Hall vest had been sent to the cleaners and had come back empty-pocketed. Even though I was a little relieved, I cried. I learned a lesson, though, and had John's stray hair laminated to the historic luncheon photo, where it stays safe in a pocket over my heart.

Nelly Weems, Come Home

Laura Hawbaker

OUTSIDE THE HALL OF MAAT, A HORDE OF ANGRY SPIRITS POUNDED UPON THE doors. It was like a deafening thunder, this constant pounding, and Anubis, fingers raised to his temples to try and massage away a ripping headache, went to the window.

His black head, with its slender, elongated nose and flopping jackal's ears, sieved past the window's curtain, his round, pebble-like eyes peering at the throng of spirits below. The spirits, ghosts of the dead, were nothing more than a swarm of humans, some carrying travel bags, others clad in their finest attire, others wearing book bags, comfortable jeans, and hiking shoes. Some were young, some old, some alone, others accompanied by hordes of family and ancestors. They were all crammed together outside the Hall of Maat, a throbbing blanket of faces that stretched out to the horizon. When Anubis appeared at the window, his human body and jackal's head silhouetted against the curtains, all of the ghosts turned their attention away from beating down the Hall of Maat's front door with identical, frazzled expressions on their faces.

Anubis stretched his arms before him, palms outward, indicating that he wanted silence. The shuffling, muttering, and movement of the crowd immediately quieted.

Clearing his throat, Anubis said, "I know you're all getting kind of antsy . . ."

"That's right!" one voice yelled, and a dozen more voices echoed their agreement.

Anubis cut them off. "But you'll just have to be patient. I promise, all of you will be judged and have your chance at the afterlife…"

A sour-faced woman near the front of the crowd batted her palm against the outside of the building, "I didn't do three years of chemo just so I could die and wait in a crowd for eternity! Why aren't you letting anyone in?" Those around her nodded and began to thump the building as well. The thrum of their pounding rattled the walls.

Anubis tried desperately to be heard over the thunder. "We've run across a little snag in the operation . . . Nothing to be concerned about!" he added quickly, seeing the faces open their mouths to protest. "Just a little snag is all. We'll have it taken care of in no time, and then we'll start letting people in again."

"When will that be?!" a middle-aged man with a beard cried out.

"We've been waiting here forever!" somebody else added.

"I say, if they're not gonna let us in, we force our way in!" another voice yelled.

There were cries of agreement, and the entire crowd surged forward like a wave, bearing down upon the door.

Sighing and shaking his head, Anubis retreated from the window. He slowly tromped down the narrow stairs until he stood in the main entranceway, a vast, splendid, gold hall lit by glowing white archways and draped in fine red tapestries. At the end of the hall, the walls widened out into a circular dome. At the top of the dome was a single skylight, a round opening that let in a cylindrical beam of sunlight. Seated at a long, circular table in the shadow around the sunbeam were forty-two judges, some scowling, some nervously fidgeting with their ebony robes.

Basking in the warm, golden center of the sunbeam was a white marble table, legs carved into identical bird claws. Beneath it, something dark and large shifted irritably but stayed out of sight. Atop that table was a scroll, a quill and inkpot, a butcher's knife, a blood-stained cutting plate, and a gleaming silver scale. Beside the table were two wood stools. Atop one of those stools perched a white ibis, its milky blue eyes blinking at Anubis expectantly. The judges, sallow-faced and lips pursed, watched Anubis approach, their arms crossed over their chests.

"So?" one of them asked.

"They're a little edgy," Anubis answered. He took his place in the center of the room, beside the marble table and the ibis. There he stood stoically, his hands clasped behind his back. He caught the eye of the ibis, and they exchanged apprehensive glances.

Another judge gazed at the walls, where the flames of a few lit candelabra quivered from the pounding outside. "Are we safe?"

"Perfectly," Anubis assured. "They can't get in, no matter how hard they try."

"Still," another judge sighed, "we can't let them wait out there forever. Perhaps we should let just one in, to quell them a bit."

"And what would we do with the one we let in?" Anubis asked. "Tell them, 'So sorry. We can't judge you because Maat's missing, and we have no way to weigh your heart?' Be serious."

"She said she'd be right back," another judge muttered.

"Well, something's obviously happened. It isn't like Maat to shirk her duties like this."

"And if we wait much longer," another judge added, uneasily pointing at the sunlight in the center of the room, "her dad's gonna have a fit."

The other judges nodded, murmured their agreement, and stared at the golden beam of sun with uneasy awe.

A dignified-looking judge with a white goatee and thick, deviled brows stood and announced, "We must send someone to find out what's happened and bring our girl home."

"Hear, hear!" the judges applauded, pounding their fists on the polished tabletop.

The white-bearded judge turned his focus to the ibis perched beside Anubis. "I nominate Thoth. As her consort, he has the best chances of finding Maat, locating who's responsible for her delay, and having Maat punish them accordingly."

"Hear, hear!" the judges bellowed in unison.

Anubis turned to face the ibis. He bowed his jackal's head slightly and whispered, "Good luck. Bring her home safely."

The ibis blinked and dipped its graceful head. Its slim neck curled, its wings stretched, and it took flight, a white beacon that soared in circles around the vaulted room before crossing the sunbeam to the dome's ceiling, where it disappeared out the opening and beyond sight.

What a terrible day this is going to be, Nelly Weems thought as she, the only senior, boarded the bus to school. Her black, pink-streaked hair was pulled back in a ponytail. She wore a torn, red hoodie draped over her favorite black anarchy T-shirt, a pair of paint-splattered jeans, two dozen clinking silver bangles, dark red lipstick, thick purple and black eye shadow, and five silver hoops: three in one ear, two in the other. She sat in a duct-taped, graffiti-slathered seat while a group of freshman boys behind her hocked spitballs at one another, a group of sophomore girls in front of her defied the bumps of the bus and applied makeup from compacts, and a googly-eyed member of the speech team persistently offered her a stick of gum. Nelly leaned her forehead against the bus window, watched the rain rivulets chase one another across the glass, and wished the day were at an end.

During home room, Nelly was made to take a state survey—she despised filling in those stupid Scantron circles with a stupid number-two pencil. Instead, she pulled out a bright green glitter pen and created diamonds on her Scantron sheet; the homeroom teacher noticed and Nelly had to retake the whole thing. An essay comparing the archetypes of Jung with characters in *Demian* was due in first-period English, which Nelly had, of course, forgotten to do. Second-period Social Studies consisted of a long, drawn-out lecture about the early American political parties. Nelly nearly fell out of her chair with boredom. By third-period Anatomy Science with Mr. Yawanis, Nelly decided to play hooky after class.

"Psst!" she leaned over her desk and hissed at Denise, her best friend who sat in front of her in Anatomy.

Denise pretended not to hear. Instead, she flicked one of her two strawberry-blonde plaits over one shoulder.

The two girls couldn't look more opposite; people saw them walking down the hall, chatting and giggling, and didn't believe they were actually friends. Nelly with her pink-streaked hair and clunky army boots was a sharp contrast to the redheaded Denise, who tended to wear polo shirts and plaid pleated schoolgirl skirts, sporting a letterman's jacket. Denise was kind of a bookworm and, with the SATs fast approaching, had become the epitome of a studious student.

Nelly kicked the back of her chair.

"What?" Denise whispered, agitated, over her shoulder.

"I'm skipping out after this class. Wanna grab a burger?"

"No way." Denise always said no way. If it weren't for Nelly constantly badgering her to break the rules, Denise would be a complete drip.

"Come on!" Nelly whined.

"Shut up!" Denise hissed, casting a nervous look in Mr. Yawanis' direction.

"Please, please, please…"

"OK! Fine! Just be quiet!"

Satisfied, Nelly sat back in her chair, folded her arms across her chest, and focused her attention on a fly circling the ceiling. Slowly, she descended into a dark lull of daydreams that brought her to the precipice of sleep.

From far away, she thought she heard the classroom door squeak open. There was a murmur of conversation and a shuffling of paper and feet, then Mr. Yawanis announced to the class, "OK guys, this is Laydon. He's joining us for the semester. Laydon, why don't you tell us where you're from?"

"Egypt."

At the word "Egypt," a collective sigh exuded from the class. Nelly's eyes snapped open and her posture whipped upright. Egypt! Egypt was so far away, so foreign, so exotic! Like the rest of the class, she craned to get a glimpse of Laydon.

He didn't look anything like how she thought an Egyptian would. She expected somebody like the ancient Egyptians, like Cleopatra, like Tutankhaman—somebody with dark, desert-tanned skin and black hair, maybe some kohl smudged around her eyes, braids and jewelry . . . that sort of thing.

By comparison, Laydon looked downright normal. Though his skin had a healthy tan, his hair was a pale shade of downy blonde. He wore a hooded shirt with a corduroy jacket, a pair of faded blue jeans, and a lumpy green book bag. In fact, the only Egyptian thing about him was the beaded choker around his neck with a small gold hieroglyphic locket glinting just visibly over his collar.

Despite the fact that he didn't look like the stereotypical Egyptian, Nelly felt a light churning in the pit of her stomach. Laydon had large, almond-shaped eyes a color so blue they bordered on ethereal. Leaning forward over her desk, Nelly kicked the back of Denise's chair.

Denise whipped around, braids flicking over her shoulders, and glared at Nelly. "What?"

Nelly beamed and, her tongue protruding slightly between her teeth, whispered, "He's cute!" She pretended to hide a girlish giggle behind one hand.

Denise glanced back at Laydon, then stared at Nelly. She shook her head and said, "He is not."

Nelly gawked at her friend. "Are you kidding? He's good looking!"

Denise rolled her eyes.

Then the most amazing thing happened. Mr. Yawanis gestured to the desks and said, "Welcome to America, Laydon. It looks like there's an empty seat next to Nelly. Why don't you sit there?"

Nelly's breath caught in her throat. She felt her cheeks blush. As Laydon approached and slung his bag onto the desk to the immediate left of Nelly's, she slowly slid down in her seat, wishing she could bury her burning face. In front of her, Denise turned around to shoot a mirthful smirk.

Halfway through Mr. Yawanis' lecture on the complexities of the aorta, Nelly became uncomfortably aware of the fact that Laydon was looking at her. No, not only looking. The boy was *ogling* her. Nelly was careful not to glance in his direction, but ten minutes before the end of the period she couldn't help it.

The second she did, he caught and held her gaze in that penetrating blue stare, and she saw his lips mouth a word, possibly "Hi," possibly something else. Was it a trick of the light, filtering gray through the raindrops on the window, or was there something a little off about Laydon's eyes, something lurking just beneath, like a shadow flickering beneath the surface of a cool blue pool . . . drawing, pulling, coercing Nelly in . . . ?

In front of her, Denise jolted her chair backward, bashing it into the edge of Nelly's desk. Nelly whipped her gaze from Laydon's and refused to flicker it his way for the remainder of the period.

After class was dismissed, just as Nelly stepped into the hall, Laydon hooked her by the elbow and pulled her aside, away from the hustle and bustle of the passing period.

"Can we talk?" he asked. Nelly noted his light, indistinguishable accent, and felt a shiver course over her arms.

Somehow, she managed to form two words, "About what?"

"Not here," his gaze shifted to the other students, "somewhere private."

"She can't," a voice interrupted. Denise appeared over Nelly's shoulder, her arms crossed, holding her schoolbooks to her chest. "We're getting burgers, remember, Nell?" She flashed Laydon a look of pure ice, which he returned, unflinching.

Nelly, standing between the two, felt caught, tied up in a ribbon of tension. In an attempt to dispel the unexplained hostility between her best friend and the new boy, she said to Laydon, "Look, she's right. We're getting some food . . . unless you want to come?"

"He doesn't," Denise snapped.

"I do."

"No," Denise's brow rose, "you don't."

"OK," Nelly interrupted, "obviously you two know each . . ."

"What do you think you're doing?" Laydon whispered to Denise, his voice hoarse and dangerous.

Nelly's mouth snapped shut, and she stepped back. There was obviously something going on here. What, she had no idea. Denise and the new boy, for one reason or another, didn't seem to like each other very much. The only logical explanation Nelly could come up with was that they must've met sometime before Anatomy and gotten into an argument. But if that was the case, why hadn't Denise told her about it? When Laydon first arrived in class, why hadn't Denise given Nelly a play-by-play of why she didn't like him and Nelly should steer clear?

Something didn't fit.

The two slid closer to one another, filling in the space where Nelly had just stood. They were face-to-face, neither blinking from the other's cold gaze. Around them, the other students continued to drift, chatter, and laugh, like an oblivious current around three rocks.

Denise snapped, "I'm not doing anything. She left on her own, remember?"

"She would sometimes, you know that. For a respite. But you've done something to her. You've turned her into this! She doesn't remember who she is or where she belongs . . ."

Denise leered, a curious curling of one lip. "I only did what she asked me to do."

This seemed to take Laydon aback. The color in his face drained and he sucked in a sharp breath. His eyes squinted and he murmured, "You lie."

"Why would I lie about that? It's so unbelievable . . . I would only say it if it was the truth."

"Where's the feather?"

Denise's eyes became big and innocent, and she cocked her head to the right, "I don't know what you're talking about, Laay-don." She said the name in a mocking sort of way.

Laydon turned around, caught Nelly by the arm, muttered, "Let's go," and started dragging her through the hall. Nelly looked over her shoulder at Denise, who watched the two leave with a half-smile before turning and disappearing into the crowd. Nelly struggled against Laydon and managed to pull herself free of his grasp. She scowled, "Listen, that's my friend back there, and if you've got some kind of gripe with her, you've got a gripe with me."

Looking left and right, Laydon steered Nelly into an alcove in the hall, next to a water fountain, and lowered his voice. "She isn't who you think she is, and I'm not who you think I am."

"Yeah, right, OK . . ." Nelly rolled her eyes and made to turn and leave. The boy was obviously insane; it must have been all that exposure to desert sun.

"I'll show you."

She glanced back at him and saw, for a flickering moment, the strangest apparition. In that instant, he wasn't Laydon. There was a flutter of white, a flapping of wings, a slender beak, and a long, delicate neck. A blink later the apparition was gone and Laydon was Laydon again.

Nelly collapsed against the wall behind her, ogling at him, her mouth gaping open and closed like a fish. She stared at the other students. Had none of them seen it? Had *she* seen it?

"Do you believe me?" he asked.

Dumb with shock, Nelly managed a nod.

"Good, then let's go." He took hold of her hand and steered her to the exit. They ran past the soccer field, rain whipping their hair and soaking their clothes. Luckily, Mr. Stills—the hall monitor who rode a green golf cart dubbed the Narc-Mobile around the school grounds to catch students playing hooky—was nowhere in sight.

There was a city bus stop at the corner, a bus just visible on the next block over. Laydon made a mad dash toward it, towing Nelly behind him like an anchor, and just managed to catch the bus before it pulled away.

They stood inside, gasping for breath and dripping pools of rainwater as they paid their fares. The bus was only half full, a barrage of half-drowned afternoon shoppers, errand runners, and businessmen on lunch staring straight ahead or gazing listlessly out the windows, refusing to make eye contact with anyone. Laydon led Nelly to two empty seats halfway to the back.

"OK," Nelly stuttered, her voice raising decibels with every word, "Now what was that all about? 'Cause let me tell you something, that was pretty friggin' freaky, OK!"

Laydon shushed her and ran a hand through his hair, shaking the water from it. "I've been looking for you for eighteen years. My name isn't actually Laydon, and Denise isn't really Denise. She's tricked you. She's taken on a different form and disguised herself. She has many names. She is Apep. She is Seth. She is the snake. She is chaos. She cannot be trusted.

"Apep is pandemonium. By stealing you, she has brought the world to the brink of anarchy. Outside the Hall of Maat, the spirits of the dead wait for the weighing of their *iebs*. It was your duty to weigh them against your feather, and thereby determine if their hearts are filled with vice or virtuosity. Because you are here, hidden in mortal form, the weighing of the hearts cannot happen. Ammut, the crocodile-hippopotamus, grows hungry without evil souls to eat. Annubis and the forty-two judges are lethargic as they wait futilely for your return. The stairway to the afterlife beckons, but no new souls descend."

A loud snort sounded just behind the two. They both turned and found themselves being scrutinized by a dowdy woman with tight, curly, gray hair, who clutched two overflowing grocery bags on her lap and had, on the seat beside her, a patchy calico in a cat carrier.

Nelly's eyes narrowed and she snapped, "You got a problem?"

The woman pursed her lips and raised her brows, but said nothing. The calico mewed.

Unfazed, Nelly returned her focus to Laydon. "So who are you?"

"Thoth, the moon God of knowledge and scribes." For a moment, it seemed he would say more but then decided against it. Instead, he added, "I'm sometimes the ibis."

Dawning. "Aahh . . . is that what that was?"

Laydon dipped his head in a nod. "It's my duty to find Maat and have her bring the one responsible for her delay to justice."

Nelly's head swum. It was all so unbelievable, so completely alien . . . any normal day, she would've called Laydon a raving lunatic, yanked the pull chord, and leapt from that bus, putting him out of reach and out of mind.

But the flickering image she'd seen in the hallway . . . for a moment, Laydon had been something else. Something not of this world at all. She hadn't imagined that. She shuddered and absently picked at the grimy, wet mass that was her hair. "Who am I supposed to be, again?"

"Maat. Truth, justice, and harmony. The Breath of Life."

Nelly sat back in her seat. Most of what Laydon was saying whisked right over her head. Why didn't she recognize any of this Egyptian mythology stuff? Then she remembered. Denise and she'd skipped school and gone to a music concert the day they'd studied ancient Egypt in sophomore World History.

Come to think of it, it was Denise who'd scored those tickets . . .

"I'm sorry, Laydon. Maybe you are this guy Thoth, and maybe even Denise is that snake thing; she can be pretty slick. But if there's one thing I know, it's me. I'm just not who you say I am."

"I can show you."

They got off at the next stop, a vacant parking lot seven blocks from the school. Rain puddles formed miniature islands out of the humps in the asphalt. A few cars splashed around the street corner, but other than that and a few scuttling rats by a trash dumpster, they were alone.

Laydon instructed her to look at him.

More than a little weirded out, Nelly obliged.

She watched his entire face go slack and his pupils dilate. He murmured something, and through the patter of rain Nelly heard a single word, "*Ba.*"

Instantly, she felt that strange pulling, like she had in Anatomy. The blue hue of his eye shifted and broke, like the cusp of waves, and the world behind him—the trash dumpster and the parking lot—dimmed to black. Then there was a silent flash of light, like a television screen had just blown out, and Laydon blinked into the black behind him.

"Laydon?" Nelly whispered, but found that her voice was no longer there. It didn't exist, her mouth, too, and her throat and her skin. She was a floating entity, unburdened by a body. Slowly, the darkness around her cleared, and she was looking at a grand temple: pillars and tapestries, old stone and white marble.

She saw a long, snaking line of people leaning against the furthest wall. Some of them read newspapers, some were asleep, their mouths gaped open and snoring; some chatted amiably, others stared listlessly ahead.

An eternity passed, the line inching step by step forward, a shuffle of bodies, a break in the lull. Then more waiting.

A wind picked up and whisked Nelly away from the line, down the temple hall, and into a circular room. There sat an imposing circle of robed men. There was also a table, and perched at the side of it was Laydon. He sat poised with a quill pen and a sheet of parchment. He gazed past Nelly and didn't seem to see her.

Standing next to Laydon was a woman, garbed in elegant finery, with a long graceful neck and beautiful, wide-set eyes, plum red lips and polished, tapered nails. Her long, black hair fell in waves down to her waist. In her hair was a single ostrich feather, white and impossibly soft, wafting in a solitary beam of sunlight as though in water. The woman, too, was staring past Nelly at something behind her.

Nelly glanced over her shoulder, back at the waiting line. She saw a frightening creature with the body of a human but the head of some sort of dog escorting the person at the head of the line, an old man in a bowler hat, into the center of the room.

The dog-headed person gestured to the bowler-hat man to lean over the table, so that the side of his midsection sat on a stained cutting plate. What then followed was the most bizarre, engrossingly gross display Nelly had ever witnessed. The dog man plucked from the table a long knife and deftly slid it into the person's chest. With an expert air he made four deep lacerations, and proceeded to scoop out the area cut as one scoops out a sliced brownie. Blood splattered to the floor, cascading over the bowler-hat man's chest like a waterfall. He didn't seem to mind. He didn't so much as flinch.

The dog man held in his palm a handful of bodily mass. He plucked free the excess flesh and muscle, picked away a few splinters of ribs, until the thing he held was wholly and completely a human heart. He handed the heart over to Laydon, then picked up a gleaming gold scale from the table.

Laydon stood up from the stool. As he did so, he casually, tenderly brushed the back of his hand against the inner crook of the woman's arm before placing the heart in one of the scale's dishes. The scale didn't move when the weight of the heart was added. It remained completely balanced.

The woman reached behind her head and plucked free the peacock feather. Her arm draped forward, the feather pinched between thumb and forefinger. She dropped it onto the scale's second dish.

Like a rock, the heart's dish clanged against the table. The momentum caused the feather to waft upward for just a moment, catch the sunlight, then drift again into the dish.

A moment later, there was a snapping of jaws, a croak, a howl of pain, a gnashing of teeth, and the man was gone, dragged beneath the table by some unseen, dark monster lurking just beneath.

Laydon made a mark on the parchment, while the judges and the dog-man watched unwaveringly, their faces passive . . . almost apathetic.

The woman, too, had that look of the daily grind. But there was something else; something indistinguishable and hidden. Something secret. As she'd watched the bowler-hat man approach, her mouth had pulled down just slightly, and her shoulders had curled forward. Her gaze flickered just once—as she pulled the feather from her hair-toward the ceiling, up at the only window in the whole of the room.

Nelly knew that expression. It was the same expression she sometimes had in class, when she'd gaze out a window at the stretch of ground outside, at the shifting leaves of trees and the bursts of clouds, at birds swooping circles in the sky, and younger children, already out of school, chasing after an ice cream truck.

It was a look of boredom.

It was a look of yearning.

And Nelly knew, with all of her being, that that woman, somehow, was *her*.

The dog-man wiped his hands clean of blood in a basin of water, then walked toward the head of the line, to fetch the next victim.

There was a flash of silent light and darkness, and Nelly was back in the parking lot. She was soaked to the bone, shivering, and Laydon stood before her, one eyebrow arched expectantly.

"So?" he asked.

Nelly felt herself sink to the curb. The gutter swirled with murky brown rainwater, and her boots sloshed in it. She nodded dumbly, "So you're right. That was me."

Laydon smiled. "Good. Now I'm not certain I'll be able to bring back your memory, but restoring you to your immortal body shouldn't be a problem at all. Then we'll return to your hall, and . . ." his voice drifted and he stared at Nelly, who hadn't said anything.

Nelly's shoulders hunched forward, her head bowed, and her hair, pulled loose from the ponytail, shielded her face like a mangled curtain.

"What's wrong?" he asked.

"It's just . . ." she shook her head, "day in and day out, the same thing. Cutting out peoples' hearts, sentencing them to be eaten by that monster-thing. An eternity of that?" She shuddered. "It seems like such a terrible life."

The rain thickened, fat drops slapping the puddles and soaking Nelly's clothes through. Laydon was still and quiet. Hands in pockets, he stared down at Nelly with a mixture of fear, repulsion, and overwhelming grief.

At long last, he sighed and muttered, "She wasn't lying, was she?"

He began to walk away.

Nelly stood and caught up with him. She gripped his shoulder, holding him back, and planted herself firmly in front of him. "What's wrong? What is it?"

"Apep . . . Denise . . . she told the truth when she said you'd asked to be made this way. You actually *wanted* this! To be mortal, a human, to give up your responsibilities, your life . . ." He cringed and turned, unable to look at her.

A stubborn flame licked up inside Nelly. To his back she spat, "So what? You were there; you can't tell me you honestly like weighing people's hearts, every day all the time for the rest of eternity . . ."

"That isn't the point."

"What is?"

He thought a moment, then gestured to the ground. Spread out in nearly parallel lines over the parking lot were thin, drowning, dying bodies of pale pink earthworms, slowly going gray.

"Why do they come out?" Laydon said. "It seems so pointless, doesn't it? They come out of the ground, where they would drown. But on the surface, if they're lucky enough to survive the rainstorm, they bake in the sun. Such a worthless organism.

"But *Maat* is the order of the universe. Everything has its place and its purpose. The earthworm breathes through its skin, taking in the air between soil particles. By doing this, earthworms break down *humus*, decaying matter in the ground. If not for earthworms, *humus* would linger, spoil, and plants wouldn't grow. The ecosystems collapse; the universe becomes chaos.

"You, Maat, are the opposite—that order, that balance—that keeps everything right. It isn't about doing something because you *like* to. This isn't about frivolous fancies. Do the earthworms like what they do? Do they dislike it? Neither. It's about doing something because it's your purpose; it's what you are meant to and made to do."

Nelly kicked a loose chunk of gravel. With the toe of her boot she pried it from its place and sent it skittering through the puddles. A few worms were mashed beneath it.

"Well," she said at long last, "I don't want to."

She saw something blink out in the blue of his eyes. They didn't seem so vibrant anymore. He looked suddenly like a bedraggled cat, half-drowned and wholly pathetic.

"Come on," he shrugged. "I'll take you back to school."

They trudged the seven blocks in silence, and passing cars occasionally spritzed them with gutter water.

At school, the grounds were empty. The buses were gone. The final class had been let out. Because of the rain, after-school sports were cancelled, and the place was utterly abandoned.

Nelly squinted through the gray fog of rain. A smear of white, like a paint stroke, seemed to be leaning against the flagpole. As she neared, the smear solidified and separate colors pieced out: a green plaid skirt, a yellow letterman's jacket, a sky blue umbrella, violent red hair . . . It was Denise, smirking beneath the protection of her umbrella as she watched the two approach. When they were near enough, she sneered, "Did I lie, *Laay*-don?"

Laydon, his head bowed and posture sunk with the weight of his wet clothes and heavy heart, could only nod once. Nelly stared at him and felt an overwhelming surge of pity course through her. He seemed so small, so insignificant now. All of his grand words, his fantastical story, his talk of myths and life and order . . . they were all now obsolete.

Denise smiled at Nelly and held out a hand. "You should come out of the rain. You're soaked, Nell. We can go get those burgers. And I promise, come tomorrow, you're not gonna remember any of this." Nelly stepped toward Denise, casting Laydon a final, apologetic look. He was still as a stone statue, gray and soaked through. Only his finger moved, a slight twitch at his side.

She remembered something. In the vision of the heart weighing, she'd seen

Laydon place the heart in the scale, and later record the results. But just before that, he'd done something small, a tiny little gesture that had gone nearly unnoticed. He'd touched Maat's arm. It had been a tender, loving little motion. A casual, intimate thing . . .

Just beyond Denise's outstretched hand, Nelly stopped and looked back at Laydon. Were Maat and Thoth lovers? How pitiful, that she didn't even remember him, and was now abandoning him for the fleeting, carefree life of a mortal. She felt sorry for him, and the girlish part of her was a little let down, but she wasn't going to chain herself to an immortal life of responsibility just because she had a crush on a cute boy.

Another thought came to her. Her life as Maat couldn't have been *all* heart weighing. That tender little gesture between lovers was proof that there was something more, a relationship beyond the duties of the temple. She'd had a life that went beyond the golden scale. There was more to Maat than feather plucking and soul condemnation.

Did she want to find out what more there was?

Sensing Nelly's hesitation, Denise said, "I should add that you begged me to make you mortal. I'm not using 'begged' as a hyperbole, here. On your knees, pleading, tears, the whole sha-bang. You want to go back to the life that reduced you to that?"

Nelly didn't know. She looked over her shoulder at Laydon, "Was there anything else? Maybe something you forgot to mention?"

He stared at her through the gray drizzle and didn't say anything. But for a moment she thought she saw a brilliant flash of blue rekindle behind his eyes.

Denise snapped, "It's a *dull life*, Nelly, an eternity of monotony. And I know you. You'd hate it. You love playing hooky too much. You love being rebellious. That's you. Not what he says. Order and balance and all that; you wouldn't be breaking the rules . . . you'd *be* the rules! The life of Nelly Weems is what you wanted!"

Nelly turned and faced Denise, her best friend in all the world. Beneath the sanctity of the brilliant blue umbrella, Denise was a vision of perfection. Unlike the soaked Laydon and frazzled Nelly, her clothes were dry and not a red hair was out of place. Nothing whatsoever about her appearance suggested there was some slithering, scaly thing lurking beneath that befreckled, ivory skin.

Nelly said, her voice sharp and edged with finality, "I made a mistake."

High above, there was a break in the gray storm clouds. A beam of warm sunlight sieved through and cast a golden glow over the flagpole.

Seething, Denise's shoulder sunk and her arm went limp. Her grip on the umbrella slackened and it dipped down, then clattered to her feet. Denise had time to give Nelly a single cold stare—the iciest, most livid look of hatred Nelly had ever borne witness to in her life—before dissipating into a curling ribbon of red smoke. Nelly watched the smoke dance up into the sunlight, thinning and spreading until not a trace of it was left. Behind her, she heard Laydon let loose a sigh of irrepressible relief.

As the sunlight warmed her wet clothes and stroked her clammy skin, a sense of overwhelming duty overcame Nelly. She recalled something Laydon had told her on the bus, something about his mission: the guilty one responsible for delaying Maat's return to the temple must be brought to justice.

Today, Nelly was the guilty one, and she knew exactly what her punishment should be. "Laydon," she whispered, "take me home."

The Room Before We Get There

Jona Whipple

THERE'S ONE OF THOSE RECHARGEABLE RAZORS BUZZING ON THE FLOOR. IT hums at full speed, tapers off to a low buzz like a cicada, stops, and takes off again. It's loosed itself from its cord, which is wrapped and tied around the white arm of the body on the floor. Broken capillaries snake out around the knot-like blue rivers under the map of his skin, a dusty, translucent color, like the stain of Kool-Aid on a child's lips at a birthday party. Hours earlier, the razor spun, fully charged, and bounced off the floor, squirming and choking against its tether.

His head is at a right angle to the rest of his body, pressed up against the wall. The body is splayed like a star, with one arm behind the toilet, one arm by the tub, and the two stiff legs sprawling against the sink and the edge of the tub. To his mother, who had the unfortunate experience of finding him lying dead in the center of her seashell bathroom, he looked almost as if he was offering himself to something, his open hands facing the ceiling, his head propped off the floor with that wild, excited look in his eyes. The shell and sand border surrounded her son, framing him as if he was just relaxing on the beach as she had been for the last two weeks. Perhaps it was her rested state of mind, or perhaps she had been expecting to find her thirty-year-old son slouched in a pool of his own piss and shit any day now, but in any case, the dispatcher found the need to ask the calm and collected woman if her son was still breathing.

"No, I don't think so," she says smoothly. "Hold on . . ." Moments. "No. No, he isn't."

Mariachi

By the time we get there, the cops are in the living room going through the necessary motions. We don't look at the family; they don't usually feel the need to look at us. The trick is just for the cops to keep them as far away from the scene as possible. The cops have poked their heads in the bathroom door and checked the man's vitals even though his exposed flesh is white and looks as if it's covered with a fine dust. One of them has placed two fingers in the hollow of the neck, between two hardened cords, although both of them have noticed the blackened skin against the floor, the pull of gravity having already taken hold of the blood within. Both of them have noticed the needle jammed into the crook of his arm, the syringe broken off and lying on the floor nearby, the bent spoon lying next to a lighter, and a Farmhouse Apple Yankee Candle on the back of the toilet, the flame sputtering at the end of the wick in a chasm of wax at the bottom.

The firemen are packing up, grumbling as they load their pickaxes and shovels and crowbars back onto the truck, anxious at the splitting smell of something burning. The EMTs feel obligated to stand around, seeing as how they got there so late, at least three minutes behind the others. "Damn dispatch," they say, shaking their heads as if they might have been able to do something three minutes ago. They are standing at the door of the bathroom when we get there, armed with our white suits and hoods and our heavy toolboxes. "He must be a whole day in by now," one of them says to me in greeting, grinning his gap-toothed grin in a spotty face, leaning his large body on one arm against the door frame.

"What's he still doing in there?" I say.

"Coroner's guys broke down. They're sending another unit."

The coroner's guys are never in a hurry to get anywhere. Everywhere they're going ends up the same way.

"It's a dirty job . . ." one of the EMTs says as they pick up their stretcher and their breathing unit. I know that one of us is supposed to finish the rest of it, but neither of us is in the mood. We sit on the edge of the tub and watch them leave.

There's a little radio on the shelf over the toilet by a large jar of cotton balls, Mason style like the ones in biology class, laced with poison for our frogs. We turn it on low so only we can hear it as we try to work around the body. The channel is set on college radio, but Sammy changes it immediately to *Que Buena*. He dusts the pool of vomit with a solidifier and scoops it into one of the waste bags. The dust is supposed to smell like citrus, but in the end it just ends up smelling like puke. And there's not a lot that can mask the odor of sweet rot that is emanating from the body as we clean, the aroma of a dumpster in the summer, a smell you inhale fully as if it's cookies baking before realizing what it actually is.

The one thing I've learned to agree with Sammy on is the music. I used to try and take my turn with the radio in the van or at the office or on a job, trying to get him interested in other kinds of music. Sometimes we'd be listening to some light jazz and I'd see Sammy tapping his hand against the desk, but it's his Mexican station that really gets him moving, so it's his Mexican station that we listen to. I put up with anything that makes him work faster.

The sounds of the mariachi always make me think of a Mexican restaurant and Mexican food, and thinking of refried beans and red rice doesn't really help when you're trying to scrape wet brains off a wall and dig skull fragments out of the plaster. I try to think instead of the four guys who come around to the tables at the local Mexican place where me and Sammy eat sometimes. I conjure up those mariachi guys so that they'll be standing around in the bathroom, the gold in their costumes glittering in the fluorescent light on the ceiling, tassels dangling from their collars and cuffs as they play their guitars. They stand there and sing while we scrub shit out from between tiles with tiny brushes, while we fill biohazard bags with the former contents of someone's stomach and intestines that have exploded from being closed up in a studio apartment for three weeks in July. These guys keep me going, if I try really hard not to think about enchiladas.

We do as much as we can around the dead guy. He's sort of covering the whole bathroom floor, so after a while we give up and sit back down on the edge of the tub and wait for the coroner's guys. It's when they come strolling through the door carrying their stretcher with the black bag on top that the family loses it (if they haven't already) and realizes what's actually happening. It's those guys they appeal to, it's the coroner's guys that they beg to bring their kids and husbands back. I guess it's because they're the guys who take them away. We can hear the mother finally freaking out, asking the cops what's going to happen to her son. The guys in black jackets come in; there's only two of them, and the thin jackets billow around them like there's air coming up from the floor.

"Jesus, he's huge," one of them says, putting his hand in his hair. It's then that I notice just how tall the dead guy really is. He'd become just a part of the floor to me. The coroner's guys lift the head away from the wall together, one pulling up on each shoulder, devising their strategy. I can tell it's going to be a difficult one, seeing as how the guy's so tall and so stiff and so very, very dead.

They figure out how to get him out from behind the toilet and the tub, and they do it by each placing a foot just above the guy's shoulders and pulling his arms up at wrong angles. The right shoulder snaps after a couple seconds of maneuvering, the pop echoes off the bathroom mirror. It sounds more like a small explosion inside a paper bag. The left shoulder is more troublesome; it takes both guys to bend it back and forth before it finally snaps. Sammy steps outside the bathroom and I help the coroner's guys lift the body, standing it up in the doorway of the room. He's heavier than I expected, too. Even with his head still bent all the way forward, his forehead could touch the frame at the top of the door. After a moment of standing there in silence, the three of us holding up this cold, hard body in the doorway, we slowly realize that there isn't a way to jimmy him through the door.

"OK," one of the coroner's guys says, "use the bathtub." I follow their lead as they lean him over toward the sink, his broken arms waving at his sides like tubes on a windchime, and lift one of his legs over the lip of the tub. One of the guys holds the torso straight against the sink while the other steps into the tub, and chunks of dried mud flake off onto the fish shapes stuck to the bottom to keep someone from falling. They flip the body around, so that the one against the sink is holding the dead man face down in his arms, and for a moment it looks like he's holding a drunken friend, someone who just needs to vomit and lament and sleep it off. His knees are on the edge of the tub, his feet against the wall. "Can you hold him here?" the one in the tub says to me, pointing at the guy's waist. I try to hold him steady around his hips as the guy with the torso pulls him closer, leaning back against the mirror and the wall to give his partner some working room.

The knees won't give. There's cartilage there that's a lot stronger, sinews that can't be torn as easily as shoulders. I want to get out of there. I start to look around the room at all the work Sammy and I still have to do, so I try to hurry the process by calling Sammy in to take my job. He does so reluctantly, because he hates helping out with stuff he doesn't get paid for. I join the guy in the tub, and together we push the knee backwards until it breaks into itself, then we do the other one. Sammy steps back again after that, but I help them slide him out the door, bending his broken arms and legs in, because the flesh and muscle are still trying to straighten them again, so that he'll fit through the frame and into the waiting bag.

We hear the van doors close after the body is loaded. We turn the music up because the family has at long last been taken somewhere else, usually to some relative's house. I start to piece together the pump sprayer, fitting the hoses and nozzles together, snapping in a new bottle of TR-32, and for a moment I look up and see Sammy leaning on his knees, staring at the wall. I think he's looking at the smeared bloodstain on the tile that was hidden behind the head before, left when the convulsions probably caused the head to smack against the wall over and over. Sammy takes off his glove and shuffles forward a little. I can see that he's looking at the magazine rack that's attached to the wall next to the toilet. He reaches out a bare hand and I see the darkened tattoo on the top of it, La Virgen de Guadalupe surrounded by her aura of stars and lightning, and with this holy hand he gently touches a magazine, an issue of *Dog Fancy*. He lifts it a little and stares at the cover, then shakes his head, slips the glove back on, and starts to work on the bloodstain.

"Main," he says, "de dogs are like us, but better."

Marla

Doug Whippo

"HERE. PUT THIS ON YOUR TONGUE."

On the tip of his index finger Mitch held a small piece of white paper. "Go ahead, Jelly. If it doesn't kill you, it just might make you free. Either way you come out a winner."

Mitch gave himself an approving smile in the rearview mirror just as the headlights of a passing car flashed across his face. I'll always remember how ghostly and white he looked in that instant.

We sat shivering in his car a week before Christmas. I watched the slowly falling snow leave a fine white layer on the limbs of trees, on the roofs of houses, on the sidewalks, and smelled the pine-forest air freshener of his car, and I was afraid. This time every year found the two of us commemorating Mom's death by doing something fucked up. Tonight Mitch had brought along three hits of windowpane acid. The finest trip you'll ever take without wings was how Mitch explained it.

Mitch *loved* acid. Mitch *loved* drugs. He *loved* alcohol, pot, coke, and speed. All the good stuff, as he put it. And for a few years he was always on something, in varying quantities, and somehow he managed to keep it all together.

Mitch nudged me with his elbow. "C'mon! What's the big deal?" He shrugged, looked out the window and whispered in despair, "Only a piece of paper, Jelly. Think Mom would like to see you behave so disrespectfully?" I rolled my eyes and gave up. I opened my mouth and Mitch stabbed that little white piece of paper onto my tongue and ordered me to swallow and told me I was a good boy.

I gulped the hit down. "How long before it starts to work?"

"In an hour we'll be flying, little brother," Mitch said, rubbing his hands with glee. I watched him as he deposited a hit on his tongue and swallowed, madly smacking his lips.

"Yummy," he crooned. "Let's grab a beer while we wait."

Out of the car and into the Blue Note, a bar in Wicker Park. The place was bathed in a soft, velvety red light. Several old men hunched over pints of beer at the bar, and as we moved past them towards the booths in the back I saw one of the cocktail waitresses, clad in black jeans and a turtleneck sweater, arguing with one of the bartenders. She stood at the service bar hurling words at him under her breath. Her voice was raspy and hurt. He glared at her with his arms folded, gritting his teeth and a comic half-smile on his face. He was the bouncer type: bushy brown goatee, tattooed forearms, shiny bald head, tight T-shirt, and sinewy shoulders. Bars and dance clubs all over Wicker Park employ his type for hipster effect. They must grow them out in the country somewhere.

We slid into one of the red leather booths along the side wall. Frantic flowing jazz music spilled out of the overhead speakers. Mitch cracked his knuckles and smiled. "Let's have a beer and some schnapps, Jelly."

The girl in black, her white skin bristling with anger, stomped over to our booth. She looked us over, then glared back at the bartender, who leaned over the bar and smoked a cigar while chatting idly with one of the old men.

"Son of a bitch!" she whispered. Her eyes were broken and watery. She peered down into her order pad and grabbed a pencil from her apron pocket. "Sorry, guys," she said. "Cocktail?"

"What's the matter?" I asked. She flung her head in the direction of the bartender. "Asshole boyfriend is tending bar tonight," she said, spitting the words out. A splash of bitterness crossed her face.

Mitch gave her a big, warm, hearty smile. "What you need, sister, is a night on the *town*. Why don't you just chuck this place in, tell the guy to fuck off, and come out with us?" Mitch reached into his coat for the leftover packet of acid he had and waved it at her, much the way a hypnotist uses a watch to put someone under a spell. "We're taking a little trip tonight, and I've got one hit left. Take it and your troubles won't seem too bad. In fact, when you come back to earth you probably won't even remember the guy's name. We could use the company." He wagged his eyebrows at her and kept his gaze steady and true right on her.

It was the kind of thing Mitch could get away with. He was the only person I ever knew who could be obnoxious, brazen, and charming at the same time, and people, especially women, would fall for it. He never said anything rude, but he pushed the envelope a lot with people and, to be fair, he took his share of rejection, but it never held him back. In fact, people loved him for that very same quality.

She looked at him, biting her lip. What he'd said was bold enough to make everyone in the bar stop what they were doing and listen in for a second. At least that's what it felt like.

She shrugged and frowned at Mitch. "Ever heard of rent, big guy? It's due in a week. I've got forty-two bucks in the bank. I haven't bought any Christmas presents for my parents, and I have a sick dog at home that needs a vet. I can't just 'chuck it in,' as you so quaintly put it." She stopped and took a breath, and a tear gathered in her eye and ran down the bright redness of her cheek. She dropped her eyes to the floor and bit her lip.

"Aww, hey," Mitch said, softening his voice. "Hey, there."

"The fucker is cheating on me. I just found out." Her face looked like it was breaking in about ten different places.

Mitch sucked in air over his teeth. "That bastard!" he said. This was funny to me, because I knew he had done the same thing to at least twelve women.

I reached out and took her hand. "My name's Jelly," I said, "that's my brother, Mitch." She looked at us blankly for a second, then gave a short laugh. "Marla. My name is Marla." She had a white pearl earring in her nose. She smiled. I'd never seen anyone smile like her. "Let me get you guys your drinks. First one is on the house. I don't care what the asshole bartender says." We ordered a couple pints and shots of peach schnapps. I watched her march off to the bar, her shoulders flung out as if readying herself for battle. She was beautiful. A few minutes later she returned with our drinks and left to look after the other customers.

We sat and nursed our beers. I kept waiting for the exact moment when the acid would kick in, expecting some grand rush of feeling, like the drug would announce itself with trumpets. Mitch calmly smoked a cigarette and watched our new friend Marla work the bar. He reminded me of a caged cheetah tracking the movements of a squirrel that danced just beyond the reach of its claws. After a while she disappeared, the bar began to fill up, and my heart started to race.

And then it began. Everything changed at once. The red lights shifted and shimmered, the floor moved slowly from side to side as if the whole bar was coasting over massive ocean waves. I felt an electric surge snake through my stomach. I looked at Mitch. He was calm and smiling, his eyes shining like rubies. His scruffy brown beard seemed alive with worms wiggling every which way. He winked at me. "It's here, Jelly. It's time. Let's go!"

He glided out from the booth and pulled me with him through the crowd. Their voices were harsh, like sandpaper. Their mouths snapped like the jaws of strange insects. I couldn't wait to get out of there.

A cool, pepperminty rush of cold winter air hit my face as we left. My fingernails tingled. Everything I touched was alive with spirits; even the door handle of the car felt skinlike and human as I gave it a pull. I giggled, my voice strange, not my own. Mitch started up the car. He said he wanted to head out to O'Hare Airport.

"The lights in the terminals are really groovy. You'll love it," he says.

He started to pull away. And then Marla burst from the door of the bar, looked up and down the street, spotted our car, and ran full out for us, waving her arms like she was fleeing the Lord's only holy fire. I rolled down the window. "Let me in! Let me in!" she shouted, pounding the roof of the car. "I want to come with. I told him to fuck off! I quit! Let's go!" I opened the door and she dove into the back seat, shivering and laughing. She smelled of patchouli.

Mitch shot me a triumphant glance. "All right! Fuck yeah!" He tossed her the little packet of acid. "Quick! Take a hit. You got some catching up to do!" Then he raced into the traffic and headed for O'Hare.

At the airport we stumbled through the terminals, threading our way through crowds of travelers: worn-out women with children in tow and solitary frowning businessmen burying their faces in paperwork. People pulled suitcases behind them or lugged massive backpacks. The floor was like snow, the overhead lights, too. I breathed the white air.

Every few minutes an incandescent voice falls from the ceiling making announcements about arrivals and departures. People scurry to and fro, their faces so serious, so *fraught*, so unhappy, I think, and I want to tell them what I now know: It will be OK. They will find love. It's right here in front of them. Love is everywhere. It's one of those absurd moments of pure truth that can only be attributed to the effects of a hallucinogen. "Love is everywhere," I say out loud, but the words sound funny and I start to laugh so hard I almost fall over. People stop and stare. I manage to control myself and run ahead.

Mitch and Marla walked together. Mitch talked and talked at her. He looked like a prophet, with his bushy beard, his long flowing hair, throwing his rap at Marla, who kept pace with him and looked up into his face with her lovely brown eyes. She seemed pulled right into his orbit, without question. It didn't surprise me. I'd seen it dozens of times. He always had a woman around. But this was different. Through the electric dazzle of the acid I felt a charge of jealousy, my cheeks flushed.

Soon the intensity of the airport, the gleaming faces, the loud voices chase us back to the car and Mitch wants to drive to the Lake and watch the sunrise. It is near dawn. Mitch drives slowly, the radio is blaring, and I turn around to look at Marla lying across the back seat. She's curled up like a baby; her hands shield her eyes and the shadows of streetlights splash across her body. Her face changes from horror to hilarity every few seconds.

"I really liked him!" she says. "I really did."

I reach over and take her hand. It feels so small, like the wing of a bird.

"I thought he loved me," she says. I lean over and touch her face; it's so smooth, cool like marble.

My heart aches and pounds. I want to fight for her, all of sudden. No one can touch her. I don't even want Mitch to so much as look at her.

She holds my hand, strokes my knuckles. "Your skin feels nice," she says. She looks up at me. Her pupils are huge, fluttering; her eyes are black as ink. "So you're the little brother, huh?"

I squeeze her hand. "I'm not so much a little brother anymore," I say. She raises herself up and stares out the window. We move past old warehouses and run-down three-flats, deserted-looking strip malls, and barren apartments. The horizon is rimmed with orange light, and soft streaks of blue shoot across the sky. Frost coats the windows of cars and sidewalks. We're almost at the Lake. Mitch is lost in the music, humming along to himself and tapping the steering wheel. He's forgotten about us.

I watch Marla. I see something unknowable and sad about her, and it's something I want to possess. She traces a finger along the window.

"You boys," she says, "you're all the same." And my heart clutches and I want to shake her and whisper in her tiny ear that no, no, that's not true, it isn't true, but Mitch breaks the moment. "Just in time," he shouts. "Sun's almost here!"

The car lurches to a stop. Mitch has parked in front of the Lake along Montrose Harbor. "C'mon. Let's go for a walk," he says, opening the door.

Cold morning air floods the car. I stretch and step out, my body stiff. The acid has mellowed a bit. I don't feel as giddy. The edge has drained off a bit. My eyes feel sharp, like needles.

We stand side by side along the lake. The sun comes up huge, glowing, burning orange fire. It's a grand, beautiful thing. Marla's cheeks turn rosy. Mitch, breathing deep, stretches his arms out wide, like he's reaching out for the sun.

"Makes you really want to love the world, doesn't it?" he says, glancing at us. Marla nods slowly. "Maybe," she says. "Maybe not."

Hitchhiking

Conrad Jacobson

IT'S THE KIND OF NIGHT THAT FEELS LIKE THE CLOSING SCENES OF A SOMBER film, something sparse and minimalistic, something heady, something French, a movie where I play the commanding lead role. Damsel in distress perhaps? Evil stepmother? Seductress? Try bumbling fool, try inappropriate comic relief.

Driving home from a weekend in the city, well, Peoria, coming to the sleepy end of a three-hour trip, I reintroduce myself to the icons, the monuments of home. The now dormant fruit stand just off the expressway with its cheery smiling apple sign: STOP ON BY, Y'ALL! the apple bellows in tall hand-painted script. The marshmallow-shaped grain elevators can be seen miles away, cylindrical silhouettes, these speechless, spooky altars of harvest, and then, past the railroad tracks, a string of small towns with dramatic, slightly mythological names: Seneca, Griffen, Fontana, and after that, East Fontana. In these towns, there are taverns where old acquaintances work long shifts, grocery stores where former students mumble greetings and give me change, libraries where old babysitters read stories to children, and cemeteries where our parents sleep.

When I reach the edge of Greyslake, my final destination, it is the tall, elegant Lutheran church I see first, the church that the highway curls around at the last moment so that, in the dark of night, it appears that the road runs straight into it, right into the sanctuary and then out the back door and into the town.

The church is illuminated from below, immaculate, unlike the rest of the murky horizon. And there is such a stifling stillness outside the car that if I squint and sort of lean back, take it all in, it feels like I am the only person in the world. It feels like that's how the movie ends, with everybody gone but me.

Which is why I am especially surprised, if not a bit startled, to see a lone figure standing against the sign that sits at the edge of the city limits, the sign that reads, in serious state-issued print, *Greyslake, Pop. 650.* But as soon as I see the outline of the figure, the tall and lanky frame, the tussle of curly hair, the slender thumb up and out, beckoning me, I know exactly who it is, and exactly what I'm going to do.

Waldo was a student of mine not too long ago—a year, two years, I can't remember—a quiet and generally unimpressive pupil who excelled at discerning what the minimum requirement was and then grounding himself to that with extreme intention—one of those kids. What set him apart was simply that he was the son of Taylor Reed, a bit of a local celebrity. Taylor was, by Greyslake standards, affluent. The owner of a construction company, most of the orange trucks that spotted the highways and small building frames bore his name and slogan: Reed Construction—When You Want it Done Right! As Mr. Jorgensen, the athletic director at Greyslake High School where I work, once put it, in his blunt and biting way, "That motherfucker's got hotels on Park Place and Boardwalk." And, most certainly, as far as Greyslake and all of surrounding Kimball County was concerned, he did.

I had always thought of Waldo as spoiled, in the dopey yet haughty way that most Midwestern teenagers are. They were like little old Southern billionaires trapped in young bodies, all full of talk and false confidence, all hollow eyes and *yahoos*. It was like part of them had grown old too fast—quite possibly the part that enjoys growing old in the first place.

Waldo was different but also the same, just a slight shuffle to the side of the rest. He had always struck me as someone who expected a little too much out of life, but in a quiet and plotting way. He was also someone who, I was sure to note on his permanent record, never took instruction from a woman well, although I secretly feared it was only me he was stubborn with.

All and all, he was harmless, he did his work in a prompt and marginal fashion, showed up on time, kept his mouth shut. But it was the looks he gave, the squinty, suspicious glances that seemed to ask, *Who do you think you are?* During a lecture, passing in the hall, he always shot me a special glare that had filled me with a dull rage, a rage that I had all but forgotten until, that is, I ease on the brake and pull my car over to the shoulder, right in front of him.

In the headlights he looks older than the eighteen or nineteen he must be. Dressed in a long coat, a Greyslake Piranhas duffel bag at his side, he walks up to the passenger window. When I roll it down and he stoops and sees me, he frowns and, turning to the side mutters, "Shit," and then with equal distaste, "hey, Ms. Patterson."

"Hello, Waldo. Hop in," and looking forward at the green town sign, *Pop. 650*, with a bemused sigh I say, "let me drive you home."

He is tall, I notice, taller perhaps then I remember him. And I am glad we are not standing, glad that it is not obvious how much and how quickly he has changed, grown, and I have not. I am glad that he slumps low in his seat, his knees spread far apart, his hands dangling on his legs near his crotch, taking up as much space as he can in what I have come to call the *sitting pose of world-weary man*. He looks up at me and says nothing.

"So where were you going?" I ask, passing my own street and driving on to the large, gated semi-mansion just outside of town.

"Just—away for a little while. Like a couple months." He does not protest or plead with me, he knows better. He has, temporarily, lost.

"What are *you* doing driving around so late?" he asks. "Don't you gotta work tomorrow?"

"I went on a little vacation this weekend myself, took a little break."

"Where'd you go?"

"Away," I say playfully, and he nods and readjusts himself in his seat, positioning himself towards me with his elbows as if about to speak, but he says nothing.

I cut to the chase: "So why don't you tell me what's up? Why are you hitchhiking in the middle of the night, huh?" I summon my no-nonsense teacher sensibility, my tough-love motherly scorn. "Do you know how dangerous hitchhiking is these days?"

I say the words, the adult script, but I don't feel it. In truth I am excited by the whole notion, strangely comforted by the fact that people are still so bold and foolish, full of irresponsible, romantic ideas like these. I feel a jittery joy in my chest rise and fall, rise and fall. And underneath that whisper of almost forgotten anger, I am glad for him. Am glad, for some reason, that he is here right now, no matter what mood he is in.

Waldo sits still and says, in a dour tone, "A lot of things are dangerous, Ms. Patterson." I can do nothing to keep from laughing at this, the extreme concern in his voice, such feigned worldliness. It just makes me laugh. "I guess that's true," I say, but he just stares forward and frowns more. "A lot of things are dangerous, but that doesn't give you an excuse to seek them out. That's like if—" I pause and think for a moment, *Why do I feel this need all the time, this obligation to explain, to teach?* "It's like if everybody else's brains were exploding, just spontaneously exploding all over the world, and then I woke up one day and blew my brains out. It's just like that. Now does that make any sense?" I think, *No, Julie, no it doesn't.* And Waldo gives me a tilted look as if he agrees. He smiles, ever so slightly.

"Well, whatever, you know what I mean."

"I do?" he asks, his tone eking towards friendliness. I hold onto that, that soft voice of his. I have heard it, but never directed towards me.

"I hope one of us does," I say. And his smile breaks into sound, a dim but very real chuckle. I glance his way and make brief eye contact.

"I just wanted to get out of here, like you said, take a little break, that's all." The whine in his voice has gone, the spoiled nasal pleading that I remember so well.

I give up. "Yeah, I know what you mean," I slip into a confidential, friendly tone, what I have come to recognize as a tone all my own, although sometimes I have doubts. "Sometimes you just need to get away from *here*."

I say *here* like it's a poison, am actually surprised at how dismal I truly sound out loud, and for a flickering second I want to turn around and take him back to that stop sign. I want to give him a few hundred bucks and drive him to the airport and send him off myself. I want to tell him that *here* is not what here used to be. I want to tell him that *here* is a joke, and a bad one at that, without a punchline or plot. Here is like a sitcom, where everyone is a sidekick, no one the lead.

"But here is also home," I say, that urge toward responsible role model forcing itself out of me, taking charge.

"I guess," he says, begrudgingly, like a true student. "How long have *you* lived here?" he asks. I am stricken by his interest, and somewhat suspicious.

"Well, I grew up here," I say. "Then I moved away. Then I, recently, came back but just kind of . . ." I try to find the right words, ". . . kind of haven't left yet."

I pause. It startles me how easily I can sum everything up, how tightly time can be compacted. But it is the truth, that is what has happened. I was here, then I wasn't, and now, I am again. Sure, there are details, but that's all they are.

I turn into his long and winding driveway. "I'll take you to the door," I say, "unless . . ."

"Naw, go ahead." He waves his hand at the house, which can be seen in the far distance, on top of a hill, towering over the trees. "Nobody's home anyway."

The house is, like the Lutheran church, illuminated from the ground, gilded, I think, like a faraway beacon. The driveway is a few miles, winding up and down and through a light forest that glows blue and black, a tunnel of trees.

"So where is everyone tonight?" I ask.

"Well, it's just me and Taylor these days." I realize now that I had never met his mother, never put a female face to Waldo's name. "And he's away on business. Well, he's in Peoria."

"Really! That's where I just came from. What hotel did he stay at?" I ask.

Waldo pulls out a scrap of paper from his inside coat pocket, examines it and says, "the Claussen, room 515."

"Oh," I say, "how nice." I don't even know why I asked. I had stayed at the Happy Trails Motel, a twenty-room place just off the exit that advertised, rather proudly, *The Closest Beds to the Interstate!* It seemed the perfect place for what I assumed would be a quick getaway. It was also forty bucks a night. I became a teacher to validate a slightly antisocial bookishness in my youth and out of a vague civic duty, not for room service and a hot tub.

"We walked past the Claussen, I think. Or around there," I say.

The Claussen is the tallest building in Peoria, not necessarily an impressive feat, but I can assume the room offered more remarkable features than the color TV and ceiling fan I was promised.

"Where did you stay?" he asks, yawning.

"Oh, just some little cheap place. You know how it is . . . teacher's salary." When you teach high school you can throw out the words *teacher's salary* like a tragic badge of honor. There was a time when I enjoyed the sacrifice, when I thought of the low material rewards of my noble calling as a commendable thing. But lately, I find myself asking, how *can* I sell out? Is it too late? Who do I see about that? What dotted line can I sign? Lately, I find myself thinking, *Once in a while, dammit, a hot tub would be nice.* What was wrong with a hot tub? In a world where less and less was sacred, a world that shrunk and soured as it did, what was wrong with wanting a hot tub. *Really?*

"Who is *we?*" Waldo asks, sitting up in his seat.

"Oh, just an old friend."

I don't know why I am holding back. Is it because he is my former student? Because I want to maintain my image? My nonconversational, curt, and generally unimpressive image?

"My ex-husband," I blurt out.

"I didn't know you were married," he says, interested, although looking out the window, careful not to seem too friendly, keeping up his *own* image, I assume.

"Yep," is all I say, thinking only, *It's just details, not much more.*

"For how long?" he asks.

"About a year, less than that."

"How old were you?"

He is feeling bold for some reason, I can tell. Or rather, not feeling young and careful, not feeling like a lesser thing to me. Which is like boldness, I assume.

"About your age," I say, navigating the curving driveway slowly, cautiously.

"Hmph," he says. But then after a long pause and a squinty look my way, he says with a snap, "Wait a second, do you have a son? Or like a nephew or something?"

I pause, for drama I guess, and am careful to keep looking forward. "I had a son when I was married, well, sort of."

"Yeah, yeah, yeah. I remember a kid, when I was in grade school. You did the summer program then, when I was . . . six years old, or around there, and I remember your kid would come and sit around during class. He was a little guy then. What was his name?"

I am surprised that he remembers, because I barely do.

"His name is Jerry," I say.

I never liked the name, I'll admit it. I would have picked something vast and slightly regal—Truman perhaps or Anthony. Something that would sound good with the word saint in front of it. But his father had chosen Jerry—*Saint Jerry?*—but that was years before he ever met me.

"Jerry," Waldo repeats, "*Jerry.* Good name, real friendly. I like it." He nods with approval, like an old man, like his word is somehow law.

"So what's the story with that?" he asks, grinning at his own forwardness. I just stare straight ahead. "Or is it none of my business?" he says.

I smile and say nothing. Not because I don't want to tell the story, but because, truly, there is no story. That was the conclusion me and my ex-husband came to this weekend, that there was not enough plot between us. Separately we were fine, with ample room to explore and have adventures, but together we just stood still, unable to move from scene to scene, just alone on stage, jabbering on and on, the same cyclical monologue. He had brought this to my attention this weekend, our dramatic incompatibility, and joked that that was the only thing we really could talk about at great length—how we never had anything to talk about. It was funny, him saying that, for a while. And I admired his perspective, admired how he had grown so much in the decade or so since I had last seen him, and admired the fact that we wanted nothing to do with each other in such a cheerful and shruggish way.

But then there is Jerry. Not my son by birth, he kept saying, but I did raise him for that year. Sure I haven't seen him since and probably never will, but he was mine for that span of time, he really was, that is, before I screamed through the silence and left for good.

Now, though, in the car, I keep my mouth shut. I think Waldo knows a thing or two about female desertion, the motherly kind, maybe a bit too much, so I keep my mouth shut so that he'll do the same.

I creep up the last and steepest hill, climbing slowly and carefully along the narrow drive and say, feeling a bit bold myself, "Why did your parents name you Waldo? Or is that none of *my* business?" I don't know why I ask, other than I am curious and am suddenly stricken by the idea, with all this son talk, that I will probably never see this person again, this boy named Waldo.

"No, it's no secret. It was my great grandfather's name," he says. "My father always intended to call me Wally or William or David, that's my middle name." He tilts his head just a bit, and peers, his eyes thin slits. "But I made them call me Waldo when I was old enough."

"Why was that?"

"I guess because that's what he didn't want to call me. My grandfather was still alive when I was born and he owned the company. It was just a gesture on my dad's part, you know? I know how he feels about my grandfather so . . . it didn't really mean anything."

I laugh again, a high squeak, and he looks surprised. "So you chose to be called Waldo *out of spite*?" I can't help but find this funny, if not, in some weird indeterminable way, admirable.

He thinks about it and then nods reassuringly, "Yeah, I guess I did. I just think of it as a reminder."

I nod, wondering what he means, but also wondering if Jerry will ever renounce his own cartoonish name.

I slow to a near stop when I reach the turnabout that curves dramatically to the front door of the house. I instinctively lean forward and look up at the four stories of bland neoclassical architecture, and I realize that I've never seen the house this close, and also that, deep down in the depths of all the other silly, insignificant wants, I have always wanted to.

"Nice place," I say when I notice Waldo watching me gawk.

"Yeah, it is nice," he shrugs. I come to a slow stop in front of the long white porch, and with a slightly impish grin he asks, "You want to check it out? The floor in the billiards room is glass. Or it's some synthetic something, I don't really know, but you can see through it."

"I thought that was just a myth," I say, and feel a strange charge in my limbs, something electrical and warm. "Actually," I say, opening the door, "I've always wanted to."

"Come on in."

He walks up the stairs, me following at what I consider a safe distance. I feel my breath quicken, and when he reaches the top step the porch light clicks on and we are suddenly bathed in light. For some reason, possibly because I've been in quiet darkness for the last three hours, I let out a stifled gasp, and when he turns around explaining about the motion sensor I blush, stop walking, and blurt out the first thing that pops into my head.

"We had one of those at my old house, on the porch. My son and I used to stand on the lawn, just outside of the sensor and when the light shut off we would run to the street and the first one who reached the light and turned it on, you know, would win."

He laughs at the story, perplexed but amused. "You'd be a pretty good mom," is all he says as he walks up to the door and jiggles the knob.

"I locked it," he says. "I forgot."

"Don't you have a key?"

"Yeah, but I left it on my dad's desk. Sort of a symbolic gesture," he says grinning, and then he turns to me and does the strangest thing—he winks at me. Just a quick wink, as if we're about to do something devious, as if he's letting me in on a dirty joke.

"You want to do me a favor?" he asks, his grin growing.

"Maybe," I say and he nods down the wall.

"You see that second window? It's open, it won't lock, but it's really heavy. I can open it and hold it for a few seconds, you think you can slide through and unlock the door from the inside?"

"Why don't I just hold the window open?" I say.

"It's *really, really* heavy."

I consider it for a moment. "Sure," I say, and then for some reason I scan the surrounding forest, making sure it's just him and me.

The window is high so I have to raise my leg over the bottom edge, swivel my body through and then slip the other leg in, but quickly because I can see the side of Waldo's face turning red, although he cannot see me, and those big veins on his neck about to pop through his skin.

"You in?" Waldo asks in a strained whisper, his body pressed against the window, which *is*, in fact, very heavy, his face turned to the side.

"Yeah," I say and he lets the window slam shut with a snap. He then shakes out his arms, looks inside squinting and points towards the door, mouthing something. With the porch light on I can tell he can't see me and is looking just above my shoulder, trying to find where I've disappeared to. So I just stand there for a second, just a moment, and look at him. He looks like a true adult, the square jaw, that serious, contemplative brow. Through the smudged window he looks different, like a different character in my story than the one he really is.

Under different circumstances, under different stars perhaps, he could have been my son, or my . . . what's the right word? . . . *companion*? I could have stayed in Greyslake and wooed the local millionaire just as easily as I could pick Waldo up at the local bar in a few years, when I am sultry and jaded, a young old maid, and he is of age, wide-eyed and hungry for something risky. He looks back, peering, wondering if I am still there, and then turns towards the door.

To the left, down the short hall, is a large room with a tall stone fireplace, leather couches, towering bookcases filled with books. Everything is dark and cold, as pristine and still as a museum exhibit.

I walk towards the front door, but once my shoes hit the hardwood floor and the heavy click and clack bounces around the emptiness, I feel a sneaking panic in my chest, like I'm breaking the rules. Still, I let out a laugh, a single high-pitched *HA!* that pops out so loud that I tiptoe across the floor for some reason, my footsteps just a patter. In the hallway, the wall to the left is lined with windows that cast squares of light onto the floor. I see Waldo walking ahead of me outside, towards the door. I walk down the hall and into a large entryway with no windows, just the front door to my left, a large spiral staircase to my right. The room, with its two-story ceilings and its drooping yet quaint chandelier, looks oppressive in its vastness. I imagine coming home to this, imagine living in this, never feeling close to anyone amongst all this—space, all this gaudy privilege.

Along the right wall, the only artwork in the room is a collection of plaques and awards and framed newspaper clippings from the local Greyslake paper. There are some from the business section: *Local Entrepreneur Draws*

National Attention one reads, *The Man Behind the Machines*, reads another, a picture of Taylor, arms crossed, standing in the raised bucket of a backhoe staring defiantly into the horizon, looking ridiculous. And then there are ones of Waldo, from his days in high school, as the baseball team captain. The picture shows him in his uniform posing before the scoreboard, his hair long, scattered across his baby face. He is not smiling but rather squinting in the intense, tough-guy, seriousness that I have always associated with young men who love their mothers too much. *Where's Waldo?* the headline reads, and then below it, *Local teen stands out in the crowd*.

Waldo knocks on the door, and the hollow snap of his knuckles echoes throughout the room. I let him in.

"You get lost?" he asks, striding through the door.

I don't say anything but am stricken at how different he looks in the picture, which is only a year or two old, and I think how he is not that kid, that stoic, eternal youth, but this strange evolving thing, blooming and wilting at the same time.

"You want to see the billiards room?" He seems eager, for him, wanting to see someone marvel at the world he has lost all marvel for, I assume. But I resist; he is, after all, not my son or my equal, not a companion in any way—although he could be, or could have been.

"Maybe some other time," I say. "I've got to get home. I have to work tomorrow."

He nods and with an "OK," shows me the door.

Out on the porch, my little car looks so beaten and familiar, so *appropriate*. I turn wondering what to say, how to end this. "I'll see you around," is all I can manage with a wave and a nervous laugh.

"No you won't," he says. There was no challenge in his voice, no threat, just fact.

"Well, then." I have run out of words. "Good luck, I guess." And then I wink, for the first time in my life, I wink at him and smile.

He nods, satisfied, and turns inside.

"Wait," I call when he is halfway in the door, and he stops but does not turn around. "Why were you on the wrong side of the road?" I say.

"What?" he asks, his back still toward me.

"Why were you on the right side of the road? If you wanted to leave town . . . why weren't you on the left side, with the leaving traffic?"

He turns his head, and for the first time he gives me a genuine smile, a wide, adult, sad smile. "I was, for a long time. But nobody was going that way."

And with that he walks inside and lets the door click shut behind him.

Outside, in the dim yellow of the porch light, I can see the hazy glow of Greyslake peeking through the distance from behind the trees. And I think of my students, my sweetly spoiled kids. I think of seeing them tomorrow morning, just going through the motions, all of them just waiting for me to be done with them.

I feel a very real, very childish need to burst forth in energy, a desire to run for the sake of running—to run to the car and just drive, somewhere. I feel a strange need for motion, even if that motion just leads to home and, let's face it, it probably will. *When the light goes off,* I say aloud, moving to the bottom stair just outside of the sensor, *when the light goes off I'm gone.*

I sit and think of Jerry, what he's like now, what he thinks of me, and imagine picking him up one day on the side of the road when we are both older and wandering elsewhere. I lean forward and watch the stars, my breath a wisp of fog. I breath in heavily once, twice, and on the third breath the light shuts off, and when it does, I run.

A Princess and a Guy Like Me

Chris DeGuire

NAOMI. SHE COULDN'T'VE BEEN GIVEN ANY OTHER NAME, COULD SHE? IT rolled off the tongue and tingled over the lips. Nigh-oh-me. She seemed as exotic as the name made her out to be, but she was more of a daddy's girl, truth be told. Daddy's *hot* little girl who liked to drink beer and smoke pot and sleep around the store. Well, with two of the third-shift stockers anyways—that was the scuttlebutt.

We occasionally took breaks together. We both worked mostly days, me in produce and her in the bakery, at opposite ends of Aisle One. I wanted her bad, really bad, but she was out of my league, *waayyyy* out. She was tall, slender, her big, curly, red hair usually tied back. She chain smoked and on most days wore too much makeup, hence the exotic-ness. And did I mention slim and slender? My dad liked big women. My brother liked big women. I preferred them slim, tiny enough to poke a hole through, if you know what I mean. I suppose that I wanted the opposite of me—shorter than average, called "big guy" by most folks on the street (and I hated that), short hair, clean-cut, wardrobe consisting mainly of old concert T-shirts—and Naomi was definitely that. And most hot girls didn't give fat guys—no matter how nice—the time of day.

One night, a rare night we both worked, in the middle of a blizzard, I went outside to find my little black hatchback buried under about five inches of snow. I fired it up and began brushing it off. Next to me, Naomi had parked her little black sports car she hadn't paid a dime for. I had forgotten my gloves and the snow swirled around me like a tornado when I saw this silver sedan pull up behind me and stop. A little old man with white hair and a long black coat jumped out and began cleaning the snow off her car. He smiled at me and happily brushed the snow clean off.

"Yep, that was my *dad*," she sing-songed the next day in the break room. She had an adorable, if ever so slight, Italian accent, but scratchy from the cigarettes.

"I don't know," I said to my manager, TJ, in our own cooler later that day. "Whaddya think? A princess and a guy like me . . ."

"No," he said with a laugh.

One day in June me and Naomi were on break discussing horoscopes and she mentioned how she was learning to read tarot cards and was into fortune telling.

"I've always wanted a tarot reading," I said, sitting across from her as she blew smoke out the side of her mouth.

"Well, I could do you, Chuck," she replied, reaching across with her free hand to smack me on the shoulder. "I need to practice." Everyone else called me Charlie.

So a week later she was at my apartment. I was a *Star Wars* geek, a collector of everything since the late 70s. And with all the new movies, you couldn't turn around in my place without knocking over an R2-D2 or a Darth Vader or even a Gandalf from *The Lord of the Rings*. I figured this geekiness was mostly to blame for my being a thirty-year-old virgin.

She sat cross-legged on the floor a few feet from the TV, the tall light behind her on low, giving the place a candlelight glow. I sat facing her, my legs stretched out in front of the TV. She had a bottle of Miller Lite on one side of her, a small paperback that she referred to every couple of cards on the other. I nursed my own beer.

She dealt out these large cards in a crosslike pattern between us, some face up, some face down. I must admit I wasn't paying too much attention to the cards, but to her. I mean, I was truly interested in what the cards told. I believed a little in magical, mystical, hocus-pocus. But what had me transfixed was Naomi, and to be more precise, her rack. She had on this tight yellow polo unbuttoned at the top, and as she dealt the cards her little butt the size of my fist would rise up ever so slightly off the floor as she leaned over, giving me a peek at her cleavage. I had this problem (is it really a problem?) of looking down women's tops. Just a peek was all I asked. And Naomi had these cute, delicious, apple-sized tits perched high up on her chest and poking right out at you, especially under that tight polo. They *invited* you to look at them. I mean, if I had tits I'd probably never leave the house, right?

And even though this was just to be an innocent tarot card reading, maybe, just maybe, tonight would be the night.

So Naomi sat there, concentrating real hard because she's only done this one other time and she doesn't want to fuck it up, and every time she leaned forward I was entranced. Gawking, probably. Salivating, actually.

She'd look up every now and then, smile, see me looking at her, and return to the cards.

When she finished she started to read them in some strange order. I wasn't watching. She translated most of them from her book, reading verbatim.

"You hold a lot of emotion in," she said, holding the book over her lap, looking up at me.

Duh!

She got some of the cards confused and we talked about the Death card, which had not come up during this particular reading.

"It doesn't necessarily mean death," she explained, "maybe the end of a relationship or a phase of your life." Then she said that it may come up during a future reading, which I should probably wait a few weeks before having.

But after learning that I'd become relatively well-off financially in some years and that I'd live a long life we went out onto the balcony because she wanted to smoke a joint.

We went out into the cool summer night and sat on the white plastic chairs and looked out across the little parking lot and the train tracks behind my building. The sky was clear and full of stars. She lit up while I started another beer. The neighbor kids downstairs shrieked and laughed every few minutes. Lights from the ball diamonds around the corner cast a soft glow down the lot.

I had some fun but I didn't really want to get high. This was as far as it was going to go, I was sure. I just wanted her to leave now. Get in her car and go. Go anywhere. My interest in the evening had passed.

Always in motion is the future, said the voice in my head.

"You're a nice guy, Chuck," she said quietly. I looked up at her and she was looking at me.

That was me, the nice guy. Nice guys finish last, I wanted to say. Or, no, nice guys *don't* finish. At all.

I laughed to myself. That was a good one. Should write that one down.

Always with you it can't be done, said the voice.

"You're thoughtful and considerate," she went on, turning to exhale across and over the railing. "You're not like most guys. Most men are dicks."

"Like Dave and Sam?" I asked, the two stockers she had been rumored with.

"You *know* about them?" she squealed, laughing.

"The whole store practically knows."

"Ha! Yeah, well . . . they were a couple of dicks all right."

I sat back and finished my beer. My feet kicked absently at the bottom of the railing, and I glanced up at her. She was still staring at me. Was she? No. She couldn't be. But she was. Totally. She sat back, too, her jeans pinching her crotch, her perky tits poking straight out like some sort of beacons.

"When do I get to see your room?" she asked.

"Beg pardon?" I asked. Had I heard right? Was she trying to develop a sense of humor or was I going deaf? How high was she? Could she get that stoned off one beer and a joint?

She got up and slid open the screen door.

"Come on," she said.

I sat there and looked at her profile in the light, her curves, her everything.

"I brought condoms if you don't have any," she replied matter-of-factly as if this had been her intention all night long—to seduce me. "It's just sex, sweetie."

Well, *there* was the understatement of the year. But she just winked, took my hand, and pulled me after her.

Well, I thought, here goes nothing.

"Oh, my God," she muttered as I flipped on the light and we stepped into my room. "Look at all this stuff."

My room was anything but romantic. Books piled on piles of books and toys everywhere, rows and rows of action figures in the packages hanging on the walls. Embarrassing.

"These are so cool," she went on, making her way to the bed in the corner. Well, maybe not so embarrassing.

"My God, how many do you have? Do you have any Princess Leias? Yep." She looked up and pointed a few out. "One . . . two. Oh, look. A whole row of them. And Yodas. I *love* Yoda. And Obi-Wan. That guy is so hot."

As much as I would've gladly given her my dissertation on the Jedi, she spun around and grabbed me by the collar, falling back to sit on my bed. She let go and I nearly fell on top of her. I switched on the little reading lamp on the desk next to my bed that I used to look at the magazines I had stashed under my bed that I jerked off to. She sat on the edge and looked at me, smiling. I went back and turned off the ceiling light and when I turned back to her she was peeling off her polo, a lacy red bra underneath. Then she stood and shimmied out of her jeans, revealing a matching thong, her skin glowing in the soft light that was as close to candlelight as I could get.

I stumbled out of my jeans as she came up to me again and pressed her body to mine, her mouth exploring mine, her tongue poking out and pushing its way into mine momentarily. She tasted good. Well, like beer. But she smelled good.

Could she tell that was my first kiss? She must've been able to sense my fear. She must've been able to feel my boner poking at her.

But I instinctively kissed her back and guided her back onto the bed, her sitting, then sweeping her legs onto the bedspread. I crawled up next to her and then straddled her. She reached back and undid her bra and flung it off to the side, the wall side where it crashed into a row of Darth Mauls and Han Solos. She leaned back against the head bars and stretched her body out and reached for the sides of her thong. But I grabbed it, too, and she let go, letting me slide it down her legs. Was she thinking that I knew what I was doing? Because *I* sure as hell didn't have a fucking clue!

I'll give this a try, I thought.

Do or do not. There is no try.

She lay on her back as I slid the thong off and tossed it aside. She was as smooth as a cue ball. I couldn't have sex with her, though. Sex was love. This wasn't love.

You are not ready, the voice said.

But I had to do something. I had this naked hottie on my bed and I couldn't pass it up. I somehow had to thank her for doing this much. So I reached behind her and took two of my pillows and slid them under her butt and then proceeded to finger her. I half-sat between her and the wall to get a good angle. She had her knees up and I kinda curled around her leg, using my right elbow as a brace against the bedspread. I traced around her lips with my right hand and used my left to steady myself on her thigh and stuck my finger in and tickled around the hood until her clit poked through. She laughed and moaned and then I dove in. I used my tongue to spell out her name – several times. She slapped at the bed and convulsed and flexed her hips a dozen times, her butt rising and falling, me almost biting my lip when she did this. She screeched and squealed and laughed so hard that I'm sure not only the rugrats downstairs were frozen in their tracks but her *dad* probably heard and was on his way over to kick my ass up through my esophagus.

I did this for about half an hour or so until she just lay still, smiling, and raised her head as far as she could to look at my face buried between her legs. My tongue ached, throbbed.

"Oh . . . my . . . God," she said, short of breath. My ears were still ringing. She swallowed. "That was the most . . . *incredible* thing anyone has ever done. Where in the *fuck* did you learn those moves?"

Like I'd tell her that was my first time. I just figured she'd get a kick out of it. God knows I've seen enough porn and read enough bad erotic fiction and seen enough Dr. Fucking Phil's to know what women might enjoy.

"Do me now," she moaned and rested her head back down. My tongue was sticky and tired and I was tired. She tasted like sweat but still smelled nice, like lilacs, not too . . . well, fishy, like I had thought. And I was so ready to come. I felt like I had been going to since she led me off the balcony. I couldn't believe I hadn't touched myself.

"No," I said after a pause. I wanted to tell her that I wanted to save the actual act for someone I loved, even if it meant waiting forever.

She propped herself on her elbows and looked at me quizzically.

"What about you?" she asked. "You want me to suck you or something, 'cause after *that* performance you can fuck my *ears* if you want."

She rolled her head around lazily, dreamily.

I flinched my lip.

"What?" she asked. "Name it."

I wanted to slide in between her tits. So I told her and she said whatever I wanted. So I straddled her and she pushed her tits together around my dick as I went to town, ejaculating in a matter of minutes, nailing her chest and face with about a gallon of sperm. She laughed, licked a bit off her lips as I sat on her belly, out of breath, for a few minutes. Then I rolled off her near the wall. She turned to me, grabbed my still hard dick, and kissed me deeply, tongue drilling me, and then she rolled the other way and out of the bed.

She showered, came back into my room and got dressed. I sat on my bed, dressed already and watched her slip back into her clothes.

"I don't know how in the world you don't have a girlfriend," she said, and leaned over and kissed me, swirling her tongue around like it was some sort of acrobat.

I told TJ about this the next day. His mouth hit the cooler floor as he stopped stacking cases of apples on his cart. I didn't give him all the details, however.

"You, my friend," he said, "are more of a stud than I'll *ever* be." And then he added, "Charlie," he put his hands on my shoulders and looked hard into my eyes, "you need to find Jesus."

Then we both laughed.

For whatever reason, after that night, Naomi made it her personal mission to get me high. She thought I'd get a kick out of it. So while on break one day I told her I'd think about it, getting high, and maybe she'd want to come over for some drinks or something that evening. Part of me was hoping we might fool around again. But a bigger part of me told me to leave her alone. Hang out, nothing else. I was kinda scared of what may happen, especially since I wasn't in love with her.

She said, yeah, she'd come by, and so she came over to my apartment on the second floor and we had some beers while we watched the Brewers' game. It was pretty hot out so I had put on the air conditioner, making it like an ice box, the way I liked it. She wasn't there more than five minutes and her nipples were poking right through her light blue pullover.

We snuggled on the side of the couch by the table with my Clone Wars figures on it. Six-legged beasts, clones, droids, Jedi, Sith, bounty hunters, maybe thirty figures fighting around this giant arena playset.

The tall white light behind the table cast a shadow on the green curtains that covered the sliding balcony doors. I set up a TV tray in front of my toy table and we set our drinks there, her handing me mine when I was thirsty. She sat against the side and I sat right up against her, my right arm draped around her slender lower back and under her top, my fingers running up and down her skin. She smoked a cigarette while we watched the game, blowing it out toward the curtain. If she was gonna break out the pot I was gonna decline. I didn't feel right. But I couldn't believe how she let me sit next to her.

Everything is proceeding as I have foreseen.

So we sat there for a bit, not talking much, watching the game. She sighed every now and then, her face kind of sad-looking, I thought, mouth overturned a bit. Or maybe she was up to something. She didn't look at me with her brown eyes and when I turned to look at her, her hair tied back, all thick and curly, all I could see was the side of her mouth, her long, thin lips that seemed to stretch on forever.

"What's up?" I asked finally.

"Nothing."

Then she turned to face me, leaned over, and kissed me quickly on the mouth and smiled, her shoulders scrunching up as she connected.

"When was your first kiss?" she asked playfully, still looking at me, hands clasped at her little crotch, the denim of her jeans worn and faded between her legs.

Like I was going to tell her that the one she just planted on me was my first real kiss. I settled, with, "Oh, jeez," and curled my lip as if in thought and looked down at her legs.

"Don't remember?" she giggled.

"Oh, I remember," I said, trying to sound cool like Fonzie.

She kissed me again.

"What was that for?" I smiled at her. Her lips tasted sweet.

She shrugged. I started getting hard.

"I like you, Chuck," she said quietly. "You're not like most guys."

"Thanks," I answered, shrugging, unsure of how to respond, "I guess . . ."

I shifted and brought my right leg up, curled it under me, knee touching her thigh as she stretched and grabbed her beer, took a swig, and set it back on the tray.

"When was *your* first kiss?" I asked as she wiped her mouth, thinking I'd turn the tables.

"Ohh," she stammered, curling herself up into the corner of the couch, hands clasped and stretching to her crotch again. "You don't wanna hear that."

"Sure I do."

She let go of herself, relaxed her legs, turned to look at me, and smiled weakly, not saying anything, and then looked down at herself again.

This sounded like it may be deep, so I said, "Hey," and put my left hand up to her, "if you don't want to you don't have to."

"No," she said, grabbing my hand softly around the wrist and setting it down on her thigh, bringing me closer to her, and held it there, not real tight, but I didn't let go. "I guess I asked you about yours because . . . well, like, I wanted to tell you something pretty personal." She took another drag and squished it out in the little glass ashtray on the tray, smoke still spiraling up.

"OK," I said, nodding that it was OK. I held my hand on her thigh a bit harder and methodically flexed my fingers on the fabric.

"I was in the fifth grade," she started, as I turned to the other side, my hand coming off her momentarily. I picked up the remote lying next to me and tapped the volume button until the TV was quiet, "and we were playing a kissing game. You know, where the girls all, like, line up against the fence and the boys all take turns smooching."

I remembered doing that in third or fourth grade myself. So I guess if she wanted to get *technical* with me about my first kiss . . .

I looked up at her and put my left hand back on her leg, but she had turned to look at the toys on the table and picked up a white-armored Republic clone trooper figure, the one on its knee, blaster poised, and held it up and brought it to her, holding it near her waist and fumbling around with it.

"It was before school even started," she continued, "middle of April, and we were all around the monkey bars. You know, the one shaped maybe like a plus sign? It goes up like this," she held up her left hand with the action figure in it, staring at it, visualizing the monkey bars, and moved the figure in a small arc up, "with, like, two, maybe, four poles to slide down from?"

She looked at me, eyes wide to make sure I was getting it and I nodded.

"I had one like that at my school," I said.

Her voice seemed to have tapped into something deep. I'd never heard her sound so serious. It was as if her Valley girl-esque dialect was just for show—when she slipped into "likes" and "whatevers." I raised my right arm behind her and traced the back of her neck with my index finger. She clutched the toy in both hands, turning it over and over, head down, staring at it, focusing on it.

"So, like I said, it was before school started at the monkey bars around the back, out of sight from most of the rest of the playground. My older brother, Antonio, had said some of the guys wanted to kiss a bunch of girls before school. I thought it'd be fun. I'd never kissed anybody before. But I get there and I'm, like, the *only* girl."

She sounded pissed. Her head nodded once when she said this last line, in her old speech pattern, as if trying to find some sort of balance. She stared at the figure as if she could see the face under the white helmet, as if it was staring back at her. Light flickered from the TV and I caught myself looking up at it out of reflex.

"And I'm, like, 'Where is everybody?' There were, like, five boys, and Antonio was sitting up on one of the arches, crouched, looking down on all of us, one hand supporting himself on the bars.

"But I'm, like, OK, whatever, ready to play, right?" She chuckled once, at herself maybe, knowing it wasn't a pleasant memory she was unspooling. "So I stood under the thing with my back against a pole, hands clasped behind it, ready to kiss a boy for the first time, and said, 'OK, who wants a kiss?' and Paul Boone, school jock, not even real cute, wearing a black sweatshirt with the sleeves torn off and a tear at the collar in the center, comes up, all smiles, and says, 'I'm going first.'"

She stopped fumbling with the figure but still hadn't looked up at me. My one hand was still behind her, pinned between her body and the cushion, rubbing her back, my other hand still on her thigh.

"He grabbed my right arm and cranked it, twisted it, causing me to spin around and face the pole, and it felt like he was gonna rip it right out of its socket. I was crying and yelling for him to stop.

"But he pressed his chest into my back as the other boys closed in around us. I could feel his breath. It was hot and my *cheek* was digging into the pole, finding the groove between my jaws as he made these smacking and slurping sounds. His tongue flicked up and down my cheek while he rubbed up and down my chest with his other hand. Then he pulled back and said I didn't have no tits and stepped back. My back stung and I tasted tears as I looked up and saw my brother silhouetted in the now rising sun, perched almost directly above me, my goddamn fucking older brother that I worshipped not doing a thing to help me.

"And then the other faceless boys all took turns groping and kissing and hurting me, and not one seemed to notice they were hurting me."

I knew she was loose and flaky and fun, but not in a million years could I have guessed any of this. I felt for her. Not quite pity and not quite love, but I was feeling something.

"I don't know how many more took turns. There were five or six of them. They all seemed like shadows. With my face pinned against that pole I never really saw them. And when my eyes *were* opened all I could see was my fucking brother who didn't do a fucking thing to stop any of it. He just crouched up there, like a vulture. He didn't smile, but he certainly didn't act as if anything was wrong."

She paused and shook the clone once, hard, between her legs. She didn't look up at me yet and her voice hadn't really cracked too much up until now. I thought she was gonna lose it.

"My legs felt numb and I could barely breathe, like I was hyperventilating in the humidity or something, and after what seemed like forever the bell rang. It sounded like a seashell to me. And then they all scrambled and jumped and raced for the door, leaving me there.

"I think I collapsed. I dunno, I blacked out because the next thing I remembered I was in the nurse's office, lying on the couch and not having a clue as to how I got there.

"Miss Rainey was leaning over me. Her big fat face that always scared the piss out of me whenever I walked past her office was the most welcome thing I think I'd ever seen. She asked me what happened, and I said I didn't know.

"My head hurt, my face hurt, and I couldn't move my legs. And it was fucking *freezing* in that office, like a damn icebox, like the air conditioner was on full blast or something. I dunno."

Her voice sounded frustrated and scared as she chose her words now more carefully, as if this part was harder to recall. Her back loosened up a bit, and I found that I had stopped scratching her back, my hand on her skin, fingertips at her waistline, curled under her jeans a bit. Her skin felt clammy.

"She stepped back a bit then reached out and grabbed my chin and turned it to her face. I winced. She turned it from side to side, but softly, looking at me. I hated when people stared at my face. She kept asking how did this happen, and I said I must've fallen off the monkey bars. She wasn't buying it. She knew I knew. All I know was I wanted to go home."

"Did she keep pressing you?" I asked. "About what happened?"

"No. But I had her call my daddy, and half an hour later he showed up. He couldn't even look at me. His eyes looked at the floor and he couldn't even come near me to give me a hug or anything, like maybe he knew all along that someday I'd be in this type of trouble."

"'I fell off the monkey bars,' I cried over and over. 'I'm sorry.'

"'Well, if my little girl says she fell off the monkey bars, then that's how it happened,' he said in this irritated voice.

"We didn't even go to a hospital or anything, and when Antonio came home Daddy asked if he knew anything and he just said, 'No, Pop,' and went to his room or something."

"Did you ever tell your dad what happened?" I asked after a minute of silence. She studied the action figure, leaned back, and then looked at the table and set it back, right where it had been, right back into the footprints in the dust.

"I never told *anyone* that happened."

"Whatever happened with your brother, then?"

"I still can't look him in the eyes," she said, finally turning to me, her eyes meeting mine, then tracking my face, a thin smile forming on her lips; then they quivered and she pursed them. "And my younger brothers don't talk to me, like I'm treating Antonio unfair or some shit. I *hate* them." She pounded a fist into her leg.

Oh, the voice was having a field day with *hate*.

I had no idea how to reply to any of that. No one's ever told me shit like that before. And because she opened up to me I wanted to tell her about my parents: my fucked-up Jabba the Hutt mom who's stuck in a nursing home because she's so fat she can't get out of bed, because she's always paid the bills, my dad has missed house payments because he's never written a check in his life. But now didn't seem like too good a time. I couldn't say anything and make it out like we'd be comparing problems. This was something traumatic for her and I had to let it be her moment for now. I was no shrink, but this had to be why her relationships with guys were fucked up, starting in her own family. Daddy's little girl . . . *Hmmpf.*

Dark and disturbing this is, said the voice.

"Kiss me," she whispered.

What?

I must've said it out loud because she repeated, "Kiss me."

She placed her left hand on my crotch and leaned in and tried to kiss me, her mouth wide open. I scooched back a bit and she stopped. Her hand remained on my crotch, and I got hard instantly.

"I'm sorry," I whispered, shaking my head at the bad idea. Our faces were practically touching. She took my hand that had been on her thigh and placed it on *her* crotch and moved back in, her tongue darting in and out of my mouth as we kissed.

I won't deny the urge I had to do whatever she wanted, but it didn't seem right. Not at all.

"Don't you want me?" she asked, our noses brushing, her eyes closed.

"Yes, but . . ."

She shook a bit, and then tears started forming in her eyes.

"I'm sorry," she sputtered and then leaned her head to my chest and began crying, her nose and face digging into me.

I reached behind her and wrapped my arm around her, stroking her shoulder and upper back as she wept, her head on my shoulder.

"Sshhhh," I said quietly, "it'll be all right."

She stopped, leaned back a bit, and sniffed hard, her eyes red, her cheeks flushed through her pale skin. Then she let go and rubbed her eyes. My arm still curled around her, her body almost on top of me, her legs turned toward me. Then she slapped her thighs.

"God, look at me, Chuck, I'm such a mess."

She shook her head quickly like she was trying to get something out of her hair, so close that her hair brushed my cheek slightly.

"Nobody knows this about me," she said, her voice a little hoarse.

I smiled weakly and sheepishly and looked down at the floor. She craned her head to look up at me.

"Hey," she said, smiling again, her left hand interlocking with my left across my lap. "You awake?"

I looked back up at her, the old Naomi, and she laughed.

But I wanted to know more. I sat back, facing her as she swung her legs up onto my lap and crossed them, her body in a sort of V. I instinctively reached for a leg and caressed it. She closed her eyes and took a deep breath.

"What about your mom?" I asked. "Does she have a clue?"

Her eyes opened as if woken from a nightmare.

"Oh, fuck no!" she roared. "She'd be all, like, wanting to know what happened, how it was her fault somehow, and then Daddy'd calm her down and say everything was fine. I don't think the poor woman's had a thought of her own since she got married."

"Well, *that's* fucked up."

"Huh. Tell me about it," she said, elbows tucked in, arms up, palms facing up. "I mean, I love my mom but she's got issues."

"So does your dad," I added as she relaxed.

"Right."

We sat and looked at each other for a few moments, the TV images still flickering.

"You wanna camp here tonight?" I asked. I figured she shouldn't drive home if she didn't want to. She didn't live that far away.

"Sure," she said enthusiastically, mouth puckered as it formed the word. Then she put her chin to her chest and looked up at me. "We don't have to do anything," she added slyly, "not if you don't want to."

I guess she thought I meant sleeping together. I looked up at her and laughed through a closed smile. I shoulda said *crash* instead of *camp*. Why did I always try to speak in movie lines? She wouldn't even know which movie that was from.

"I'll hold you," I offered.

She bent forward and placed her hands on my shoulders and kissed me softly, no tongue, no forcefulness, just nice.

"Let's see what happens," I replied after she backed off.

"OK," she said.

We sat and held each other for a bit, and then we both yawned. I let her sleep in my bed. I kissed her goodnight on the cheek and then passed out on the couch with the TV still on, dreaming of an army of Naomis in white stormtrooper armor but without the helmets. I always kinda prided myself on not being like everyone else, on being an individual, and I think she kinda felt that way about herself, too.

Colophon

HAIR TRIGGER 28 WAS PRODUCED ON A DELL OPTIPLEX GX260 WITH INTEL Pentium 4 CPU (2.40 GHz) using QuarkXPress 5.0. (The cover and photo pages were produced on an Apple Macintosh G5 using InDesign CS2 and Adobe Photoshop CS2.) They were submitted to Sheridan Books, Ann Arbor, Michigan, camera-ready on Imation 100MB Zip Disks for printing.

Images were provided by the artist in a digital format. They were submitted to Carqueville Printing Company, camera-ready, on Imation 700MB CDR for printing. All photo titles are ITC Franklin Gothic Book.

The cover copy is ITC Franklin Gothic Demi and ITC Franklin Gothic Book. The text on the first photo page is ITC Franklin Gothic Book Oblique. All photo titles are ITC Franklin Gothic Demi.

Body copy is Bembo 11 point. Author names are in Franklin Gothic Book Compressed 14 point. Page footers are in Franklin Gothic Book Compressed 9 point.

Paper stock for cover is 12 PT Carolina C-1-S. Paper stock for photo pages is 100# Sterling Gloss Text. Print specs for photo pages are four-color process plus overall aqueous satin coating. Print specs for cover are four-color process and one PMS color with matte laminate.

Print run 1,500.